AMERICA'S FAILURE IN CHINA, 1941–50

AMERICA'S FAILURE IN CHINA

1941-50

Volume II

TANG TSOU

Phoenix Books

THE UNIVERSITY OF CHICAGO PRESS
CHICAGO AND LONDON

This book is also available in a one-volume clothbound edition from
THE UNIVERSITY OF CHICAGO PRESS

Standard Book Number: 226-81515-3 (clothbound);
226-81518-8 (paperback)
The University of Chicago Press, Chicago 60637
The University of Chicago Press, Ltd., London
© 1963 by The University of Chicago
All rights reserved
Published 1963. First Phoenix Edition 1967
Fifth Impression 1969
Printed in the United States of America

CONTENTS

Volume I

CHAPTER IX

MARSHALL'S

CHINA POLICY:

INTELLECTUAL

PROCESS

AND

POLICY

DECISIONS

A. Civil Strife and Armed Intervention

In China, General George C. Marshall confronted a range of alternatives: armed intervention; provision of massive military assistance and operational advice to China; support for the Nationalist government short of armed intervention and without providing military assistance on such a scale as would, in his opinion, escalate into armed intervention; standing aloof from the military-political conflict between the Kuomintang and the Communists but granting economic aid to the recognized government; and finally, total withdrawal from China. Marshall did not choose to undertake armed intervention in China. His negative decision rested on the widely shared assumption that American interests in China were not worth a war. This estimate of American interests in China naturally reinforced other assumptions and considerations which predisposed the United States against armed intervention in the Chinese civil war. In turn, the decision against armed intervention shaped or controlled such crucial elements in Marshall's China policy as his efforts to effect a truce between the Kuomintang and the Chinese Communists, his program to bring about a coalition government, his decision to limit the activities of the United States Army Advisory Group, his rejection of General Wedemeyer's recommendations for an expanded program of military assistance, and his negative response to Ambassador John Leighton Stuart's suggestion that the American government advise Generalissimo Chiang to retire.

When Marshall's policy is thus seen as an integrated whole, the relative importance of the various assumptions and considerations in influencing policy decisions can be determined, and the various elements of his policy fall into their proper place. Such a reconstruction enables us to see clearly that all the characteristic ambiguities of America's traditional policy toward China persisted in Marshall's policy. The withdrawal of the United States from China between 1947 and 1949, following President Franklin D. Roosevelt's wartime policy of making China a great power, can then be understood as another phase of the cycles of advance and retreat of the United States in China. In short, Marshall's China policy was a continuation of the traditional policy of the United States and met the same fate that befell its precursor.[1]

1. The Structure of Ends and Means in Marshall's Policy

Soon after Ambassador Hurley abruptly resigned on November 27, 1945, and made public his letter of resignation,[2] President Truman appointed General Marshall as his special representative in China with the personal rank of ambassador.[3] The policy which Marshall was to implement was thoroughly discussed by him and top officials in the State Department. It was again reviewed by him and Secretary of State Byrnes in a meeting with President Truman and Admiral Leahy on December 11 [4] and was outlined in a group of papers, supplemented by an oral understanding. The papers consisted of a letter of instructions from President Truman to General Marshall and three attached documents: a document entitled "United States Policy toward China," a public statement by the President, and a memorandum from Secretary Byrnes to the War Department.[5]

[1] For an account of the cycles of advance and retreat from 1899 to 1937, see A. Whitney Griswold's classic work, *The Far Eastern Policy of the United States* (New York: Harcourt, Brace & Co., 1938).

[2] Chap. viii, above.

[3] Department of State, *United States Relations with China* (Washington, D.C.: Government Printing Office, 1949), p. 132 (hereafter cited as *United States Relations with China*). See also Harry Truman, *Years of Trial and Hope* (New York: Doubleday & Co., 1956), pp. 66–77. The name of General Marshall was suggested by Clinton Anderson, the secretary of agriculture, in a cabinet meeting on November 27 (Walter Millis, *The Forrestal Diaries* [New York: Viking Press, 1951], p. 113).

[4] Truman, *op. cit.*, p. 67; Herbert Feis, *The China Tangle* (Princeton, N.J.: Princeton University Press, 1953), pp. 413–15, 418–20.

[5] General Marshall's role in the writing of his directive and in the formulation of the China policy at this stage was, for a time, a subject of controversy. In the hearings on his nomination as secretary of defense, General Marshall told the Senate Committee on Armed Services on September 19, 1950: "While I was in this room for a week undergoing the Pearl Harbor investigation, the policy of the United States was being drawn up in the State Department, and that was issued when I was on the ocean, going over there" (Senate Committee on Armed Services, *Hearings on the Nomination of General George C. Marshall to be Secretary of Defense*, 81st Cong., 2d sess. [1950], p. 21). In the MacArthur hearings, Marshall, on May 10, 1951, gave a slightly more

The superficially simple program laid down in these papers and in the oral understanding actually comprised an elaborate structure of interrelated ends and means. The "long-range goal" of the United States was defined as "the development of a strong, united and democratic China."[6] This was a continuation of the policy adopted during the war; the words themselves had been popularized by General Hurley. The overriding short-term objective was to support the Nationalist government and to establish its authority, especially in Manchuria, as far as its military capabilities and limited American assistance would permit.[7] This intention found expression in the press release which declared that the United States recognized "the present National Government of the Republic of China as the only legal government in China" and as "the proper instrument to achieve the objective of a unified China."[8] The aim of establishing its authority as widely as possible was revealed in the following statement:

> The United States and the United Kingdom by the Cairo Declaration in 1943 and the Union of Soviet Socialist Republics by adhering to the Potsdam Declaration of last July and by the Sino-Soviet Treaty and Agreements of August 1945, are all committed

detailed account of the writing of the directive. It also minimized his own role and concluded with the statement that "my preparation for going to China was largely a matter in this room of the investigation regarding Pearl Harbor" (Senate Committee on Armed Service and Committee on Foreign Relations, *Hearings on the Military Situation in the Far East*, 82d Cong., 1st sess. [1951], p. 468. [hereafter cited as *Military Situation in the Far East*]). In the same hearings, Secretary of State Acheson gave a different version of the events relating to the preparation of the instructions. It shows that Marshall participated in the task from the beginning (*ibid.*, pp. 1848–49). Acheson's account was fully substantiated by Feis' meticulous narrative of that episode (Feis, op. cit., pp. 413–20).

In his attack on General Marshall, Senator Joseph McCarthy took full advantage of Marshall's erroneous testimony. See the speech made by McCarthy on the Senate floor on June 14, 1951 (*Congressional Record*, XCVII, 82d Cong., 1st sess. [1951], 6580). See also, Joseph McCarthy, *Story of General George C. Marshall* (1952). For a contemporary analysis see Norman Palmer, "Marshall's China Mission," *Current History*, September, 1951, pp. 145–46.

The letter of instructions, the memorandum from Secretary Byrnes to the War Department, and the press release can be found in *United States Relations with China*, pp. 605–9. The statement of policy was printed in Truman's memoirs (Truman, op. cit., pp. 68–71). The press release omitted several significant passages from the statement of policy.

[6] Memorandum from Secretary Byrnes to the War Department, December 9, 1945, *United States Relations with China*, p. 609.

[7] See pp. 352, 355, below. Testifying in the MacArthur hearings, Secretary of State Acheson stated that the American policy was "to give important assistance of all sorts to the Chinese Government and to assist in every way in the preservation of peace in China and the working out of the agreements which were so necessary to enable the Chinese Government to establish itself in those parts of China where it had been before and to get, for the first time, into areas of China where it never had been" (*Military Situation in the Far East*, p. 1842).

[8] Statement by President Truman on United States Policy toward China, December 15, 1945, *United States Relations with China*, p. 608.

to the liberation of China, including the return of Manchuria to Chinese control.[9]

To achieve this objective, which was justified by the formulas regarding the unification of China and the evacuation of Japanese troops still remaining in that country,[10] the American government adopted positive measures, but these, as we shall see, were counterbalanced by the negative decision that "United States support [for the Chinese government] will not extend to United States military intervention to influence the course of any Chinese internal strife"[11] and that "incidental effects of American assistance upon any dissident Chinese element should be avoided as far as possible."[12] On the positive side, various types of military assistance were provided to the Nationalist government. United States military and naval forces were to be maintained in China for the time being[13] — a decision which had been made in a cabinet meeting on November 27. General Wedemeyer was instructed to "put into effect the arrangements to assist the Chinese National Government in transporting Chinese troops to Manchurian ports, including the logistical support of such troops," and to perfect immediately "arrangements for transportation of Chinese troops into north China."[14] It was also decided to establish a United States military advisory group in China at the appropriate moment.[15]

At this time, the generally accepted view, shared by General Wedemeyer, held that the extension of the authority of the Nationalist government into Manchuria and North China would be impossible without either a political settlement with the Chinese Communists or American military intervention.[16] Thus, the American government adopted measures designed to achieve such a settlement. General Marshall was instructed "to persuade the Chinese Government to call a national conference of representatives of the major political elements to bring about the unification of China and, concurrently, to effect a cessation of hostilities."[17] In the public statement

[9] *Ibid.*

[10] At the time of Marshall's arrival only some 200,000 out of approximately 3,000,000 Japanese troops and civilians had been returned to Japan (*ibid.*, p. 690).

[11] Statement by President Truman on United States Policy toward China, December 15, 1945. This was the press release, reprinted in *ibid.*, p. 608.

[12] "United States Policy toward China," reprinted in Harry Truman, *op. cit.*, p. 70. The press release cited in n. 11 is a public version of this statement, with several important omissions.

[13] *Ibid.*, p. 71, and *United States Relations with China*, p. 608.

[14] Memorandum from Secretary Byrnes to the War Department, December 8, 1945, *ibid.*, p. 607.

[15] President Truman to General Marshall, December 15, 1945, *ibid.*, p. 606.

[16] For Wedemeyer's view, see *ibid.*, pp. 129–30; Feis, *op. cit.*, p. 402; see also chap. viii, above.

[17] President Truman to General Marshall, December 15, 1945, *United States Relations with China*, p. 605.

of American policy, President Truman told the warring parties in China: The Government of the United States believes it essential:

1. That a cessation of hostilities be arranged between the armies of the National Government and the Chinese Communists and other dissident Chinese armed forces for the purpose of completing the return of all China to effective Chinese control, including the immediate evacuation of the Japanese forces.

2. That a national conference of representatives of major political elements be arranged to develop an early solution to the present internal strife — a solution which will bring about the unification of China.[18]

It was in this choice of means to re-establish the authority of the Nationalist government that a basic conflict of policies developed between the United States and Generalissimo Chiang Kai-shek. The strategy adopted by the American government was to use the proposal of a broadly representative government, including the Communists, as a bargaining counter for gaining control over the Communist armies, and thus to check Communist influence. President Truman in his public statement declared:

The United States is cognizant that the present National Government of China is a "one-party government" and believes that peace, unity and democratic reform in China will be furthered if the basis of this Government is broadened to include other political elements in the country. . . .

The existence of autonomous armies such as that of the Communist army is inconsistent with, and actually makes impossible, political unity in China. With the institution of a broadly representative government, autonomous armies should be eliminated as such and all armed forces in China integrated effectively into the Chinese National Army.[19]

Since the development of a united and democratic China was not only a long-term goal but also a means to extend and strengthen the authority of the Nationalist government, it became an immediate objective of American policy. As President Truman told General Marshall in his letter of instructions, "Secretary Byrnes and I are both anxious that unification of China by peaceful, democratic methods be achieved as soon as possible."[20]

In contrast, the strategy of the Generalissimo was, as subsequent events suggested, to crush the Communists by force, or, at least, to drive them

[18] *Ibid.*, pp. 607–8.
[19] *Ibid.*, p. 608.
[20] *Ibid.*, p. 605.

out of the strategic regions and to reduce them by military means to a negligible factor. For the Nationalist leaders, the elimination of the Communists was a matter of utmost urgency. As Mr. Ch'ên Li-fu, the leader of the C.C. clique was reported to have said later, the Chinese Communists were like a "bad appendix that has to be removed to preserve life."[21]

The American government was aware of this conflict of views over methods of solving the problem of China. Speaking of the necessity of broadening the government to include all major political groups, Secretary of State Byrnes told the War Department:

> This problem is not an easy one. It requires tact and discretion, patience and restraint. It will not be solved by the Chinese themselves. To the extent that our influence is a factor, success will depend upon our capacity to exercise that influence in the light of shifting conditions in such a way as to encourage concessions by the Central Government, by the so-called Communists, and by the other factions.[22]

Thus, the United States government adopted a policy of conditioning large-scale support for the Nationalist government upon the cessation of hostilities and the achievement of unity. President Truman instructed General Marshall:

> In your conversations with Chiang Kai-shek and other Chinese leaders you are authorized to speak with the utmost frankness. Particularly, you may state, in connection with the Chinese desire for credits, technical assistance in the economic field, and military assistance (I have in mind the proposed United States military advisory group which I have approved in principle), that a China disunited and torn by civil strife could not be considered realistically as a proper place for American assistance along the lines enumerated.[23]

The American government further realized that the prospective American military assistance and the Nationalist hope for American intervention would embolden the Nationalist government to seek a military solution to the Communist problem. President Truman's press release specifically ruled out American military intervention.[24] The sentences in the statement of policy concerning the decisions to continue to furnish military supplies, to assist the Nationalists to re-establish control over the liberated areas, including Manchuria, and to set up an American military advisory group

[21] *New York Times*, July 22, 1946, p. 2.
[22] *United States Relations with China*, p. 606.
[23] *Ibid.*, p. 606.
[24] *Ibid.*, p. 608.

in China were omitted from the press release.[25] General Wedemeyer was told that pending the outcome of Marshall's discussions with Chinese leaders he was to hold in abeyance further transportation of Chinese troops to North China, except to such North China ports as might be needed for the movement of troops and supplies into Manchuria. He was also instructed that arrangements for transportation of Chinese troops into North China might be immediately perfected but not communicated to the Chinese government.[26] These precautions were also necessary in order to preserve the impartial position of the United States as mediator in the internal Chinese conflict.

The program adopted at this time exerted pressure on the Chinese Communists too, for they had to face the possibility that rejection of the American plan might bring the United States to intervene actively on the side of the Nationalists. As it turned out, however, American pressure on the Nationalist government was far stronger than that on the Communists, because the American program for peace and unity coincided with Communist demands of the moment. Furthermore, American unwillingness to undertake armed intervention in China set a narrow limit on the amount of pressure which the United States could exert on the Chinese Communists.

It cannot be too strongly emphasized that, these facts notwithstanding, the *overriding* objective of the United States was to support the Nationalist government and to establish its authority as far as possible. In the deliberations leading to the final adoption of the program, it was decided that, if the Generalissimo failed to make reasonable concessions to obtain a cease-fire and a political settlement, the United States would continue to support him "to the extent of assisting him to move his troops into North China in order that the evacuation of the Japanese might be completed." [27] This element of Marshall's program was agreed upon but not written into any of the official papers. The rationale behind this decision was stated by General Marshall in the following terms, according to the notes of a meeting on December 11:

> If the Generalissimo . . . failed to make reasonable concessions, and this resulted in the breakdown in the efforts to secure a political unification, and the United States abandoned continued support of the Generalissimo, there would follow the tragic consequences of a divided China and of a probable Russian reassumption of power in Manchuria, the combined effect of

[25] Compare the two statements respectively in Truman, *op. cit.*, pp. 68–71, and in *United States Relations with China*, pp. 607–9.

[26] *Ibid.*, p. 607.

[27] Notes by General Marshall on a meeting with the President, Byrnes, and Leahy, December 11, as quoted in Feis, *op. cit.*, p. 419, n. 15.

this resulting in the defeat or loss of the major purpose of our war in the Pacific.[28]

Marshall recognized that to continue to support Chiang under these circumstances the American government "would have to swallow its pride and much of its policy."[29] But in fact, it was this basic policy of supporting the Nationalist Chinese government, within what were judged to be the capabilities of the United States, which General Marshall endeavored to implement at the beginning of his mission to China and which, according to the State Department White Paper, governed American actions from 1946 to 1949. The establishment of a coalition government including the Communists was only a means to support the Chinese government, one element of a broad political program. To see this element as the over-all purpose of American policy, as the critics of Marshall frequently did, is a gross oversimplification.

Rather, the basic and controlling element in Marshall's policy was the decision against armed intervention and the related decision to refrain from action in China which might escalate into armed intervention. Despite the total collapse of the negotiations between the Kuomintang and the Chinese Communists in November, 1946; despite the rapid deterioration of the political and military position of the Nationalist government in the summer of 1947; and despite Marshall's recognition in February, 1948, of the possibility of an early defeat of the Nationalist government,[30] this decision was strictly adhered to. Nor was its modification effected by the formal repudiation in March, 1948, of the concept of a coalition government including the Communists; the Communist conquest of Manchuria and North China between November, 1948, and January, 1949; the retirement" of Generalissimo Chiang from the presidency in January, 1949; the imminent crossing of the Yangtze River by the Communist forces in April, 1949.

2. The Decision Not To Undertake Armed Intervention

In the complex events from 1945 to 1949, the decision not to undertake armed intervention in China was inextricably intertwined with other factors: first, a misjudgment of the nature and intentions of the Chinese Communist party; second, the incompetence of the Nationalist government and its obstinate resistance to American advice; and third, America's anxiety over the growing influence of communism in Europe and the intensification of disputes with the Soviet Union. There are indications that

[28] *Ibid.*
[29] *Ibid.*
[30] Marshall's testimony before the Committees on Foreign Relations and Foreign Affairs in executive session, *United States Relations with China,* p. 382.

in late 1945 the Chinese Communists were still judged by some high officials in the State Department to be something other than dedicated Communists. In Byrnes' memorandum of December 9, 1945, one of the three documents attached to President Truman's letter of instructions to General Marshall, the term "so-called Communists" was used.[31] But according to his own testimony, General Marshall had no illusions about the Chinese Communists, at least after his arrival in China.[32] Similarly, John Carter Vincent, the director of the Office of Far Eastern Affairs from 1945 to 1947, was, according to his own account, led by the difficulties confronting Marshall in his negotiations with the Chinese Communists to the "definite conclusion" that they were Communists and part of the international Communist movement guided by Russia.[33] Although in the early months of 1949 some American officials probably entertained the idea that Mao would become a Tito,[34] Secretary of State Dean Acheson, in his characterization of the Chinese Communists as a party serving the "interests of a foreign imperialism"[35] in the letter of transmittal in the White Paper, showed that he did not subscribe to this view. The idea of a Chinese Tito was a negligible factor in the decision against armed intervention.

In contrast to the rapidly diminishing influence of the initial misjudgment of Communist intentions, the incompetence of the Nationalist government and its resistance to American advice assumed increasing importance in strengthening America's decision not to intervene by armed force. No one knows to what extent the United States could have been effective in reforming the Nationalist regime, had she actively intervened in Chinese politics. But the fact remains that after the termination of the embargo on arms in May, 1947, the American government did not again resort to strong pressure or intervene actively in Chinese politics, apart from Ambassador John Leighton Stuart's gentle advice and personal activities. One reason for this omission was obviously General Marshall's opinion that no Chinese leader could replace Chiang[36] and that there was no alternative to supporting him within the reasonable limits of American

---

[31] Truman, *op. cit.*, p. 72, and *United States Relations with China*, p. 606.

[32] Testifying before the MacArthur hearings, Marshall declared: ". . . when . . . I got out to China and looked the ground over, from the very start, . . . there was no doubt that the leadership of this group [the Chinese Communist party] were Marxist Communists, and they so stated in my presence, and insisted, in my presence, that they were" (*Military Situation in the Far East*, p. 378; see also p. 379).

[33] Senate Committee on the Judiciary, *Hearings on the Institute of Pacific Relations*, 82d Cong., 1st and 2d sess. (1951–52), p. 1708 (hereafter cited as *Institute of Pacific Relations*).

[34] *New York Times*, February 14, 1949, p. 10; February 15, 1949, p. 12; February 18, 1949, p. 8; February 21, 1949, p. 5; April 24, 1949, Sec. 4, p. 3.

[35] *United States Relations with China*, pp. xvi–xvii.

[36] Pp. 385–87, below.

capability. But, as we shall see, another reason was American refusal to assume the moral and political commitment to do whatever was necessary to preserve the Nationalist regime in at least a part of China.[37] This commitment would have flowed from active intervention in Nationalist politics. But it would not have been compatible with the prior decision not to use American armed forces in China and the related decision not to give massive military assistance and operational advice in the field. Thus, the decision to refrain from armed intervention inhibited actions to make the Nationalist regime viable. In retrospect, it stands out as the fundamental decision governing China policy from 1945 to 1949.

The decision not to intervene with American armed forces in China stemmed also from considerations other than the misjudgment of Communist intentions and the perception of Nationalist failings. This is evidenced by the fact that such Republican critics of Marshall's policy as Senator William F. Knowland, Senator Owen Brewster, and Representative Walter H. Judd, who were bitter foes of the Chinese Communists and stalwart friends of the Nationalist government, nevertheless concurred in the decision not to use American ground forces in China for combat duties, or at least never publicly advocated such an action.[38] Thus, the decision not to undertake armed intervention must be examined in its own terms.

It should be remembered that events in China moved toward a climax during America's intensified struggle with the Soviet Union over the fate of Europe. Her concerns in Europe formed an increasingly significant element in America's decision against armed intervention in China. America's vital interests in Europe and the Mediterranean decreed that available resources should be devoted to these regions first. In the fifteen weeks of revolution in American foreign policy in 1947, the policy of containment was proclaimed, the program of aid to Greece and Turkey was enacted, and the general concepts of the European recovery plan were formulated. As the Soviet Union continued to push forward with the coup in Czechoslovakia and the Berlin blockade, the United States responded with the North Atlantic alliance and the airlift. These moves were undertaken at a time when the Chinese civil war was entering its decisive phase. Confronted with historic tasks in Europe and a hopeless situation in China, the administration steadfastly adhered to its decision against armed intervention and the related decision against any action which would degenerate into armed intervention. While its critics advocated granting increased military and economic assistance to China, none of them publicly proposed sending American ground forces to China. There was no basic conflict during 1945–49 between "internationalists" and "isolationalists" over the

[37] Pp. 389–90, below.
[38] Pp. 363–64, below.

issue of armed intervention on the Chinese mainland. This phenomenal lack of disagreement on a basic issue obliges us to search for the deeper reasons for the decision to refrain from armed intervention which underlay the other elements of Marshall's policy.

3. The Basic Assumption behind American Policy

Armed intervention in civil strife usually involves heavy commitment of a nation's resources, entails a grave risk of counterintervention by a third power, and points only to an uncertain outcome. In the classic balance of power in eighteenth- and nineteenth-century Europe, intervention was admitted to be legitimate only insofar as it was intended to protect the security and vital interests of the intervening power.[39] For the independence and sovereignty of the nation-state were the cornerstones of the international system and non-interference in the internal affairs of another nation was a principle for preserving national independence and for maintaining the flexibility of alignment. The doctrine of non-intervention, however, did not apply to weak nations outside Europe. On the contrary, the powers interfered actively in the internal affairs of these weak nations and, not infrequently, turned them into dependent states or colonies.

By her principle of respecting the territorial and administrative integrity of China and its corollary of non-intervention in Chinese internal affairs, the United States sought to extend the application of the doctrine of non-interference to China. Meanwhile, Wilsonian idealism, the Good Neighbor policy, the Atlantic Charter, the Moscow Four-Power Declaration, and the United Nations Charter — all gave the doctrine of non-intervention the appearance of a self-sufficient and universal principle, seemingly dissociated from the multiple system of balance of power on which it was originally based.

This trend in American thinking was still strong at the end of the Pacific war when the multiple balance of power was being replaced by a bipolar system. Under the new system, each of the two superpowers was the center of a particular philosophy and way of life. The rigid alignment of

[39] Commenting on the principle of intervention in the classical system of balance of power, Lord Brougham, an early nineteenth-century statesman and writer, wrote: "Whenever a sudden and great change takes place in the internal structure of a state, dangerous in a high degree to all neighbors, they have a right to attempt, by hostile interference, the restoration of an order of things safe to themselves, or, at least, to counterbalance, by active aggression, the new force suddenly acquired.

"The right can only be deemed competent in cases of sudden and great aggrandizement, such as that of France in 1790; endangering the safety of the neighboring powers, so plainly as to make the consideration immaterial of the circumstances from whence the danger originated" (Lord Brougham, *Works*, VIII, 37–38, as quoted in Edward Vose Gulick's *Europe's Classical Balance of Power* [Ithaca, N.Y.: Cornell University Press, 1955], p. 63).

the two blocs and the ideological dimension of the conflict vitiated the historic reasons for non-intervention under the multiple system. Thus, while the long tradition of American thinking continued to restrain the United States, changes in the international system and the theory and practice of the Communist movement were placing a premium on intervention as a method in the world-wide struggle for power. More than ever, non-intervention became a policy designed to hold the ring against possible intervention by a third power while indigenous forces favoring the non-intervening nation maintained the upper hand in an internal conflict.

In any case and under any international system, the military and political risks involved in armed intervention can be justified and the commitments entailed can be successfully discharged only if the intervening power has made a prior political decision that her security and vital interests, or at least essential interests, are at stake. Generally speaking, this decision ought to be based upon long-term considerations reflecting geopolitical reality, which find expression in the historic policy of the nation. Once a positive decision is arrived at, the feasibility of armed intervention and its timing, limits, and methods can be determined by weighing the factor of cost and the chances of success in the light of the estimate of the interests at stake.

As we have noted, American policy toward China in the twentieth century contained two contradictory elements: espousal of the principles of the Open Door and refusal to go to war on behalf of China. America's pronouncements gave the impression that she had very important stakes in China. But her concrete actions up to 1941 had consistently been governed by a low estimate of her interests in China.[40] The acceptance of war with Japan represented only a temporary resolution of the contradiction in favor of the principle of upholding the integrity of China. The inconsistency in the traditional policy persisted in the wartime policy of making China a great power. This grandiose policy was in practice a political means to keep China in the war. It was meant to be a substitute for America's military presence in the Far East after the war. It implied nothing more than the circular notion that, to the extent China could become a great power, America would have important interests in China; otherwise she would not.[41] After the Stilwell crisis, American officials, including President Roosevelt, entertained serious doubts that China would soon become a great power.

Thus, after the Pacific war, the assumption that American interests in China were not worth a war continued to govern American policy. It

[40] William L. Neumann, "Ambiguity and Ambivalence in Ideas of National Interest in Asia" in Alexander DeConde (ed.), *Isolation and Security* (Durham, N.C.: Duke University Press, 1957), pp. 133–58. See chap. i, above.
[41] See chap. ii, above.

found expression in the reluctance of the State Department to define the minimum American interests in China which would be defended by military power. On November 1, 1945, Secretary of War Patterson sent a memorandum to Secretary of State Byrnes requesting political guidance on the question: "What, if any, corollary involvement in *continental* affairs in the Far East do we foresee or accept?"[42] He wanted an answer to this question to determine what military plans must be made against unacceptable aggression in the Orient. Specifically, he suggested that "it would be most valuable to have a clear-cut statement of *minimum interests from which the United States will not retreat in the event of a clash of interests* in the Far East, particularly concerning *Manchuria, Inner Mongolia, North China and Korea.*"[43] The State Department returned a vague reply which plainly revealed its lack of a definite answer to this vital question. It read:

> As to your request for a statement of minimum interests from which the United States will not retreat in the event of a clash in interests in the Far East, the [War] Department might determine in advance the military steps to be taken against possible aggression in the Far East. Department's contribution to political guidance to the Armed Forces can best be made by consistent and close cooperation between the Departments concerned.[44]

[42] "The State Department's Answers to Questions contained in the Memorandum Dated November 1, 1945, from the Secretary of War to the Secretary of State," printed as Appendix XV in John C. Sparrow's *History of Personnel Demobilization* (Washington, D.C. Department of the Army, 1951), p. 493.

[43] *Ibid.* It is interesting to note that Captain H. E. Yarnell asked very similar questions in 1919 (Louis Morton, "War Plan ORANGE," *World Politics*, January, 1959, p. 225).

[44] Sparrow, *op. cit.*, p. 494. As early as 1946 some American officials approached the Chinese scene with the assumption that China could not be a strong ally against the Soviet Union. In a conference of experts on American foreign policy held at the University of Chicago in the late spring of 1946, Mr. Joseph C. Ballantine, who had resigned not long before from his position of special assistant to the secretary of state, assured one of the conferees who had expressed his skepticism of the worth of China as an ally: "I think we would be doing a marked disservice to China, not only to our relations with Russia, if we attempted to build her up as a sort of buffer against Russia. Not only do we have the Russian suspicions, but you have an expectation that cannot be realized. I don't think that anybody in the State Department has any such conception in its plans in connection with military aid to China" (Quincy Wright, *A Foreign Policy of the United States* [Chicago: University of Chicago Press, 1947], p. 160).

True to the pattern of the traditional policy, the public pronouncements of American officials stressed the vital interests of the United States in China, although the crucial term, "vital interest," was used in contexts that rendered it virtually meaningless. In his statement of December 15, 1945, President Truman said, "It is thus in the most vital interest of the United States and all the United Nations that the people of China overlook no opportunity to adjust their internal differences promptly by means of peaceful negotiation" (*United States Relations with China*, p. 607). In a statement issued in March, 1946, Marshall referred to a "stable" government in China as being "vital" to the United States (*New York Times*, March 17, 1948, p. 26). Like the repeated invocation of the principles of the Open Door, this type of statement empha-

The basic assumption regarding American interests in China played a part in cultivating three considerations which in turn exercised discernible influence on policy decisions. The first was the military postulate that American ground forces should never be used on the mainland of China. The second was the existing military capability at particular times. Both the military postulate and the existing military capability reflected a low but unpublicized estimate of the interests at stake in China. The avowed objective, whether it was the integrity of China or the preservation of the Nationalist government, was beyond the reach of the United States. The third consideration concerned the policies and actions of other powers, who were fully conscious of their interests in China. Toward them, American policy represented merely belated and inadequate responses; and the action or non-action of a third power became too weighty a factor in shaping American decisions. Thus, Japanese aggression in China in the thirties led to war with Japan only after the political and military foundations of the Nationalist government had already been undermined. The lack of direct Soviet support for the Chinese Communists was regarded as an important reason for American abstention from direct military intervention.[45] When the total bankruptcy of American policy seemed imminent, the course of action followed up to that time was justified by pointing to the unimportance of China and by stressing the limits of American capability, which had been set in part by the low estimate of American stakes in China.

4. The Influence of a Military Postulate

In the years between 1946 and 1949, one important consideration governing American policies and actions was that American ground forces should never be used for combat duties on the mainland of China. Testifying in the MacArthur hearings on his thoughts in 1946, General Marshall stated that "I was not only skeptical, but alarmed at the possibilities of the ground involvements in connection with China."[46] The same postulate determined his policies in 1947 and 1948. As he testified in another context, "The real issue was how you would meet this situation without a tremendous commitment of this government on the land area in Asia."[47] The United States Army Advisory Group in China was under specific instruction not to assign its officers and enlisted men to combat units of the

---

sized the importance of a goal which could not be achieved by a policy based on official thinking. Their only effect was to increase the public's subsequent disappointment in the results of official policy and to magnify the political consequences of America's failure.

[45] Pp. 367–69, below.
[46] *Military Situation in the Far East*, p. 383.
[47] *Ibid.*, p. 465. Emphasis added.

Nationalist forces.[48] In his now famous report, made after a fact-finding mission to China in the summer of 1947, General Wedemeyer recommended a vast expansion of American military and economic aid to China. However, he rejected "active participation in operations by American personnel" as "contrary to current American policy."[49] The American supervision of Nationalist forces which General Wedemeyer envisaged was to be carried on "outside operational areas."[50]

Marshall's reluctance to use ground forces in combat duties on the Asiatic mainland reflected an almost universal feeling in the United States. In the deliberations leading to the enactment of the China Aid Act of 1948, Senator Arthur H. Vandenberg, chairman of the Senate Foreign Relations Committee, stated in his report to the Senate that the broad language of the bill "should not be interpreted to include the use of any of the armed forces of the United States for combat duties in China."[51] Even the most outspoken critics of the Marshall-Truman policy never proposed publicly the use of American ground forces in China for combat duties. In the debate leading to the adoption of the China Aid Act of 1948, Representative Walter H. Judd stated in the House: "Not for one moment has anyone contemplated sending a single combat soldier in. . . . So it is important to make clear when we speak of military aid . . . it is supplies, training and advice, nothing further."[52] In the hearings Mr. William C. Bullitt testified that "you would not send an American soldier except in an advisory status. I do not propose that American troops be sent to China."[53] In reply to the question put by Representative Mike Mansfield whether the sending of military aid might eventually lead to active military participation on the part of the United States, General Claire Chennault said that "there is that possibility, I believe, but I do not feel that it is very probable that that would occur."[54] In a debate on China policy in June, 1949, Senator Tom Connally, a staunch defender of the administration's policy, asked Senator Owen Brewster what he or other Senators would have done to save China and whether they would have sent an army into China. Senator Brewster answered, "I never proposed to send an army into China."[55] On the same occasion, Senator William K. Knowland stated without contradiction that "there has never been a proposal on the

[48] *Ibid.*, pp. 558–59.
[49] *United States Relations with China*, p. 811.
[50] *Ibid.*, p. 813.
[51] *Ibid.*, p. 388.
[52] *Congressional Record*, XCIV, 80th Cong., 2d sess. (1948), 3442.
[53] House Committee on Foreign Affairs, *Hearings on United States Foreign Policy for a Post-war Recovery Program*, 80th Cong., 2d sess. (1948), p. 1918 (hereafter cited as *Foreign Policy for a Post-war Recovery Program*).
[54] *Ibid.*, pp. 2222–23.
[55] *Congressional Record*, XCV, 81st Cong., 1st sess. (1949), 8296.

part of those who are critical of the policy we have pursued in the Far East to send an army to China. . . ."[56] General Marshall was right in his estimate that the Nationalists could not win the civil war without direct armed intervention on the part of the United States. He was probably also right in his judgment that providing massive military assistance and operational advice to Nationalist combat units would lead to full-scale intervention. Most of his critics, on the other hand, espoused the ambitious goal of saving China from communism but shrank, for reasons of their own, from publicly advocating the means which would have been indispensable to the achievement of their objective. They did not face squarely the probability that military assistance alone would not enable the Nationalists to defeat their foes.

As the situation in China rapidly deteriorated, this basic military postulate found an additional justification in the tremendous effort necessary to prevent a Communist triumph. It became, to some extent, a self-validating principle. When in December, 1948, the Chinese Communists were annihilating the main Nationalist forces north of the Yangtze and were making preparations to cross the river, Major General David Barr, head of the United States Military Advisory Group, reported to the Department of the Army that he "emphatically" would not recommend a policy of unlimited aid and the immediate employment of United States armed forces, which alone would enable the Nationalist government to maintain a foothold in South China.[57] In rejecting the proposal made by Senator Patrick McCarran to extend a loan of $1.5 billion to China, Secretary of State Dean Acheson wrote Senator Tom Connally, chairman of the Senate Committee on Foreign Relations, on March 15, 1949:

> To furnish the military means for bringing about a reversal of
> the present deterioration and for providing some prospect of suc-
> cessful military resistance would require the use of an unpredict-
> ably large American armed force in actual combat, a course of
> action which would represent direct United States involvement

---

[56] *Ibid.*, p. 8297. A possible exception to this generalization was General Wedemeyer, who made the following cryptic statements in the hearings leading to the China Aid Act of 1948: "I do not believe that military participation is necessary *at this time,* sir. I could not develop this subject intelligently for you in open session" (*Foreign Policy for a Post War Recovery Program*, p. 2070). Emphasis added.

In another context he said: "When one is talking about the expenditure of money to accomplish international objectives, one must think in terms of *blood* as well as treasure" (*ibid.*, p. 2068). Emphasis added.

In academic circles, there were advocates of direct military intervention. Professor David Rowe proposed such a policy as early as 1947 (*Institute of Pacific Relations*, pp. 3985–86).

[57] *United States Relations with China*, p. 336.

in China's fratricidal warfare and would be contrary to our traditional policy toward China and the interests of this country.[58]

5. The Factor of Existing Military Capabilities

The belief that it was contrary to the American interest to commit ground forces on the mainland of China should be understood against the background of the rapid demobilization after the Second World War. At the time of the surrender of Germany, the United States Army consisted of approximately 8,290,000 persons.[59] The estimates made by the War Department before Japan's capitulation envisaged the reduction of this mighty force to 2,500,000 men by July 1, 1946, with a figure of 900,000 for the Pacific. The plan for rapid demobilization did not satisfy Congress, nor did the current rate of discharging army personnel. General Marshall had to assure the congressmen in September, 1945, that the War Department was releasing the largest number of men from service as rapidly as possible and that there was "no relationship whatsoever between the rate of demobilization and any future plan of the Army."[60] By the end of 1945, when General Marshall set out on his ill-starred mission to China, the total strength of the army had been reduced to 4,228,936.[61] Although at one time in the second half of 1945 the American armed forces in China were at their peak strength of some 113,000 soldiers, sailors, and marines,[62] the estimate made by the War Department of the authorized strength of the entire Pacific region as of July 1, 1946, envisaged a reduction from 830,000 to less than half that number. Of these, six thousand were to be designated for service in China, and General Wedemeyer feared that reduction by discharges would reduce the available forces to barely three thousand men.[63] By June 30, 1946, when the sporadic fighting in Manchuria began to spread to various points in China proper[64] and when the Soviet press started to give attention and praise to the activities of the Chinese Communists and to express confidence in their potentialities,[65] the total strength of the United States Army had fallen to 1,889,690 men, which represented a decrease of 6,133,614 in a period of nine months since V-J Day.[66] By the

[58] *Ibid.*, p. 1053.

[59] Sparrow, *op. cit.*, p. 359.

[60] *Demobilization of the Army*, Senate Document No. 90, 79th Cong., 1st sess. (September 20, 1945), pp. 1–10.

[61] Sparrow, *op. cit.*, p. 360.

[62] Statement by President Truman on United States Policy toward China, December 18, 1946, *United States Relations with China*, p. 694.

[63] Feis, *op. cit.*, p. 423.

[64] *United States Relations with China*, pp. 170–71.

[65] Charles B. McLane, *Soviet Policy and the Chinese Communists* (New York: Columbia University Press, 1958), pp. 252–56.

[66] Sparrow, *op. cit.*, p. 360.

end of 1946, when General Marshall abandoned his efforts to bring about a political settlement in China, the United States with her world-wide responsibilities had an army of only 1,319,483 men, with 12,000 soldiers and marines in China.[67] On June 30, 1947, shortly before General Wedemeyer embarked on his fact-finding mission to China, the total strength was 989,664 of which the effective strength was only 925,163.[68] In February, 1948, when in Secretary of State Acheson's retrospective view the United States had the last chance to commit her armed forces to the struggle in China,[69] the actual size of the army and air force was 898,000 men, with 140,000 men deployed in the Far East.[70]

No one was more conscious than General Marshall of the limits imposed by military weakness on the policies of the United States. Recalling the fruitless fourth meeting of the Council of Foreign Ministers in Moscow in March and April, 1947, General Marshall told an audience in the Pentagon in November, 1950:

> I remember, when I was Secretary of State, I was being pressed constantly, particularly when in Moscow, by radio message after radio message to give the Russians hell. . . . When I got back I was getting the same appeal in relation to the Far East and China. At that time, my facilities for giving them hell — and I am a soldier and know something about the ability to give hell — was 1⅓ divisions over the entire United States. That is quite a proposition when you deal with somebody with over 260 and you have 1⅓rd. We had nothing in Alaska. We did not have enough to defend the air strip at Fairbanks. . . .[71]

With reference to the situation in China in 1947 and 1948, particularly in regard to General Wedemeyer's recommendations in September, 1947, that the United States extend large-scale military and economic assistance to the Nationalist government, General Marshall testified in the MacArthur hearings:

> There, the issue in my mind, as Secretary of State, was to what extent this Government could commit itself to a possible involve-

[67] Ibid., p. 352; *United States Relations with China*, p. 604. The number of marines and soldiers in China at the end of 1946 was twice as large as the estimate of 6,000 men to be stationed in China by July, 1946. This change was due to the need for the use of American marines and soldiers to supervise the truce and to keep open the lines of communication.

[68] Sparrow, *op. cit.*, p. 360.

[69] *Military Situation in the Far East*, p. 1869.

[70] Millis, *op. cit.*, p. 375.

[71] Remarks by the Secretary of Defense at the National Preparedness Orientation Conference, November 30, 1950, p. 15, as quoted in Sparrow, *op. cit.*, p. 380.

ment of a very heavy nature in regard to operations in China itself. . . .

We would have to make a very considerable initial contribu-
tion, and we would be involved in the possibility of very extensive continuing responsibilities in a very large area.

At that time, our own military position was extraordinarily
weak. I think I mentioned the other day that my recollection is
. . . we had one and a third divisions in the entire United States.

As I recall General Wedemeyer's estimates, about 10,000 officers and others would be necessary to oversee and direct those
various operations.

In view of our general world situation, our own military
weakness, and the global reaction to this situation, and my own
knowledge out of that brief contact of mine in China, we could not
afford to commit this government to such a procedure.

Therefore, I was not in agreement with undertaking that, nor
were . . . the chiefs of staff.[72]

American weakness in conventional forces was not fully compensated
by the atomic monopoly which the United States enjoyed. At least up to
the time of the Berlin blockade, American officials had not resolved the
question of how to turn atomic monopoly into diplomatic bargaining power. This failure was forcefully pointed out by W. Phillips Davison: "The
bomb was the only real power the United States had, but no one knew
under what circumstances it could be used, or indeed whether it could be
used at all." [73] But even if American officials had devoted serious thoughts
to the problem of maximizing the political and military utility of the atomic
bomb, the ultimate weapon would still have appeared to have no relevance
to the civil strife in China. Thus, there was no discussion of its implications,
or the lack of them, for the Chinese situation either in the published records concerning America's postwar policy or in Marshall's retrospective
accounts.

6. The Soviet Policy of Non-intervention

In steadfastly adhering to a policy of refraining from direct military
intervention in China, the United States was influenced at once by the
Soviet policy of non-intervention and by the fear of Soviet counterintervention. Direct military intervention on the part of the United States could
be justified, in the American view, only by direct, overt Soviet intervention

---

[72] *Military Situation in the Far East*, pp. 465–66.
[73] W. Phillips Davison, *The Berlin Blockade* (Princeton, N.J.: Princeton University
Press, 1958), p. 155.

or, at least, by large-scale Soviet assistance to the Chinese Communists. But the Chinese Communist armies had already been immensely strengthened by captured Japanese arms and ammunitions in Manchuria which the Soviet Union had allowed to fall into their hands. They had extended their control over the greater part of Manchuria, thanks to the subtle and inconspicuous help rendered by Soviet authorities and to Soviet maneuvers in obstructing Nationalist attempts to take over that region. Against American advice, Generalissimo Chiang moved his best forces deep into Manchuria when the Russian forces withdrew in the spring of 1946. In the fighting which followed, the Chinese Communists proved able to survive the Nationalist offensive in the first phase of the civil war and then to counterattack with increasing ferocity in the later phases. There was no need for the Soviet Union to intervene or to help them with supplies on a large scale. In adhering to the policy of non-intervention, the Soviet Union was following a policy of holding the ring for the Chinese Communists and of discouraging the United States from intervening on the side of the Nationalist government. She was confident of the ability of the Chinese Communists to fend for themselves.

As evidence of Soviet aid or intervention was lacking,[74] the United States found an additional reason for her reluctance to intervene with her armed forces. American officials had an intense fear that, confronted by the Soviet policy of non-intervention, the United States would be condemned by world opinion for her active intervention. Recounting his thoughts on the Chinese situation, General Marshall told a Round Table Conference held in October, 1949, to discuss China policy:

> When it came to Soviet assistance at all, I never could get my hands on it. . . . What did worry me more seriously than anything else was it seemed apparent to me that the Soviets were

[74] Marshall's testimony, *Military Situation in the Far East*, p. 543. See also report of Marshall's statement in the *New York Times*, January 12, 1947, p. 44; and reports of Ambassador John Leighton Stuart to Secretary Marshall, October 29, 1947, and December 16, 1948, in *United States Relations with China*, pp. 832, 895.

General Marshall made this point even more explicitly in an informal remark at a Round Table Conference, called in October, 1949, by the State Department to discuss China policy: "I had officers pretty much all over North China, along the Yangtze and Manchuria, and I always felt that the reports I got were far better than those the Generalissimo received. He was being fooled time and again because the fellow would defend himself, if he withdrew in an ignominious situation, he always made it a great battle with Russian tanks and Russian soldiers. The only thing they did not introduce was the Russian paratroops; they had everything else. I would find out from my people it was a patrol encounter and that went on all the time. Always I was trying to find out anything you could put your finger on that was authentic as to Soviet influence or Soviet help in all this; I never got anything except the influence of what I would call the spiritual or something akin to that" (Transcript of Round Table Discussion on American Policy toward China, as reprinted in *Institute of Pacific Relations*, pp. 1551–1682; the quotation appears on p. 1653).

leaning over backwards . . . in their attitude out there [in China]. . . . Well as far as I could see, what they were preparing themselves for was a case before the United Nations, where they could appear clean as the driven snow and we would have our hands muddied by every bit of propaganda they could put on it. I would probably be the particular lump of mud they would throw on it, and that worried me.[75]

Marshall's sensitive conscience played a part in the vital decision to terminate the China theater of operations and to reduce the strength of the marines in China. General Marshall wrote President Truman from China in February, 1946:

We must clear our hands out here as quickly as possible in order to avoid the Russian recriminations similar to those today regarding the British troops in Greece. I mean by this, we must terminate the "China Theatre of Operations" and in its place quickly develop the military advisory group. . . . Also in this connection, we must move all the Marines out of China but some reconnaissance and transportation and some housekeeping and local guard units.[76]

In explaining the differences between the Greek and Chinese situations, Secretary Marshall told the Committee on Foreign Affairs in February, 1948: "In Greece you have a force which is being supported, according to the report by the United Nations Commission, by bordering states. Now in China we have no concrete evidence that it is supported by Communists from the outside."[77]

7. The Fear of Soviet Counterintervention

The success of the Soviet Union's policy of non-intervention followed a classic pattern of *Realpolitik*. By inspiring a fear of her counterintervention, the Soviet Union managed to hold the ring for the Chinese Communists.[78] Apprehension of possible Soviet actions was intensified by the

[75] Transcript of Round Table Discussion, *ibid.*, p. 1654.

[76] Truman, *op. cit.*, p. 77.

[77] *Foreign Policy for a Post-war Recovery Program*, p. 1555. In explaining the active American policy in Greece, Marshall stated at the MacArthur hearings: "The situation in Greece, however, Senator, I think, was a little different from that in China, because of the proximity of the satellite states which were openly supporting this operation, which we knew were equipping it almost entirely, and which also were protecting these Communist forces, guerrilla forces, by permitting them to retreat across the border and be armed and re-equipped and returned to the fight" (*Military Situation in the Far East*, p. 557).

[78] For a discussion of non-intervention, see Martin Wight, *Power Politics* (London: Royal Institute of International Affairs, 1954), pp. 49–51.

geographic position of the Soviet Union and her posture of strength, despite the American atomic monopoly. When Assistant Secretary of War John J. McCloy returned from China and met with the secretaries of State, War, and Navy on November 6, 1945, he described the American dilemma in the following words: "The Kuomintang must have our support to be able to cope with the situation. If the Russians, however, decide to give active support to the Chinese Communists, then we are in a real mess." [79]

One of the main arguments which General Marshall used in his vain attempts to dissuade Generalissimo Chiang from trying to solve the Communist problem by military means was that the Chinese Communists "would be driven to seek and be dependent upon outside support such as Russian aid" and that the spread of the civil war would afford an ideal opportunity "for the U.S.S.R. to support the Chinese Communists, either openly or secretly."[80] As a soldier, General Marshall was intensely conscious of the strategic position of the Soviet Union. He reminded the Generalissimo that, if Russian aid were given to the Communists, their supply line would be much shorter than his own and much more secure from attack.[81]

There was another political reason for the fear of Soviet intervention in China. Since the United States was refusing to give the Soviet Union a share in the control of Japan, she was apprehensive that the Soviets might disturb the situation in China as a reaction to American policy in Japan.[82] American armed intervention in China or even the mere presence of American troops was thought likely to increase the danger of Soviet intervention.

While the decision not to use ground forces on the Chinese mainland and the rapid demobilization of America's once powerful army were self-imposed limitations, the possibility of Soviet counterintervention in combination with the political and military strength of the Chinese Communists set an external limit to American power and policy. Given a clear recognition of interests at stake, a solution of the problem of American policy toward China would have been to seek a strategic settlement. But the conscious search for a strategic settlement with the Soviet Union was not a predominant mode of thought immediately after the Pacific war. In any case, it presupposed a prior political decision that the United States had certain minimum interests in China important enough to be defended by her armed forces and that a line must be drawn somewhere in China to

[79] Memo of meeting, Byrnes, Patterson, Forrestal, McCloy, Matthews, and Gates, November 6, 1945, in Feis, *op. cit.*, p. 389.

[80] *United States Relations with China*, pp. 176, 189.

[81] Truman, *op. cit.*, p. 88.

[82] Feis, *op. cit.*, chap. xxxiv.

protect these interests. This prerequisite for positive action in China was the very opposite of the basic assumption behind American policy.[83]

Insofar as can be ascertained from published records, there was never a broad strategic plan to hold China or any part of it.[84] In his prepared statement on American policy toward China made at the MacArthur hearings, Secretary of State Dean Acheson outlined three alternatives open to the United States in 1945–46: "to pull out of China"; "to put into China unlimited resources and all necessary military power to try to defeat the Communists, remove the Japanese, and remove the Russians from Manchuria"; and, finally, "to give important assistance of all sorts to the Chinese Government and to assist in every way in the preservation of peace in China and the working out of the agreements [between the Kuomintang and the Chinese Communist party]."[85] Absent from this statement of alternatives was a program to work out, either explicitly and openly or implicitly and under the guise of a loose confederation, a boundary between American-Nationalist and Communist zones of influence which would have fully protected the minimum security interests of the United States and at the same time reflected the relative military and political strengths of the two sides.[86]

8. The Decision Not To Intervene and the Policy of Establishing a Coalition Government in China

General Marshall's program of establishing a coalition government including the Chinese Communists and of unifying the partisan armed forces into a national army was a continuation of the wartime policies of the United States, which Ambassador Clarence E. Gauss and General Patrick J. Hurley had endeavored to implement without success. Holding that the civil war in China could be settled by an elaborate set of formal agreements between the two sides, it assumed that the conflicts could then be confined within a democratic, constitutional framework.[87] But Marshall's postwar program of seeking a political settlement between the Kuomintang and the Chinese Communist party was intimately and explicitly related to the decision not to intervene by the use of American forces. It rested upon the correct military estimate that, without direct American military intervention on a large scale, the Nationalist attempt to suppress the Communists by military means "might end in the collapse of the Government" and "would probably lead to Communist control in China," as

---

[83] See pp. 359–62, above.

[84] *Military Situation in the Far East*, p. 2759.

[85] Ibid., p. 1842, see also *United States Relations with China*, p. x.

[86] For a perceptive contemporary view, see Paul M. A. Linebarger, "The Complex Problem of China," *Yale Review*, Spring, 1947, p. 513.

[87] For the sources of this erroneous assumption, see chap. vi, above.

General Marshall repeatedly warned Generalissimo Chiang in 1946.[88] Or, to use Secretary of State Acheson's succinct statement, "There was not available force in China to settle these problems by force and therefore you have to resort to negotiations."[89]

It was the hope of some American officials that the political-military settlement sponsored by General Marshall would curb the growing power of the Communist party. As the White Paper on China stressed, the political and military agreements signed by the Kuomintang and the Chinese Communist party during the first three months of the Marshall mission "recognized the preponderant strength of the Kuomintang position in the National Government."[90] In the hearings on the Institute of Pacific Relations, John Carter Vincent, who had played an important role in formulating policy, explained his thoughts in 1945 and 1946: "My concept was that the Communists would come into the Government on a minority basis and that . . . through support of the Chiang Kai-shek government . . . [and] with help from us we could eventually strengthen the Chinese government enough to eliminate the Communists."[91] In other words, the tactic was one of "taking the Communists in in more ways than one by bringing them into a government on a minority basis."[92] At this time, the Communist parties in France and Italy were participating in their governments on a minority basis, and they were later successfully ousted. Responsible American officials may have been influenced at the time by the analogy with the French or Italian situations. Certainly, some tried to justify the Marshall mission by pointing at this parallel. As President Truman wrote in his memoirs, "There was no reason why the Nationalist Government could not be successful in this struggle, as non-Communist governments had been in Europe, if it attended to the fundamental needs of the people."[93]

But this superficially attractive program suffered from a serious flaw. Given the political weakness of the Nationalist government and the popular support enjoyed by the Communists, the political and military settlement between the Nationalist government and the Communists which was indorsed by Marshall might well have worked out to the over-all advantage of the Chinese Communist party, rather than the Kuomintang. The provision for the popular election of the provincial governors and the principle

[88] *United States Relations with China*, p. 176; see also pp. 173–74.
[89] *Military Situation in the Far East*, p. 1897.
[90] *United States Relations with China*, p. 143.
[91] *Institute of Pacific Relations*, p. 1714.
[92] *Ibid.*, pp. 1713–1714. Vincent testified that this idea of "taking the Communists in in more ways ways than one" dated back to a report written by him in 1942, when he was the counselor at the American embassy in Chungking.
[93] Truman, *op. cit.*, p. 90. Mr. Vincent also alluded to this parallel in his testimony before the McCarran Committee (*Institute of Pacific Relations*, p. 1714).

of "a fair distribution of power" between the central government and the provinces as "the highest unit of self-government" [94] would certainly have given the Chinese Communists actual control over several of the most important provinces in North China, Manchuria, and Inner Mongolia. In this respect, the provision for popular election of provincial and local officials would have given the Communists a much greater advantage than their own proposal made in the summer of 1945 for actual control over a specific number of provinces. From the provinces which they would have controlled through elections, the Chinese Communists could have reached out to capture the central government, utilizing the political advantage given them by their participation in a coalition government in the transitional period and the freedom for propaganda and organizational activities granted them under the proposed constitutional principles. The importance which the Communists attached to control over local governments, to their participation in a coalition government, and to the political settlement in general was demonstrated time and again in the controversies leading to the final breakdown of the truce. The political advantages which the political program would have given to the Communists might not have been offset by the military advantages conferred on the Nationalists by the military agreement which was arrived at with Marshall's advice.[95]

General Marshall himself recognized this possibility in his subsequent account of his mission. In explaining what he termed the Communist anxiety to go through with the political agreement, he stated in October, 1949:

> They [the Chinese Communists] undoubtedly felt they could win politically and therefore, if they could avoid the military effort, they were very much better off politically, because they had discipline and indoctrination and they had a solid party; whereas they felt the Kuomintang was just an icing on the top and all its foundations of public support had become almost non-existent . . . so if they could ever get the thing in the political arena they would win, and . . . it would not have been so hard but a rather easy thing for the Communists to dominate the government.[96]

According to Secretary of Navy Forrestal, General Marshall himself also admitted in July, 1946, that the truce of January, 1946, which he had succeeded in obtaining as a preliminary to a general settlement, "had worked out to some extent in favor of the Communists."[97]

[94] Resolution on the Draft Constitution Adopted by the Political Consultation Conference, January, 1946 (*United States Relations with China*, p. 621).

[95] *Ibid.*, pp. 161, 164–66, 168–69, 175–76. For details, see p. 410, below.

[96] *Institute of Pacific Relations*, p. 1656.

[97] Millis, *op. cit.*, p. 174.

B. The United States and Power Relations in Nationalist China

The political and military settlement which some American officials thought would curb the influence of the Communists might have strengthened them unless the unpopular economic and political policies of the Nationalist government had been changed and the Kuomintang rejuvenated, or unless new political forces had been brought into being. In the light of the dynamism of the Chinese Communist party and the weakness of the Kuomintang and other political groups, one is tempted to suggest that the Chinese Communists might even have won in a contest with a reformed Kuomintang and the liberal forces unless the latter had been aided by American economic and military assistance on a large scale, not excluding direct armed intervention. But a new political force could have brought into existence a Chinese government which could have effectively used American aid and which would have given the United States a fair chance of holding a line somewhere in China by direct military intervention.

To bring about these political changes it was necessary to put the greatest possible pressure on the leadership of the Nationalist government. If direct pressure failed to bring about the desired reforms, it was then necessary to effect a change in that leadership, curbing or destroying the influence of some of the groups in control and building up the power of others. Undoubtedly General Marshall saw the urgent need for some fundamental changes in the policies and composition of the Chinese government. Testifying in the MacArthur hearings, General Marshall said:

> And the hope in the matter so far as I saw it was that other parties — the Young China Party, Democratic League and so on . . . and the non-party group could coalesce and the Generalissimo back them, and they would be a group which I would think [*sic*] have drawn strength from both the other parties, those that were outraged at the character of the operations of the Nationalist Party in its lower echelons, and those that had gone into the Communist Party, who were not real Communists . . . but they were violently antagonistic to the present regime of the Nationalist Government. And it looked as though there would be enough drawn from those groups, together with what existed in the way of an independent group, which was a very small group, to hold the balance of power between the two, along-side of the evident factor to me and to my associates that the Kuomintang Government was utterly incapable of suppressing the Communists by military means.[98]

[98] *Military Situation in the Far East,* p. 638.

The general principle underlying Marshall's remarks, as distinguished from his specific program, was entirely valid. To bring about a change in the balance of force among various political elements in Nationalist China was not only imperative but feasible. Given the rapid disintegration of the Nationalist regime and the Nationalists' dependence on the United States for survival, it would not have been impossible for the United States to bring about drastic changes in the composition and policies of the government if she had adopted a positive program for China and if American officials had been experienced in the art of political maneuver.

1. The United States and the Third Force

Unfortunately, the specific program adopted by General Marshall had several serious flaws both in conception and in execution. His hope that the influence of the small parties and non-party groups would increase depended on his success in achieving a political settlement between the Kuomintang and the Chinese Communist party, under which the liberal groups would become holders of the balance of power. By persisting in his scheme to suppress the Communists at this time, Generalissimo Chiang, intentionally or otherwise, also dealt a fatal blow to Marshall's plan to strengthen the small parties and non-party groups.

Moreover, while General Marshall realized the importance of exerting strong pressure on the Nationalist government to change its policies,[99] American influence and power were, during the larger part of Marshall's mission to China, dissipated in his attempts to seek a settlement on terms which the Kuomintang could not have accepted and which, if implemented, might have benefited the Communists. Little was done at this time to bolster the position of the small parties and other political groups and to curb the arbitrary power of the reactionary groups. Marshall was most careful to avoid partiality toward any group.[100] It was during his mission that two of the most prominent leaders of the Democratic League were assassinated and other liberal leaders were forced to seek asylum in the American consulate in Kunming. It was only after his mission to bring about a political settlement had failed that General Marshall attempted to persuade the small parties and groups to unite and form "a single liberal patriotic organization."[101] He also endeavored to use his influence to bolster the political position of these groups by his informal talks with govern-

---

[99] *United States Relations with China*, pp. 186, 226.

[100] Letter from Professor Knight Biggerstaff, August 31, 1962. For perceptive comments on this failure to support the liberal groups, see John K. Fairbank, "Our Chances in China," *Atlantic*, September, 1946, pp. 37–42; "China's Prospect and United States Policy," *Far Eastern Survey*, July 2, 1947, p. 148; "Can We Compete in China?" *Far Eastern Survey*, May 19, 1948, p. 117; "Toward a Dynamic Far Eastern Policy," *Far Eastern Survey*, September 7, 1949, p. 210.

[101] *United States Relations with China*, pp. 213–14.

ment leaders and his public statement of January 7, 1947, which was issued after his departure from China.[102]

But by this time the small parties and political groups were already badly divided between those who refused to participate in a government dominated by the Kuomintang and those who would enter the government to obtain a nominal share of power and prestige. The former group, oppressed and persecuted by the Nationalist government, had already come increasingly under the influence of the Chinese Communists. The latter group, which, generally speaking, consisted of less capable and influential men, failed to play the role envisaged by Marshall. A program to build up a third force might have had a better chance for success if it had been vigorously implemented at the very beginning of the Marshall mission.

2. The United States and the Various Factions in the Kuomintang

Unlike the Chinese Communist party, the Kuomintang had never been a monolithic organization. Divided into sharply antagonistic factions, it was rent by constantly changing alignments among them. The Generalissimo himself had captured and then retained control over the party by building up the military and political power of a personal following. The Whampoa clique was the personal, military instrument with which he undercut the power of his potential rivals — such men as Generals Li Tsung-jên, Pai Ch'ung-hsi, and Fu Tso-yi — even at the cost of dissipating the over-all strength of the Kuomintang vis-à-vis the Communists. In the political field, the extreme right wing C.C. clique was his principal pillar of strength. Various other groups in the Kuomintang — the Political Science group, the "elder statesmen," and the followers of Sun Fo — served the Generalissimo with varying degrees of loyalty and enthusiasm. But there was a constant struggle for power and maneuvering for position among all these groups, a state of affairs that did not totally displease the Generalissimo, for even among his personal following he maintained control by balancing one faction against another.

Since the Whampoa group and the C.C. clique were factions in control, respectively, of the army and the party, they were the strongest opponents of the changes in government and policies which General Marshall deemed essential to the survival of the Nationalist regime. Yet, with minor exceptions, American equipment and supplies went to the armies commanded by the Whampoa generals and thus, unintentionally, strengthened them vis-à-vis the other military leaders in the Kuomintang. In spite of their better equipment, the armies commanded by Chiang's lieutenants did not, however, distinguish themselves in either the Sino-Japanese War or the

[102] *Ibid.*, pp. 215–18, 686–89.

Chinese civil war, with the exception of the first few months in both cases. In contrast, the provincial armies, poorly equipped but placed in desperate positions where they had to fight for their own survival, frequently gave good accounts of themselves. In the political field, the C.C. clique was just as ineffective in its fight against the Communists. While few Chinese were more fervently anti-Communist than the leaders of the C.C. clique, their narrow intellectual outlook and their determination to monopolize political power led them to pursue restrictive and repressive policies which drove the liberals and intellectuals into the arms of the Communists. While engaging in a life-and-death struggle with the Communists, they were also preoccupied with checking the power of other factions within the Kuomintang. Their tactics played into the hands of the Chinese Communists.[103] The C.C. clique and the Whampoa faction were thus the main obstacles to the pursuit of an effective American policy in China. The success of General Marshall's program to change the composition and policies of the Chinese government hinged upon curbing the power of both groups, remaking them into useful elements in a broad anti-Communist coalition, if possible, and eliminating their most reactionary leaders, if necessary. This was clearly recognized by Marshall. In conversations with several high-ranking government officials shortly before his departure from China, he stressed "the necessity of removing the dominant military clique and the reactionaries from the Government structure" and of creating "an opportunity for the better elements in China to rise to the top." [104]

In late 1946 and the early part of 1947, American actions had the effect of exerting pressure on the Nationalist government to curb the power of the reactionary groups, particularly the C.C. clique, and to strengthen the other groups. In his statement of January 7, 1947, announcing the failure of his mission, General Marshall denounced "a dominant group of reactionaries" in the Kuomintang as severely as he condemned the Communists.[105] In his numerous dispatches, Ambassador Stuart showed that

---

[103] To cite one specific example, the C.C. clique organized in May, 1947, a series of student demonstrations and strikes to discredit the government which, partly as a result of American pressure, was then under the nominal leadership of the Political Science group. It hoped that the disorders would provide the justification for the establishment of "a strong-arm, right wing government" either through a coup d'état or through winning the elections to be held in the coming autumn (*ibid.*, p. 730). But the leadership in the disturbance organized by the C.C. clique soon passed into the hands of the Democratic League and the Communists. In reporting this incident, Ambassador Stuart commented: "This development [in student agitation] can hardly be displeasing to the CC-CC[sic] clique, which can now claim that lack of public order is attributable to their enemies. Just how much of the agitation is now under Communist leadership is debatable, but it must be assumed that the Communists are present and, if not already active, are prepared to exploit the situation should it become necessary or desirable" (*ibid.*).

[104] *Ibid.*, p. 218.

[105] *Ibid.*, pp. 687–88.

he was clearly aware of the destructive influence of the C.C. clique. Against the background of the embargo on arms and ammunition, the American "wait-and-see" policy followed by General Marshall in early 1947 militated against the reactionary group and bolstered, to some extent, the influence of the liberal groups. But for several reasons American actions and policies in this direction were too hesitant to be decisive and their effects sometimes neutralized each other. The reactionary groups dominated the Kuomintang long enough to bring about the downfall of the Nationalist regime; and the other factions did not gain sufficient power soon enough to enable them to combine with the liberal groups outside the Kuomintang into a new, effective political force.

3. The American Desire To Introduce Western Institutions to China

American officials in their desire to introduce Western institutions to China did not realize, first, that these Western institutions might have no application at all in China, at least for some time to come; second, that the intended effects of an institutional change might easily be nullified by adroit political maneuvers and other factors; and third, that an institutional change, desirable in itself, might have the consequence of weakening the groups which the United States intended to help. An illustration of the first point is General Marshall's attempt to establish the principle of civil control of the military or at least to check the further development of the domination of civilian authorities by the military. He proposed the setting up of a system of basic military training in China south of the Yangtze River and worked out an arrangement under which he hoped "it would be done in such a manner [that] it would not revitalize the military control of the civil authority." [106] No matter how anxiously the Generalissimo and other Nationalists wanted a system of basic military training to strengthen their own armed forces, the adoption of the system proposed by General Marshall would have gravely weakened, if not destroyed, the basis of their power. In China, the realistic alternatives open to the United States were not civilian control of the military on the one hand or military domination of civil authorities on the other. Rather, the choice was between the continuation in power of a group of generals, including the Generalissimo, who had proved unable to co-operate effectively with the American government, and another group of generals who could probably have acted in concert with the United States and who had showed a greater willingness to work with the liberals, intellectuals, and civilian administrators in China. Naturally, General Marshall's plan came to nothing.[107]

[106] *Military Situation in the Far East*, p. 698.
[107] *Ibid.*

To illustrate the nullification of the intended effects of an institutional change by adroit maneuvers, the following example can be cited. There began in June, 1946, a major military reorganization in China, made partly as a gesture to demonstrate the government's willingness to undertake administrative reforms and partly in pursuance of the resolutions of the Political Consultative Conference of all Chinese political parties and groups — a conference which was held soon after General Marshall arrived in China and which had his blessing. A major objective of those who advocated the change was to establish the principle of civilian supremacy over the military and to enable the other political groups and parties to control the Whampoa clique through the civilian authorities. The military reorganization involved the abolition of the National Military Affairs Commission which had existed outside the Executive Yüan, the highest civilian administrative organ. In its place, a Ministry of Defense was established under the Executive Yüan. The detailed structure of the new ministry closely followed the American concept of unity of control and the organizational pattern of the United States Department of War. Superficially it was based upon American advice.[108] It had the approval of American officials.[109] But in one crucial aspect it departed from American practice: the chief of staff was empowered to ignore or even counteract the directions of the minister of defense.[110] With an eye to American opinion, General Pai Ch'ung-hsi, a leading member of the Kwangsi group and reputedly the best strategist of China, was appointed minister of defense. But General Ch'ên Chêng, a ranking member of the Whampoa clique, was appointed chief of staff. While the chief of staff had direct access to the President — Generalissimo Chiang himself — the new minister of defense had to act through the Executive Yüan. Thus, the hope of establishing civilian control over the military and of promoting the influence of General Pai was largely frustrated.

Sometimes the institutional reforms suggested by American officials had the unintended effect of strengthening the reactionary group whose influence they hoped to curb. After his failure to bring about a political settle-

[108] Ch'ien Tuan-sheng, "The Role of the Military in the Chinese Government," *Pacific Affairs*, September, 1948, p. 249.

[109] During his mission in China, General Wedemeyer told a meeting of the top officials of the Nationalist government: "There must be a streamlined organization and clear-cut enunciation in [sic] the duties of all the ministries and bureaus of the government. April a year ago I discovered that there were over 60 sections in the National Military Council with duplicating functions and conflicting authorities. There was little coordination between the various groups or sections. Actually there were some groups within the National Military Council that were handling matters which had nothing whatsoever to do with national defense matters. Today in the Ministry of Defense we have grouped 60 sections under 6 general heads and reduced the personnel about 50 per cent" (*United States Relations with China*, p. 760).

[110] F. F. Liu, *A Military History of Modern China, 1924–1949* (Princeton, N.J.: Princeton University Press, 1956), p. 231.

ment between the Kuomintang and the Chinese Communist party, General Marshall made a strong effort to persuade the Kuomintang to terminate its one-party rule and to inaugurate a constitutional regime. In the period of political tutelage, the Kuomintang was financed openly and directly from the treasury of the government. The group in control of the party machinery, the extreme right-wing C.C. clique, whose members in general showed no special competence in financial affairs, obtained a relatively small share in the control of the monopolistic and semi-monopolistic economic enterprises of the government. The prospective termination of political tutelage raised the grave problem of financing the hypertrophied party organization and its numerous activities. The only solution was for the C.C. clique to gain control of certain of these economic operations and to venture into commercial and economic activities with an initial capitalization from the treasury or through purchase of government-owned enterprises at a low price.[111]

This expansion of the influence of the C.C. clique into the economic and financial field tended to strengthen its position at the expense of the Political Science group, which the United States sought to help. As Ambassador Stuart reported to Secretary Marshall on April 5, 1947, on the result of the Third Plenary Session of the Kuomintang Central Executive Committee:

> The Chen brothers [leaders of the C.C. clique] are now attempting to insert themselves into the economic field and . . . Chen Li-fu desires to become vice-Chairman of the National Economic Council. . . . [The Political Science group] failed in its objectives to consolidate its hold in financial affairs because the C.C. clique was successful in gaining leadership of the Central Trust. . . . Wong Wen-hao [a leading member of the Political Science group] has said if Chen Li-fu did become vice-Chairman of the National Economic Council, it would be impossible for him, and perhaps others around him, to continue on the Council. . . . On balance, it would appear that the struggle will be continued between the liberals who will control most of the high government positions and have a major interest in the economic world and the C.C. clique largely controlling the Party organization and an influential section of the army, and attempting to inject itself into finance.[112]

The conclusion reached by Ambassador Stuart was that "in the struggle between factions . . . the C.C. clique seems to have emerged in a stronger

[111] Richard E. Lauterbach, *Danger from the East* (New York: Harper & Bros., 1947), p. 357.
[112] *United States Relations with China*, pp. 735–36.

position, to the detriment of other factions."[113] The expansion of the C.C. clique into the financial and economic field had far-reaching consequences, for it weakened confidence in the government among commercial and banking groups,[114] whose active support was a necessary condition for the survival of any non-Communist government in China. This development completed the monopolistic and semi-monopolistic hold of the members of the Kuomintang on the economic life of the country. It gave color to the Communist charge that China was under the merciless and exploitative control of four big families: Chiang, Soong, Kung, and Ch'ên.[115]

Another example of the unintended effect of a new institution was the strengthening of the C.C. group by the pending elections in connection with the inauguration of the constitutional regime. The C.C. group was by far the most disciplined faction in the Kuomintang. By its control over the appointment of magistrates in the *hsien*, the basic unit of local government in China, and by its domination of the party organization reaching still further down, the C.C. group was the only faction in the Kuomintang which could get out the vote and manipulate the electoral machinery throughout Nationalist China, particularly in the rural areas. Thus, it was not accidental that, as Ambassador Stuart reported on April 5, 1947, "the C.C. clique was putting its main effort into preparation for the elections which would precede the coming into effect of the constitution on December 25, 1947."[116] Commenting on the dependence of Generalissimo Chiang on the C.C. clique, the American ambassador noted:

> The paradox of his position, of which he may be unaware, is that he is being compelled to utilize the qualifications which the C.C. clique can offer. At the same time this clique exploits its preferred position to render more firm its hold on the Party and the country; and with time the Generalissimo therefore may well become less and less able to dispense with them or to circumscribe their activities, which can only serve to aggravate those social conditions basically giving rise [*sic*] and strength to the Communist movement."[117]

As the date of the elections approached, the American consul general in Shanghai reported on September 22, 1947, according to the White Paper:

[113] *Ibid.*, p. 735.

[114] Ambassador Stuart reported on March 12, 1947: "Evidence of C.C. clique expansion into the financial field will not increase banking and business confidence in government. . ." (*ibid.*, p. 243).

[115] See the book written by a leading Communist theoretician, Ch'ên Po-ta, *Chung-kuo ssŭ ta chia-tsu* ["China's Four Big Families"] (Hsin-hua shu-tien, 1946).

[116] *United States Relations with China*, p. 736.

[117] *Ibid.*, p. 735.

The C.C. clique there was increasing its power and dominating the Kuomintang's preparations to ensure that the successful candidates in the coming elections were "elite" party supporters plus such few political beggars as it may seem expedient to accept as window dressing.[118]

Summing up the outcome of the elections, the China White Paper put it this way: "In the end it was apparent that majority influence in the new National Assembly and the Legislative Yüan would lie with the C.C. clique, the extreme right-wing faction of the Kuomintang."[119] Thus, in their endeavors to introduce into China a set of institutions taken for granted in the West, American officials diverted their energy and influence from the principal task of building up a new political force and of checking the influence of the reactionary group.

When the first National Assembly was meeting to elect a president and vice-president, the American embassy reported to the State Department that "the party bosses of the Kuomintang regarded the establishment of the constitutional government as an exercise in machine politics."[120] On April 26, 1948, Ambassador Stuart cabled Washington:

Interference of Generalissimo and party machine with elections to Assembly and the new Yuan, with deliberations of Assembly on constitutional amendment question and flagrant intervention in vice-presidential election has [sic] thoroughly convinced those desiring effective constitutional government that Generalissimo intends to use the new constitution as vehicle for continuation of his personal rule in close cooperation with C.C. Clique-dominated party machine and Whampoa clique-dominated High Military Command as has obtained in past.[121]

In the end, however, the military defeats suffered by the Nationalist armies and the general dissatisfaction with the policies of the government created such a widespread resentment against the groups in control that not even Generalissimo Chiang and his following could prevent the election to the vice-presidency of General Li Tsung-jên, the leader of the Kwangsi group and the candidate of the groups demanding reforms. On the surface, it seemed as if the constitution had served as a vehicle for political reform. As a matter of fact, however, the political realities in China did not undergo significant changes, as the impotence and helplessness of the new vice-president clearly demonstrated.

[118] *Ibid.*, p. 263.
[119] *Ibid.*, p. 268.
[120] *Ibid.*, p. 908.
[121] *Ibid.*, pp. 853–54.

4. The Illusion about Generalissimo Chiang

In the postwar years as well as during the Pacific war, Chiang maneuvered the United States into the dilemma of either giving him economic and military assistance on his terms or risking the loss of China. At first, American officials were handicapped by their illusions about the Generalissimo. Chiang did not always flatly reject American advice. Frequently, he accepted American suggestions so long as they could be modified and put into practice in such a way that his power position and that of his personal following would not be affected. After the negotiations with the Communists collapsed, the Generalissimo lent his influence to promote the adoption of a constitution in reasonable accord with the resolutions of the Political Consultative Conference — a step which General Marshall urged strongly on Nationalist leaders.[122] In so doing, Chiang appeared to have exercised a determined personal leadership and worked in concert with all other groups and individuals to oppose the extreme right wing.[123] The adoption of the constitution, which is in many ways an excellent document,[124] was considered by General Marshall to be a great moral victory for the Generalissimo, which "had rehabilitated if not added to his prestige."[125] Thus General Marshall advised the Generalissimo that "he must by his own indirect leadership father a coalition of the minority groups into a large liberal party" and that "the organization of the minority parties into a large liberal group would assist him greatly and he could place himself in the position of the father of his country rather than continue merely as the leader of the Kuomintang one-party government."[126] This advice was given in pursuance of his plan of "building up of the liberals *under the Generalissimo* while at the same time removing the influence of the reactionary."[127]

In April, 1947, the Nationalist government proclaimed the end of the period of political tutelage by the Kuomintang [128] and brought several members of the two minority parties into a reorganized government. In this reorganization, members of the Political Science group were given many of the top positions in the government. These changes brought a certain amount of satisfaction to American officials. As Ambassador Stuart

[122] *Ibid.*, p. 213.
[123] *Ibid.*, p. 214.
[124] The most interesting features of this constitution are the provisions regarding the relations of the president of the Republic, the president of the Executive Yüan, and the Legislative Yüan. This arrangement combines elements from both the presidential system and the cabinet system. In this respect it resembles loosely the constitution of the Fifth Republic of France.
[125] *United States Relations with China*, p. 216.
[126] *Ibid.*
[127] *Ibid.*, p. 213. Emphasis added.
[128] *Ibid.*, p. 245.

reported on April 19, 1947, "The composition of the State Council is as regards the Kuomintang and independents as good as could be expected in the circumstances."[129] On June 18, 1947, the American ambassador informed the State Department:

> He [Generalissimo Chiang] has gone so far in discarding his earlier preconceptions and adopting progressive ideas that I believe he can be influenced to further advance. This will perhaps be slower and much less satisfactory than a more spectacular procedure but it has real possibilities and is perhaps by all odds the most hopeful solution.[130]

Unfortunately, these superficial changes did not modify the actual control of the C.C. clique over the party machinery and the Whampoa clique over the bulk of the armed forces. They did not decrease the dependence of Generalissimo Chiang on these two groups or his trust in them. It is significant that the members of the Kwangsi group and other provincial leaders, such as General Fu Tso-yi, who offered a realistic alternative to the Whampoa clique gained little genuine advantage in the reorganization. It is true that the Political Science group gained the premiership and several important ministries, but this hopeful development was offset by the expansion of the influence of the C.C. clique into the financial and economic field.[131] Under these circumstances, the reorganization meant very little.

American officials were not unaware of these political realities in China as the reports sent by diplomatic and consular representatives in this period clearly showed. But at this time they were still sufficiently impressed with the empty gestures of Generalissimo Chiang to believe that somehow a new political force could be developed under his leadership. This policy of building a new political force under Generalissimo Chiang assumed that he could undergo a moral conversion, abandon his lifelong ideas on government and politics, and sever his relationship with the following which he had relied on to gain and retain control of China — all this without great pressure from the United States. Inevitably, political developments in China disabused them. On February 6, 1948, Ambassador Stuart reported that "increasingly it must be the Generalissimo who must make the decisions and he continues to be the slave of his past and unable to take the drastic measures required."[132] When Generalissimo Chiang relieved General Pai Ch'ung-hsi of the Kwangsi group of his post as minister of defense and rejected his idea of organizing local militia, the American ambassador informed the State Department on June 24, 1948, that "he [Generalissimo

---

[129] *Ibid.*, p. 746.
[130] *Ibid.*, p. 241.
[131] Pp. 380–81, above.
[132] *United States Relations with China*, p. 267.

Chiang] seems suspicious that the Kwangsi clique have designs against him and is thus alienating, or at least losing the effective cooperation of, men who by every test have been loyal both to him and to the national cause."[133] On August 10, 1948, Ambassador Stuart reported:

> [L]ong experience with him [Chiang] suggests that he is no longer capable of changing and reforming or discarding inefficient associates in favor of competent ones; . . . it [the Nationalist government] ignores competent military advice and fails to take advantage of military opportunities offered, due in large part to the fact that the Government and the military leadership continue to deteriorate as the Generalissimo selects men on the basis of personal reliability rather than military competence.[134]

In a policy review in October, 1948, Secretary Marshall himself told the ambassador that in the light of past experience pressing the Generalissimo for removal of incompetents would not produce promising results.[135]

5. Chiang as the Indispensable Man

After the failure of the Marshall mission, it should have been clear that the Kuomintang and the Chinese Communists could not be brought together under a constitutional regime. If at this time the United States had not been under the illusion of Chiang's indispensability, if she had considered her interests in China vital, and if she had been determined to prevent the Communists from extending their control over the whole of China, the logical course would have been to use her tremendous influence to effect a complete change in the leadership of the government, substituting some other leaders for Chiang. Such a step might have been taken after Generalissimo Chiang's offensives failed to achieve their objectives, when his armies began to suffer reverses, and when the military, economic, and political crisis deepened to such a degree that the Chinese government had to depend upon immediate American assistance for survival.

Certainly, Generalissimo Chiang himself was preoccupied with the thought that it was the policy of the United States in the summer of 1947 to remove him. When the mounting crisis in China led General Marshall to dispatch General Wedemeyer on a fact-finding mission to China, Generalissimo Chiang on August 25, 1947, called Philip Fugh, a Chinese who was Ambassador Stuart's personal secretary, to his residence and asked the American ambassador's confidant whether the dispatch of the Wedemeyer mission meant that the United States wished to force his retirement or re-

[133] *Ibid.,* p. 275.
[134] *Ibid.,* p. 284; see also *Military Situation in the Far East,* p. 698.
[135] *United States Relations with China,* p. 284.

moval.[136] More than a year later, the possibility of advising Chiang to retire did occur to Ambassador Stuart, who by this time was totally disillusioned with Chiang.

As a matter of fact, even without strong pressure or positive advice from the United States, Generalissimo Chiang was forced by political and military events in China to retire from the presidency in January, 1949, though he succeeded in using what remained of his power to prevent his successor from gaining really effective control over Chinese affairs. The real question is not whether American pressure and maneuvers could have been the catalyst in a movement to replace Chiang, but whether the political forces opposing Chiang could have been developed with American help rapidly enough, and whether Chiang could have been replaced soon enough, to make a salvaging operation in China feasible.[137]

But, to the very end, the alternative of building a new political force in China without Generalissimo Chiang was never even seriously considered, let alone implemented. At the time of the Wedemeyer mission, the illusion that Generalissimo Chiang could lead a new political force had not yet dissipated. When disillusionment about Chiang set in, American officials were troubled by the idea that Chiang was the indispensable man whom no one could replace. On April 23, 1948, Ambassador Stuart told Secretary Marshall:

> I do not believe he [Chiang] is conceited or intoxicated with power in the usual sense. Yet he is dangerously self-opinionated and confident that he understands the situation better and has more experience than anyone else. This is all the more tragic be-

[136] *Ibid.*, pp. 258, 826.

[137] Commenting on this problem, Professor George E. Taylor observed: "There was a time when by more purposeful intervention we might have turned the tide in the Kuomintang and have brought about an alliance between the Chinese intellectuals and the modern-minded military on the Nationalist side. This would have meant countenancing what would in effect have been a plot to get rid of Chiang Kai-shek. Today, we have no organized social group to work with at all. The time has long since passed when American assistance could be given to anyone who could use it" (George E. Taylor, "An Effective Approach in Asia," *Virginia Quarterly Review*, Winter, 1950, p. 35). See also Franz Michael, "A Revolutionized Kuomintang," *Far Eastern Survey*, July 28, 1948, pp. 161–64; Woodbridge Bingham, "American Responsibility in China," *Far Eastern Survey*, February 9, 1949, pp. 28–31.

Hanson Baldwin wrote in the *New York Times* that there should be a "thorough clean-up and reformation of the Nanking government" or, alternatively, the present government should be replaced by one or more governments "less wedded to archaic political and military measures." He thought that the United States might have to support individual governors or commanders (*New York Times*, November 9, 1948, p. 4). Later he wrote: "We have it in our power to insist upon reforms in Generalissimo Chiang's Government or to back individual provincial governors or warlords. Aid previously given also could have been on our terms; we have only to review recent events to see that" (*New York Times*, December 4, 1948, p. 4).

cause he is so largely right in these assumptions, and because there really seems to be no one else who could take his place.[138]

The dilemma confronted by the United States as American officials saw it was succinctly stated in the following words of Ambassador Stuart as late as August 10, 1948:

> Universally the Generalissimo is criticized for his ineffective leadership and universally no one can suggest any one to take his place. He is the one who holds this vast country together. Without him disintegration seems inevitable yet . . . unless he can summon the resources to reverse the present trend he will inevitably and in time be discarded.[139]

General Marshall never succeeded in finding a solution to this central dilemma. As he told a conference on China policy sponsored by the State Department in October, 1949, "there was constant pressure to eliminate Chiang Kai-shek, but no one ever suggested anyone [who] could take his place; at least, they never made a suggestion to me that made any impression on my mind, of a man who can handle the situation."[140] Looking at the Chinese scene with this fixed idea, General Marshall found the problem of China insoluble.[141]

This dilemma confronting the United States was no doubt real. But it was also largely created by the political maneuvers of Generalissimo Chiang himself with unintentional help from the United States. While fighting the Communists, he was at the same time trying to undercut the political and military power of the other Nationalist leaders who did not unquestioningly obey him. His policy was the familiar one of rule or ruin. In his domination of the Kuomintang over a period of twenty years, he had built up a powerful following which placed personal loyalty to him above all else. When in early 1948 there was a possibility of General Li Tsung-jên's challenging his absolute control by running for the vice-presidency against Chiang's wishes, the Generalissimo announced his desire to withdraw from the presidential race. Almost immediately, the C.C. clique made known its refusal to co-operate with any government not headed by

[138] *United States Relations with China*, p. 851; see also p. 854.

[139] *Ibid.*, p. 886. Earlier, on June 12, 1948, the American embassy reported to the State Department: "The Generalissimo has dominated the scene for so long, no one stands out as capable of replacing him. . . . We find it difficult to believe that the Generalissimo can be removed from the scene except at the expense of national unity. . . . Should he leave the scene and should regionalism result, the Communist task would be made much more easy" (*Ibid.*, p. 912).

[140] Transcript of Round Table Discussion on American Policy toward China held in the State Department, October 6, 7, and 8, 1949, *Institute of Pacific Relations*, p. 1657.

[141] *Military Situation in the Far East*, pp. 397, 466; see also Millis, *op. cit.*, p. 372.

the Generalissimo and the Whampoa group threatened to go over to the Communists rather than serve under any president other than Chiang.[142] In these circumstances, he naturally appeared to be the only person who could hold China together.

Furthermore, the passive American policy played into his hand. Generalissimo Chiang never allowed the United States to attach any truly effective political conditions to American assistance even when the survival of the Nationalist government depended on large-scale American aid. When in November, 1947, the State Department was considering a program of American assistance to China to the amount of $300,000,000,[143] the Nationalist government handed Ambassador Stuart a memorandum which stated, among other things, that "the American aid to China plan shall contain no political condition other than what may be stipulated in the aid plan for Europe."[144] It informed the American government that while China would, of her own accord, employ American personnel to assist her in planning for financial, monetary, and other administrative reforms, "the employment of these personnel will not, however, be made an international legal obligation of the Chinese government in order to avert infringement on China's sovereignty and administrative integrity."[145] While Congress was debating the China aid bill, Dr. Sun Fo was reported as having said on March 13, 1948, that he feared American aid might infringe on Chinese sovereignty and that China "must insist on the right to reject advice if it is unacceptable."[146] In the end, the China Aid Act of 1948 did not contain any political conditions, though there were provisions regarding the use of economic aid which insured some direct benefits to the Chinese people.

Under these circumstances, the mere prospect of American aid strengthened Generalissimo Chiang's determination to hold on to his power despite the rapidly deteriorating situation. Commenting on the possibility of Chiang's retirement from the government so as to facilitate a political settlement of the civil war, the American embassy reported on March 18, 1948, to the State Department that "we feel sure that he will not do so [*i.e.*, retire] as long as he has any hope that our military assistance to him will be of a scale and scope sufficient to allow him to gain a military decision or to prolong the civil war until such time as other events may force us to intervene decisively in his favor."[147] At this time, the China aid bill had been under consideration in Congress. The subsequent flow of American

[142] *United States Relations with China*, p. 850.

[143] *Ibid.*, p. 374. This figure was subsequently raised to $570 million in the State Department's proposal. Congress actually appropriated $400 million under the China Aid Act of 1948.

[144] *Ibid.*, p. 377.

[145] *Ibid.*

[146] *New York Times*, March 14, 1948, p. 13.

[147] *United States Relations with China*, p. 907.

economic and military assistance strengthened him vis-à-vis the other dissident Nationalist leaders controlling various provinces. The American embassy reported to the State Department on August 24, 1948:

> The reluctance of the dissidents to make an open break [with Chiang] very likely stems from a new realization that the present Government still performs for them certain indispensable functions. Principal among these at the moment is Nanking's role in channeling American aid to the Provinces. We have made it abundantly clear that we support the Nanking Government. We have also made it plain that we intend to consult the Nanking Government on the allocation of our economic aid, and it is a well-known fact that the disposition of military aid is Nanking's responsibility. In this situation the potential dissident, who cannot dispense with American aid, is bound to Nanking by very strong ties.[148]

6. Intervention and the Problem of Responsibility

The American failure to bring a new political force into existence also arose from American unwillingness to assume the responsibilities that would have come with the exercise of power and the pursuit of an active policy in China. These responsibilities could have been discharged only if the United States had been willing to give large-scale economic and military assistance to China and, if necessary, to intervene with her armed forces to preserve the authority of a pro-American government in at least part of China. Since General Marshall based his policy on the axiom that American ground forces should never be used on the Chinese mainland and since he did not plan, after the failure of his mission, to give large-scale assistance to China, the United States shrank from any action which might have decisively changed the political conditions in China.

On July 17, 1948, Ambassador Stuart called on Generalissimo Chiang to urge him to reconcile his differences with other Nationalist leaders and to unite with them to save China from communism. After having reported his conversations with Generalissimo Chiang, the American ambassador told Secretary Marshall that he could not go further than giving his advice in trying to influence the political development in China. He explained that "any effort to urge him further than I have done would either have to imply much more American aid than is possible or would over-persuade him to relinquish his own judgment."[149] In October, 1948, Changchun, one of the most important cities in Manchuria, was lost to the Communists, and the authority of the government began to disintegrate very rapidly. Ambassa-

[148] *Ibid.*, p. 916.
[149] *Ibid.*, p. 786.

dor Stuart sought instructions on a number of hypothetical questions. One of them was:

> Would we advise the retirement of the Generalissimo in favor of Li Tsung-jen or some other national political leader with better prospects of forming a republican non-Communist government and of more effectively prosecuting the war against the Communist rebels?[150]

To this inquiry, Secretary Marshall replied:

> [T]he United States government cannot place itself in a position of advising the retirement of the Generalissimo or the appointment of any other Chinese as head of the Chinese Government. To offer such advice is to accept responsibility for developments arising from the acceptance thereof and inferentially to commit the United States Government to support the succeeding regime regardless of United States interests.[151]

7. Chiang's Threat To Go It Alone and To Ask for Soviet Help

In his dealings with the United States, Generalissimo Chiang acted on the unshakable conviction that China was indispensable to the United States and that he was indispensable to China. Against the background of the wartime policy of making China a great power and the principles of the Open Door, the passive American policy and American refusal to assume the responsibilities for Chinese affairs failed to make Chiang aware of the possibility of the United States leaving China to her fate. As a result, he felt confident enough to threaten to go it alone in his fight against the Communists and to come to an understanding with the Soviet Union when he hoped to exert pressure on the United States. Thus, the United States was confronted with a paradoxical situation as the military, economic, and political position of the Nationalist government rapidly deteriorated. On the one hand, most of the Nationalist officials and anti-Communist leaders showed an attitude of almost complete dependence on American assistance as the sole means of saving the regime.[152] On the other hand, the Generalissimo frequently proclaimed his determination not to be dependent on American aid. Ambassador Stuart reported on March 3, 1947:

> [T]he Generalissimo is not without hope that the United States will in due course come in some fashion and to some degree to the Government's assistance. There is no doubt he is now increasingly concerned about the rate of financial deterioration and the ability

[150] *Ibid.*, p. 285.
[151] *Ibid.*
[152] *Ibid.*, pp. 246, 255, 262, 275, 823, 831.

of the Communists to prolong the struggle and create havoc. However, he has made a point of telling Chinese who call upon him that China must stand on its own feet and face the future without American assistance.[153]

Toward the end of General Wedemeyer's mission to China, when it was apparent that unconditional American assistance would not be immediately forthcoming, Generalissimo Chiang proclaimed before the Central Executive Committee of the Kuomintang on September 9, 1947, that China would never again be dependent on the United States for assistance.[154]

To threaten to go it alone was only one aspect of Chiang's tactics. In trying to exert pressure on the United States, Nationalist officials employed the same technique that they had used during the Pacific war. When they were asking for large-scale American assistance, they played upon the American fear of a Soviet-dominated China just as they had exploited the American anxiety over a total collapse of Chinese resistance against Japan. When American assistance was not readily granted, they threatened to seek a rapprochement with the Soviet Union just as they had capitalized on American apprehension of a separate peace between China and Japan. Thus, immediately before the dispatch of the Wedemeyer mission to China, Nationalist officials stressed the material assistance given to the Chinese Communists by the Russians, the Russian aggressiveness in the border regions of China, and the probability of a Russian-dominated China unless large-scale American aid was granted China soon.[155]

Yet when General Wedemeyer's strong criticisms of the Nationalist government aroused their ire and when it was apparent that no large-scale American aid would immediately be given to China, Nationalist officials soon forgot their statements about Soviet ambitions and Soviet support for the Chinese Communists. Instead, they threatened to seek a rapprochement with the Soviet Union. On September 9, 1947, Generalissimo Chiang told the Central Executive Committee of the Kuomintang that China's policy toward Japan was in accord with that of the Soviet Union and that China would have to strengthen her ties with Russia while preserving her traditional friendship for the United States.[156] The Generalissimo's gentle reference to the Soviet Union was expanded upon by the "thinly-veiled suggestions from senior officials of the government obviously intended to convince the [American] Embassy that if aid is not soon forthcoming from

[153] *Ibid.*, p. 235.

[154] *Ibid.*, p. 262.

[155] *New York Times*, June 8, 14, 21, 25, 27, and July 5, 1947, pp. 12, 8, 9, 21, 14, and 4, respectively. See in particular Tillman Durdin's dispatch on the statements made on June 20, 1947, by Dr. Sun Fo, the president of the Legislative Yüan (*ibid.*, June 21, 1947, p. 9).

[156] *United States Relations with China*, p. 262.

the United States, it may be necessary for China to seek assistance from the Soviet Union."[157] Ambassador Stuart further reported that "it has even been suggested to the Ambassador that the Soviet Ambassador to China . . . might be asked to mediate the civil war and that he would be glad to accept."[158] The American ambassador concluded that such talk was "primarily for effect on the United States."[159]

Public statements made by Nationalist officials had an ominous tone. With obvious reference to the Wedemeyer mission, Mr. Ch'ên Li-fu, the leader of the C.C. clique, was reported to have said on September 2, 1947: "Man needs material help but if that help hurts his self-respect, he had better give up material help. If a man keeps his dignity, he can get help, *if not from one source then another*."[160] Dr. Sun Fo declared that the results of the Wedemeyer mission "will tell China whether it would be better for her to side with the United States or Russia."[161] He explained: "China in the struggle between the powers must adapt herself where it is most advantageous immediately and in the long run. Countries do not ally for the sake of sentiment. Each must consider her national interest."[162] In contrast to their success during the Pacific war, the threats of Chiang and other Nationalist officials failed to achieve their primary objective, which was to draw the United States into the Chinese civil war or, at least, to obtain large-scale economic and military assistance from the United States. Instead, this tactic had the opposite effect and made American officials even more reluctant to pursue an active policy in China.

8. Chiang's Policy of Rule or Ruin

Chiang's policy of rule or ruin was an important factor in his failure to counter successfully Mao's political strategy of isolating the "die-hards," winning over the "middle-of-the-road forces," and developing the "progressive forces." With his narrow outlook and his determination to monopolize all power regardless of consequences, the Generalissimo made it impossible for the Nationalist government under his control to survive on the mainland. With his political and diplomatic skill, he made it equally impossible for other political leaders to replace him. With his recalcitrance and maneuvering he succeeded in implanting a profound sense of despair in the minds of American officials. General Marshall time and again expressed the view that the problem of China was insoluble. According to Secretary of Navy James Forrestal, Secretary Marshall stated at a meeting

[157] Ambassador Stuart to Secretary Marshall, September 20, 1947, *ibid.*, p. 830.
[158] *Ibid.*
[159] *Ibid.*
[160] *New York Times*, September 2, 1947, p. 11. Emphasis added.
[161] *Ibid.*, September 17, 1947, p. 18.
[162] *Ibid.*

of the secretaries of State, War, and Navy on June 26, 1947, that the United States was confronted "by the dilemma created by the incompetence, inefficiency and stubbornness of the Central Government — qualities which made it very difficult to help them."[163] In explaining the difference between American policies in Greece and China, General Marshall stated that in Greece the United States exercised "quite an influence on the Greek Government" through her program of economic and military assistance while in China American effort brought little result.[164] When Marshall, one of the chief advocates of the *quid pro quo* policy during the Pacific war, was giving up that policy in 1947 and 1948, he was also approaching the point of writing China off as a lost cause. To Secretary of State Acheson, the only alternative to the actual policy pursued was "full-scale intervention in behalf of a government which had lost the confidence of its own troops and its own people." [165] This was precisely the alternative which Chiang's political and diplomatic maneuvers presented to the United States. Commenting on this situation, Ambassador Stuart cabled:

> [The] view is not infrequently expressed that he [Chiang] is best asset Communists have. It is ironical therefore that he refuses to turn over active direction of affairs as he has been repeatedly advised to do because this would be in his opinion tantamount to allowing Communists [to] overrun country. [The] issue is thus confused in his mind as apparently in case of many in United States as though American military aid to him were only alternative to complete Communist domination of China. [To maintain in power a man who has lost support of his own people] would arouse greater sympathy for [the Communist] cause and violent anti-American feeling.[166]

Generalissimo Chiang's hold on China also spoiled the case of the American champions of the Nationalist regime. Throughout the period 1946–49, the Chinese government could not make effective use of American assistance, would not wholeheartedly co-operate with the United States, did not accept American advice, and refused to carry out necessary reforms. Even after the military debacles in Manchuria and North China forced Generalissimo Chiang in January, 1949, to step down from the presidency and General Li Tsung-jên took over its formal duties, the Nationalist armies loyal to Chiang refused to take orders from General Li, and Chiang himself in his capacity as leader of the Kuomintang tried to manipulate the political situation from behind the scenes. The result of

---

[163] Millis, *op. cit.*, 285–86; see also *Military Situation in the Far East*, pp. 282, 284, 287, 887, 889.
[164] *Ibid.*, p. 663.
[165] Letter of Transmittal, in *United States Relations with China*, xv.
[166] *Ibid.*, p. 898.

all this was to make it impossible for General Li to defend any part of China.[167] Only purposeful intervention in Nationalist politics over a long period of time by the United States might have forced an early retirement of the Generalissimo and brought about the conditions necessary for successful armed intervention, efficient use of military aid, and effective implementation of American advice. Yet the proponents of Chiang's cause thought, as Marshall did, that there was no alternative to Chiang and drew diametrically opposite conclusions.[168] Thus, the United States debated her policy toward China along lines drawn by the Generalissimo himself.

C. An Examination of the Basic Assumption

When the China debacle was in the making, it became clear that the United States was acting on the assumption that American interests in China were not essential, that China was a liability to her ally, and that she could not possibly be a menace to the United States. In February, 1948, Secretary Marshall told the Committees on Foreign Affairs and Foreign Relations in executive session:

> China does not itself possess the raw material and industrial resources which would enable it to become a first-class military power within the foreseeable future. The country is at present in the midst of a social and political revolution. Until this revolution is completed — and it will take a long time — there is no prospect that sufficient stability and order can be established to permit China's early development into a strong state.[169]

In 1948 and 1949, expert opinions were overwhelmingly on the side of Secretary Marshall. It seemed inconceivable that China after eight years of war with Japan and an immensely destructive civil strife could be a menace to the United States. The task of rehabilitating the devastated country would be tremendous. Even assuming that the Chinese Communists gave the country a relatively efficient and honest government and brought the country some stability, the Chinese would still be confronted

---

[167] Just prior to his retirement, Generalissimo Chiang had shipped the gold and silver reserve of the government to Formosa, which was under the control of one of his chief lieutenants. Arms and ammunition destined for China under the United States aid program had also been diverted from Shanghai to Formosa (*New York Times*, February 15, 1949, pp. 1 and 12; Yin Shih, *Chiang Li kuan-shih yü Chung-kuo* ["The *Chiang-Li Relationship and China*"] [Hong Kong: Freedom Press, 1954], pp. 114–21; Liang Shêng-chün, *Chiang Li tou-chêng nei-mo* ["The Inside Story of the Struggle between Chiang and Li"] [Hong Kong: Union Asia Press, 1954]).

[168] Some of the American advocates of large-scale American assistance to Generalissimo Chiang openly expressed the view that instead of being a precondition for the effective use of American aid, reform in China was impossible before victory over the Communists was achieved. See *Foreign Policy for a Post-War Recovery Program*, p. 2042.

[169] *United States Relations with China*, p. 383.

with long-range problems of immense proportions. Basic among these would be the reconstruction of the national economy so as to insure a decent livelihood to the Chinese people and the acquisition from the nation's production of a surplus for the support of the government. Evaluating the ability of the new regime to meet these "minimum requirements," the American embassy told the State Department on November 8, 1948, that "here we may fairly question whether the new government has this capacity, and from all indications it would appear that the answer is in the negative."[170] Even if the new government passed this fundamental test of survival, an impoverished and unindustrialized China could not be a menace to the United States and would probably be a liability as an ally. James Reston reported on April 24, 1949: "For China, as the Administration sees it, is not a 'strategic springboard' but a 'strategic morass.' . . . It is a vast unconnected, poorly organized continent of a country, populated by undernourished, highly individualistic people."[171]

Rapid industrialization in China could not be achieved without a revolutionary change in the basic patterns of culture which for thousands of years had been those of an agricultural, family-centered civilization. Admittedly, these basic patterns had been in the process of breaking down in the last hundred years under the impact of the West. But many of the traditional attitudes lingered on, and the development of new social, economic, and political institutions had always lagged behind the demands of the times. In the light of the difficulties that had plagued the Nationalist government and obstructed American efforts to help China, it was easy to conclude that the Chinese Communists would not be able to overcome the cultural obstacles to rapid industrialization.[172] Furthermore, the Chinese Communists would approach the task of industrialization with their imported ideology. As communism clashed violently with the traditional culture of China at many points, it was natural to conclude that the ideological baggage would be an additional impediment to Communist success.[173]

[170] *Ibid.*, p. 918. James Reston reported in April, 1949, that the official information was that the Communists "do not have the administrative personnel to deal effectively with the economic problems of the country. Winning the war, the State Department feels, will be easy for the Communists; running the country will be extremely difficult. . ." (*New York Times*, April 24, 1949, Sec. 4, p. 3).

[171] *Ibid.*, April 24, 1949, Sec. 4, p. 3. Reporting on the views of Washington, C. L. Sulzberger wrote earlier that, "instead of gaining an area replete with the sinews of power, the U.S.S.R. is tending to acquire a major interest in a morass of misery where famine is a calendrical occurrence" (*ibid.*, February 18, 1948, p. 8).

[172] For a most interesting discussion of this question, see Marion J. Levy, Jr., "The Problem of Our Policy in China," *Virginia Quarterly Review*, Summer, 1949, pp. 348–64. Levy's analysis was eminently sensible. No one foresaw the efficiency with which the Chinese Communists swept aside these hindrances.

[173] The American embassy reported on November 8, 1948, that the basic problem of the new regime would "involve the organization of the economy in terms of a new economic and social philosophy which is altogether an import and has no real roots

In contrast to the United States, the Soviet Union, and Western Europe, China was believed to be poor in the natural resources necessary to a high level of industrial development. More important, China was so impoverished that she was considered to lack the ability to accumulate the capital needed for the immensely large initial outlay in any program of rapid industrialization. The Soviet Union was thought to be incapable of supplying China with the necessary amount of economic and technical aid.[174] Thus, the prospect for the rapid industrialization in China was so dim that there was no cause for alarm.[175] From this evaluation of Chinese and Russian economic capabilities flowed an exaggerated notion of the economic dependence of China on the United States. Some thought that the Chinese Communists would have to depend on trade with the United States for the success of their program of rapid industrialization and that their dependence on United States trade and the long tradition of American friendship might serve as a basis for a modus vivendi between the two nations.[176]

There is a kernel of truth in all these analyses. In spite of the amazing initial success of the Communist program of industrialization, the stress and strain stemming from the basic poverty of China and insufficient foreign aid have begun to show. The system of communes, based partly on practical considerations and partly on ideology, contributed to three consecutive years of agricultural crisis. The great leap forward has turned into the great retreat. There is certainly a limit to human endurance even for a people traditionally accustomed to hard work and thrift. Neverthe-

in the country," and that "deep and vital changes will be difficult without doing violence to the Communists' basic, underlying dogma" (*United States Relations with China*, p. 918).

C. L. Sulzberger reported in February that in Washington analysts were reasoning that the Communist program of revolutionizing China was "an issue of such fundamental and vast scale [that] no compromise is permissible: that the Kuomintang . . . had a revolutionary program. But it foundered upon the reef of Chinese realities" (*New York Times*, February 18, 1949, p. 8).

[174] George Kennan, then head of the Plans and Policies Division, told a round table conference held in October, 1949, to discuss China policy: "It has been my own thought that the Russians are perhaps the people least able to combine with the Chinese in developing the resources of China and producing anything which in a physical sense would be dangerous to us. . . . China is a competitor with Soviet Siberia for such things as the Soviet government may have to give — and I have heard Stalin express this same thought and I think with complete sincerity" (*Institute of Pacific Relations*, p. 1558).

[175] C. L. Sulzberger reported in February, 1949: "The State Department view — which is prevailing policy — is that the U.S.S.R., even if it establishes truly cozy relations with Mr. Mao, cannot provide the necessary cadre and assistance for the Chinese to face her fundamental problems and that the Communists will wear themselves out in the slough of misery, just as did General Chiang" (*New York Times*, February 18, 1949, p. 8).

[176] For example, Derk Bodde, *Peking Diary* (New York: Henry Schuman Co., 1950), p. 265.

less, what these analyses failed to take adequately into account was a new political factor: The ability of a totalitarian party, using all the levers of social control, to manipulate mass attitudes, to organize social life, and to tap surplus labor as a source of capital for the paramount purpose (until 1959, at least) of rapid industrialization. It is a new dimension which American specialists and officials, immersed in the liberal, democratic environment of a free society, naturally failed to gauge. The trend of the social sciences up to that time, which emphasized the determining effects of social forces on political actions, also left them unprepared to appraise correctly a situation in which the political actors deliberately and methodically sought to manipulate the social environment to achieve a preconceived purpose. This deterministic bias, which was a measure of the separation of knowledge from practice, led the West at once to overestimate the difficulties confronted by the Communists and to underestimate the ability of the free world to work out its own destiny. This was one of the basic sources of its complacency as well as its incapability to undertake a bold program to meet the Communist challenge.

These analyses of the difficulties confronting the Chinese Communists were not the only reasons for the absence of a sense of profound crisis. Because of America's traditional friendship for China and her support for Chinese nationalism, many Americans underestimated the hostility of the Chinese Communists toward the United States. Others overestimated the restraining effect of Chinese nationalism and pro-American sentiments in China on the Chinese Communists in their conduct of foreign affairs. Correspondingly, they failed to give adequate weight to ideology as a factor in determining the international behavior of the Chinese Communists. Rightly or wrongly, they expected a conflict between a Communist China and the Soviet Union to take the form of a clash between Chinese nationalism and Soviet domination. As C. L. Sulzberger reported in February, 1949, "Quite plainly the policy makers of the United States are counting upon the historic forces of Chinese nationalism to assert themselves as strongly under a Mao Tse-tung government vis-à-vis the U.S.S.R. as they did under a Chiang Kai-shek government vis-à-vis the United States."[177] Furthermore, the year 1948 witnessed not only the decisive military defeats sustained by the Nationalists but also the sudden rupture in the relationship between Tito and Stalin. This unexpected schism in the seemingly monolithic Communist bloc encouraged some Americans to anticipate the development of a Chinese Titoism, for which all the necessary conditions seemed to be present. As James Reston reported, "Some of our officials believe that Mao Tse-tung and the other Communist leaders will probably show signs of 'Titoism' once they are in control," though "the top officials" discouraged

[177] *New York Times*, February 15, 1949, p. 12.

this idea.[178] Since then, a dispute between the Soviet Union and Communist China has indeed developed. But the widening breach has assumed the form of a conflict over revolutionary strategy against the West, with Peking urging the adoption of a more militant policy toward the United States.

While Marshall's basic assumption of the unimportance of China has been refuted by events since Peking's intervention in the Korean War, it is a partisan view to attribute to him or other administration officials personal responsibility for the failure of American policy. His program was based on his estimate of the existing limits of American capability and on his judgment of what the American people were willing to do for China. There is every reason to believe that his calculations of these two constraints on American action were correct. The rapid demobilization of the armed forces, the unwillingness of the American people to send their boys to fight in China for a decadent government, and the reluctance to use force without both an unambiguous moral issue and an immediate threat to survival were conditions totally beyond his personal control. The large-scale military assistance proposed by the Republicans was, in Marshall's view, beyond the existing capability of the United States and would entail a serious risk of involving the United States in armed intervention. Armed intervention or any action entailing serious risks of developing into armed intervention could have been a feasible alternative only if the United States as a nation had followed a different approach in foreign affairs and had entertained a different set of assumptions and considerations. Even if there had been such a revolutionary change in thinking, no one can prove conclusively that armed intervention and active interference in Chinese politics could have maintained a non-Communist government in a part of mainland China, or that these actions would have served the national interest rather than courted an even more serious defeat. History may still prove that America's failure in China was a blessing in disguise.

Assuming that the objective constraints on the use of force in China could not have been changed, Marshall's policy of withdrawal from China in order to concentrate American efforts in Europe was the only feasible policy. Immediately after the statement, quoted above, in which Marshall disparaged the importance of China, he added:

[178] *Ibid.*, April 24, 1949, Sec. 4, p. 3. See also reports written by C. L. Sulzberger explaining why some officials expected the development of Titoism in China (*ibid.*, February 14, 1949, p. 10; February 15, 1949, p. 12; February 18, 1949, p. 8; February 21, 1949, p. 5).

In his letter of transmittal in the White Paper on China, Secretary of State Dean Acheson clearly showed that he did not subscribe to this view. He spoke of the Chinese Communists as a party serving the "interest of a foreign imperialism" (*United States Relations with China;* xvi–xvii).

On the side of American interests, we cannot afford, economically or militarily, to take over the continued failures of the present Chinese government to the dissipation of our strength in
more vital regions where we now have a reasonable opportunity
of successfully meeting or thwarting the Communist threat, that
is, the vital industrial area of Western Europe with its traditions
of free institutions.[179]

Marshall's program of establishing a coalition government in China was
a way to avoid military entanglement. It would have enabled the United
States to disengage gracefully from China, although it was not designed
to achieve such a purpose. It is not unlikely that the Chinese Communists
would, sooner or later, have won control of China under the settlement
indorsed by Marshall. But, to use the words of Professor John K. Fairbank, "It seems pretty plain that civil war brought Communist domination
in China more rapidly than the alternative of coalition could have done."[180]
The avoidable mistake which Marshall committed was that, after events
in China had proved the impossibility of a coalition and his mediation effort had collapsed, he failed either to find firm bipartisan support for his
policy of limiting American commitments to China or, failing that, to disclose all relevant information and make his policy a subject of public debate
at the earliest possible time. In 1947 and 1948, his policy and views, regardless of their intrinsic merits, would in all probability have been indorsed
by the American people. Unfortunately, he suppressed the Wedemeyer
report of September, 1947, for almost two years and did not take his case
to the American public at the appropriate time. His omissions led to a
breakdown of bipartisanship and enabled the critics of the administration
to charge it with sole responsibility for the China debacle.[181]

No matter what one's evaluation of Marshall's policy and his freedom of
action, there cannot be any doubt that Marshall's decision not to undertake
armed intervention and the related decision not to provide large-scale
military assistance and operational advice to Nationalist China constituted
the crucial element of his policy and exercised perceptible influence on its
other components. If one cannot demonstrate that armed intervention or
massive military assistance could have prevented a total Communist victory, one can at least conclude that the lack of immediate military capability to intervene was a decisive factor in the failure to sustain the Nationalist
government, an objective which Marshall sought to achieve. To the extent

[179] *Ibid.*, p. 383.
[180] John K. Fairbank, "America and the Chinese Revolution," *New Republic*, August 22, 1949, p. 13.
[181] For an able analysis of this point, see A. Bradford Westerfield, *Party Politics and
Foreign Policy* (New Haven, Conn.: Yale University Press, 1955), chaps. xii–xvi.

that this lack of military power was a product of the rapid demobilization after V-J Day, it was a function of the American people's inability to anticipate the postwar situation in China and to maintain the necessary capability to influence it. To the extent that the political and military developments in China were anticipated by individual officials, the lack of capability was a product of the nation's unwillingness to develop and use military power purposefully to achieve her objectives in China.

One may argue that even if she had been willing to use her armed forces in China, the United States, primarily a naval and air power, could not have done anything effective against the ground forces of the Soviet Union and the Chinese Communists. In other words, it was not merely the existing military capability but also the absolute limits of America's military potential or at least, to use the words of the White Paper, "the reasonable limits" of America's capabilities, which were the ineluctable condition of American policy since the end of the Pacific war. From this point of view, the present balance of power in the Far East, which rests on the confrontation between the ground forces of the Communist bloc on the continent and America's air and sea power based on the island perimeter, was an inevitable development. This line of argument, likewise, cannot be proved or disproved. But one wonders whether this estimate of America's military potential was not itself an expression of the unwillingness of the United States to achieve her political purposes in China by military power. If one directs one's attention beyond the postwar years to American policy toward the Far East since the dispatch of the Hay notes, one finds that its persistent and crucial feature was not the absolute limit set by America's military potential but the unwillingness or, at times, the inability of the United States to develop and use her military power purposefully to achieve her avowed political purpose. After all, in the twenties and thirties, the United States could have developed her immense potential naval power to uphold the Open Door principles against infringement by the island-empire of Japan. During the Pacific war, it was the military objective of securing the unconditional surrender of Japan which shaped political policy rather than the political objectives which guided military strategy. It seems unlikely that this persistent feature of failing to use force purposefully to achieve political objectives should suddenly have disappeared in the postwar years. Seen from this perspective, Marshall's China policy can be interpreted as a new manifestation, under a different set of circumstances, of a persistent feature of American policy and as one more link leading to the present balance of power in the Far East, which was foreshadowed by the abandonment in 1944 of any thought of waging a major campaign on the mainland of China.

In the last chapter, the examination of Marshall's China policy, in order to answer the question of Marshall's failure to achieve his objective of sustaining the Chinese government, was presented in a logical rather than a chronological order. In this and the next two chapters, Marshall's China policy and its continuation under Acheson are viewed in their natural, historical setting. The treatment follows, in the main, the conventional chronological order and will, it is hoped, clarify the question of why the United States did not disentangle herself completely and promptly from China after Marshall's mediation efforts had collapsed. The treatment of substantially the same subject matter first in terms of a logical structure and then in the form of a historical narrative will necessitate a certain amount of repetition. But this will facilitate analysis of the complex problems involved and give a more adequate explanation of why the United States rejected, on the one hand, armed intervention and massive military assistance and, on the other, complete and prompt withdrawal.

A. American Policy and the Foredoomed Settlement in China

1. The Impact of American Policy on Chinese Politics

Marshall arrived in China on December 20, 1945, carrying with him the elaborate program described at the beginning of the last chapter. To understand the impact of Marshall's program, it is necessary to recapitulate briefly the policies of the Kuomintang and the Communists in their political-military struggle. At this time, the Nationalist government enjoyed a five to one superiority in armed forces vis-à-vis the Communists. Thanks to the military assistance given by the United States in airlifting and transporting its troops to Japanese-occupied areas, it was able to re-establish its authority in the big cities and was in a position to reopen important lines of communication in North China. At the same time the position of the Chinese Communists was also strengthened by the extension of their control in the countryside of North China and, above all, by their acquisition of Japanese arms in Manchuria. But the military superiority still lay with the Nationalists. Therefore, Generalissimo Chiang pressed forward his military campaign to drive the Communists from important regions, while continuing to negotiate with them, partly with a view to satisfying the public clamor for peace and partly with the hope that under intensified military pressure the Communists might accept a settlement on his terms. On their part, the Communists countered the attacks by effectively cutting Nationalist lines of communication. At the same time, they demanded an unconditional cease-fire and a cessation of the movement of Nationalist troops into North China. The Nationalist government would agree to a cease-fire only on condition that communications between key points be restored first and that the Communists withdraw their troops from places along the railways.

In the political sphere, the Nationalist government insisted that the establishment of "unity of military command" i.e., integration of the Communist forces into a national army, was a precondition to the cessation of its military attacks and that it had to come before the inauguration of constitutional rule and a democratic regime. As the survival of the Chinese Communists depended on their possession of an autonomous army, their acceptance of the Nationalist demands would have meant political suicide. Thus, the Communists argued that the integration of the Communist forces into a national army could take place only after the establishment of a democratic coalition government and a constitutional regime. Since the narrow power base of the Kuomintang contrasted sharply with the popular support enjoyed by the Communists, the establishment of a genuinely democratic regime would have doomed the Nationalists to political defeat in the near future. The Kuomintang thus proposed to end its political tutelage and to inaugurate constitutional rule only in accordance with its own procedures and on its own terms, making certain that nothing really important would be changed.

To do this, it took steps to convene a National Assembly which had been elected in 1936 when the Kuomintang was the sole legal party. This constituent assembly would adopt a constitution, drafted by the Nationalist government, which provided for an all-powerful president, a weak legislative branch, and a highly centralized unitary government with very little power left to local governments. These features would guarantee the continued domination of the Kuomintang. In contrast, the Communists called for a conference of representatives from all parties and groups to discuss and to pave the way for the adoption of a constitution. This conference would terminate the one-party rule of the Kuomintang and become the source of a new legitimacy. As the Communists knew that they could not hope to capture the executive branch at once, they wanted to have a powerful legislature which would check the powers of a Nationalist cabinet. As they also knew that they could not dominate the central government immediately, they demanded large powers for the provinces and the popular election of provincial governors and other officials on the lower levels of the local governments, feeling that their grass roots support would give them control over important regions.

Maneuvering to gain a semblance of public support for their program to establish a constitutional rule, the Nationalists were not inflexibly opposed to the calling of a conference of all parties and groups, provided that this conference could take place under such political and military circumstances that it would give its stamp of approval to the Nationalist plan of convening the old National Assembly and of adopting a constitution which would enable them to perpetuate their dominance. When its military campaign was gaining momentum in October and November of 1945, the Nationalist government pressed for an early meeting of a Political Consultative Conference of all parties and groups. In contrast, the Communists at this particular time refused to name their delegates to the Conference, so as to avoid negotiating under military pressure; and they used their refusal to back up their demands for an unconditional cease-fire. The deadlock was complete. These impasses reflected the absence of principles shared by the two sides and showed the existence of basic conflicts of interest.[1] While it might have been possible to achieve a temporary modus vivendi on the basis of a division of zones of control or even to set up a coalition government or constitutional regime as a temporary arrangement to gain time, any attempt to achieve a permanent settlement within a constitutional framework was doomed to failure. But this was precisely what General Marshall set out to do.

[1] For the Communist views, see *Hsin-hua jih-pao*, editorial, December 21, 1945, as reprinted in *Hsin Chung-kuo ti shu-kuang* ["The Dawn of New China"] (Hsin-hua jih-pao, 1946), pp. 30–32; "Press Conference of Chou En-lai and General Yeh Chien-ying, Dec. 18, 1945," *ibid.*, pp. 35–41; "The Proposal of the Chinese Communist Delegation for an Unconditional Cease-fire," *ibid.*, pp. 42–43; "Chiang Kai-shek's Speech on New Years' Day and the Political Consultative Conference," editorial in the *Chieh-fang jih-pao*, January 7, 1946, as reprinted in *Chung-kuo wên-ti wên-hsien*, Hsiang Chün (ed.), ["Documents on the Problem of China] (Ta-chung ch'u-pan-shê, 1946), pp. 71–85.

For the Nationalist views, see "Generalissimo Chiang Kai-shek's Speech on New Year's Day," as reprinted in K'ang Tan, *Chung-kuo chih hsin-shêng* ["The New Birth of China"] (Hong Kong: Hsin-shêng Chung-kuo shê, 1948), pp. 163–72; editorial in the Central Daily News, January 17, 1946," as reprinted in Li Hsü (ed.), *Chêng-chih hsieh-shang hui-i chih chien-t'ao* ["An Appraisal of the Political Consultative Conference"] (Nanking: Shih-tai ch'u-pan-shê, 1946), pp. 102–3; editorial in the Central Daily News, January 26, 1946, in *ibid.*, pp. 113–14.

See also chap. viii above; Department of State, *United States Relations with China* (Washington, D.C.: Government Printing Office, 1949), pp. 107–12 (hereafter cited as *United States Relations with China*).

The events in the first three months after Marshall's appointment created the pleasant illusion that the seemingly immense power of the United States, reinforced by his own great prestige, might be able to break the deadlock. Soon after the announcement of the appointment of General Marshall, Wang Ping-nan, the Chinese Communist representative in Chungking, informed the American embassy on December 3 of Yenan's decision to participate in the Political Consultative Conference. The adoption by the Chinese Communists of this more co-operative attitude suggests that they were gravely concerned over the future of American policy. As Wang told the embassy, future developments in China depended even more on American policy than on the meeting of the Political Consultative Conference, and the Communists were eagerly awaiting the arrival of General Marshall and the clarification of the American position. In this conversation, the Communist representative also emphasized the independence of Yenan from Moscow.[2] On December 17, an official spokesman of the Central Committee of the Chinese Communist party in Yenan released a statement which welcomed the Truman declaration of December 15 and pledged its support for the American policy of obtaining a cessation of hostilities, convoking the Political Consultative Conference, terminating the party tutelage of the Kuomintang, and establishing a democratic and united China. He expressed the approval of the Chinese Communist party for the proposal to turn the Communist troops into "a component part of the armed forces of a democratic state."[3] He foresaw "prolonged resistance, misinterpretation and sabotage" on the part of the "anti-democratic" forces.[4] The Nationalist government also expressed its approval of the Truman declaration but, like the Communists, interpreted American policy in its own way.[5] On December 31, 1945, the government announced that the Generalissimo had decided that the Political Consultative Conference would convene at Chungking on January 10, 1946.

But there was also an undercurrent of intensification of the civil strife. In an important political broadcast on New Year's Day, Generalissimo Chiang reiterated his determination to convoke the National Assembly. He did not mention the Political Consultative Conference,[6] which, after President Truman's declaration of December 15 urging an immediate cease-fire and the broadening of the base of the Chinese government, might have had to meet under circumstances quite different from those in October and November, 1945. This significant omission on Chiang's part

[2] *Ibid.*, p. 111.
[3] "The Statement of the Spokesman for the Central Committee of the Chinese Communist Party, welcoming President Truman's Statement," December 17, 1945, as reprinted in *Hsin Chung-kuo ti shu-kuang*, pp. 18–19.
[4] *Ibid.*, p. 19.
[5] *New York Times,* December 16, 1945, p. 1.
[6] The text of the speech is printed in K'ang Tan, *op. cit.*, pp. 168–72.

and his program of convening the National Assembly called forth a harsh attack in the official Communist newspaper at Yenan.[7] Meanwhile, the government declared that it was making preparations to take over the province of Jehol, which was partly occupied by Soviet troops and partly by Chinese Communist forces. Nationalist troops were deployed for an attack. The Communists said they would resist and urged an end to the invasion of that province.[8]

2. The Military-Political Settlement of January and February

a. Marshall and the cease-fire agreement of January 10. — In spite of all difficulties, General Marshall succeeded in helping to construct an elaborate structure of agreements to end the internal conflict of China. This edifice consisted of three closely interrelated parts: the cease-fire agreement of January 10, 1946; a set of five resolutions passed by the Political Consultative Conference, meeting from January 10 to 31; and the military reorganization agreement of February 25.

In the formal and informal negotiations leading to the cease-fire, General Marshall exerted his influence to settle two disputes. In the first and more important, he acted decisively in support of the Nationalist position. On January 4, one day after General Wedemeyer had announced that the United States would transport additional Nationalist forces to Manchuria, General Marshall told Chou En-lai, the chief Communist representative, that the United States was committed to the movement of Nationalist troops to Manchuria. Chou then gave his agreement to the inclusion of an exception in the proposed cease-fire order, which permitted the movement of Nationalist troops into that important region. On the second and less important matter, General Marshall supported the Communists. On January 9, the Nationalist government unexpectedly demanded, as a precondition to issuing a cease-fire order, that its forces occupy Chihfeng and Tolun, strategic points in the provinces of Jehol and Chahar respectively. The Communists resolutely refused to accept this demand, arguing that these two places were deep in territory controlled by them since V-J Day. Marshall interceded on behalf of the Communists.[9]

[7] Editorial in *Chieh-fang jih-pao*, January 7, 1946, as reprinted in *Chung-kuo wên-ti wên-hsien*, pp. 71–86.

[8] *New York Times*, January 3, 1946, p. 1; January 5, 1946, p. 5; January 6, 1946, p. 28.

[9] For a contemporary report of General Marshall's role in settling this dispute, see Feng Tzŭ-chao, *Chung-kuo k'ang-chan shih* ["A History of China's War of Resistance against Japan"] (Shanghai: Chêng-chi shu-chü, 1946), p. 282. For an account of General Marshall's position on the question of Chihfeng, see Carsun Chang, *Third Force in China* (New York: Bookman Associates, 1952), p. 147.

The various dispatches appearing in American newspapers at the time corroborate

On January 10, the Nationalist government and the Chinese Communist party announced an unconditional and immediate cease-fire, with a provision for simultaneous restoration of communications.[10] With regard to Manchuria, it was stipulated in the minutes of the conferences published in the joint statement that the relevant provision in the Order for Cessation of Hostilities "does not prejudice movements of the forces of the National Army into or within Manchuria which are for the purpose of restoring Chinese sovereignty."[11] The agreement also provided for the immediate establishment of an executive headquarters to be composed of three commissioners: one representing the Nationalist government, one representing the Chinese Communist party, and one representing the United States, who was also to be the chairman. Its decisions were to be made by a unanimous vote.[12] Its function was to implement the Order for the Cessation of Hostilities. This was to be discharged by a number of "supervisory and reporting teams."[13] These field teams, consisting of Nationalist, Communist, and American members, were to be sent to areas of conflict or threatened conflict to halt or prevent hostilities.[14] The decision of a field team was to be made by a unanimous vote of its members. During the negotiations for a cease-fire, a committee had been set up consisting of General Marshall, one Nationalist, and one Communist, which was subsequently known as the Committee of Three.

   b. The Political Consultative Conference and the future political balance in China. — The announcement of the cease-fire furnished a favorable background for the Political Consultative Conference (the PCC), which met from January 10 to January 31. This conference was composed of eight

the statement made by the writer. In his memoirs, President Truman wrote that Marshall persuaded "Chiang Kai-shek to issue an order without reference to Jehol and Chahar" (Harry Truman, *Years of Trial and Hope* [Garden City, N.Y.: Doubleday & Co., 1956], p. 73).

   Largely following Freda Utley's account, Senator McCarthy magnified the importance of this episode out of all proportion. He listed it as one of Marshall's four actions in which the American general intervened on the side of the Communists in order to promote their interests (*Congressional Record,* CXVII, 82d Cong., 1st sess. [1951], 6581–82, 6587; Freda Utley. *The China Story* [Chicago: Henry Regnery Co., 1951], pp. 11–12). Senator McCarthy failed to mention Marshall's support for the Nationalist position on Manchuria. The *United States Relations with China* did not mention the Chihfeng episode.

[10] Press release on Order for Cessation of Hostilities, January 10, 1946, in *ibid.,* pp. 609-10. By another agreement, the cease-fire was to be implemented not later than three days after the proclamation of the cease-fire order on January 10. The truce came into effect on January 13.

[11] *Ibid.,* p. 610.

[12] *Ibid.,* and Agreement on Establishment of the Executive Headquarters, January 10, 1946, in *ibid.,* pp. 627–28. Mr. Walter S. Robertson, chargé d'affaires of the American embassy, was named the American commissioner.

[13] *Ibid.,* p. 628.

[14] Memorandum on Operations of the Executive Headquarters, *ibid.,* p. 630. By September, 1946, there were thirty-six teams (*ibid.,* p. 631).

delegates from the Kuomintang, seven from the Communist party, nine from the Democratic League, five from the Youth party, and nine representing the non-party people of the nation, with a total of thirty-eight members.[15] It was held amidst widespread popular desire to end the intermittent civil war which, coming after eight years of war against Japan, was causing immense suffering. Meeting not long after President Truman's statement calling for broadening the base of the government, it was an important link in the American policy of seeking a political settlement in China. Any party taking an intransigent and uncompromising stand would incur the onus of obstructing a peaceful solution of China's problems and risk the displeasure of both the Chinese people and the American government.

Under these circumstances, the conference adopted a political program unfavorable to the Kuomintang. With regard to the procedures leading to the adoption of a new constitution, the PCC resolutions envisaged a thorough reorganization of the government, pending the convocation of the National Assembly. The existing and actually impotent State Council of the Nationalist government was to be reconstituted into a multiparty body and to become "the supreme organ of the Government in charge of national affairs."[16] It was to have both supreme legislative and executive powers. There were to be forty state councilors, half of whom would be Kuomintang members and the other half members of other political parties or prominent social leaders. They were to be nominated by the parties concerned. Any resolution which involved a change in "administrative policy" had to be passed by a two-thirds vote of the state councilors present. This provision was subsequently interpreted to mean that any resolution modifying the PCC resolutions could be passed only by a two-thirds vote. Thus, any party which together with its allies had fourteen seats in the State Council could veto any revision of the PCC resolutions.[17] According to one source, an oral promise was given by Nationalist authorities to the Communist party and the Democratic League that they would have enough seats in the State Council to avail themselves of a veto.[18]

Pending the inauguration of the constitutional regime, the Executive Yüan, the highest executive organ under the State Council, was to be reorganized. This coalition government with a new State Council and a reorganized Executive Yüan was to rule China until the establishment of the constitutional regime. The National Assembly was to meet on May 5 to adopt a constitution, and elections under the new constitution were to

[15] Tuan-sheng Ch'ien, *The Government and Politics of China* (Cambridge, Mass.: Harvard University Press, 1950), p. 376; *United States Relations with China*, p. 111.
[16] Resolution on Government Organization adopted by the Political Consultative Conference, January, 1946, in *ibid.*, p. 610.
[17] *Ibid.*, pp. 139–40, 183–85.
[18] Ch'ien, *op. cit.*, p. 378.

take place six months after its adoption. As for the composition and procedures of the projected National Assembly, the PCC resolutions assured the Communists and their friends, in effect, of a veto on any proposals inconsistent with the PCC resolutions regarding the future constitution and designed by the Kuomintang to perpetuate its power.[19]

The principles laid down by the PCC to govern the revision of the draft constitution drawn up by the government embodied the quintessence of liberal thought in China. But given the nature of the Kuomintang and the Chinese Communist party and the relative strength of the parties in China, a government structure built on the basis of these constitutional principles would very probably have given the Communists a strong position from which they could have proceeded to capture control of the government in the not too distant future. These principles provided for a cabinet form of government with the Executive Yüan responsible to the Legislative Yüan, thus repudiating the Nationalist concept of a government with a strong presidency and an impotent legislature. In the proposed constitutional setup, the province was to be the highest unit of local government, with a provincial constitution. The powers of the province and the central government would be divided according to the principle of "a fair distribution of powers." The provincial governor was to be elected by the people of the province.[20]

These principles were further reinforced by provisions in the Resolution on the Program for Peaceful National Reconstruction which was to serve as a guide for the reorganized government pending the inauguration of constitutional rule. One provision stated that local self-government should be actively pushed forward and that popular elections beginning from the lower administrative units and gradually ascending to the highest unit should be carried out. Provincial, district, and municipal councils were to be established throughout the country at an early date, and district magistrates to be elected by the people.[21] Another provision in this resolution bore directly on the hotly disputed issue which had been the immediate cause of the spread of civil war after the Chiang-Mao negotiations in the late summer of 1945.[22] This stated that, in areas recovered from the Japanese where local government was under dispute, the status quo should be maintained until a settlement was made by a reorganized government, according to the provisions regarding popular election of local governing bodies and the "fair distribution of powers" between the central

[19] *Ibid.*, pp. 319–20. For details, see *United States Relations with China*, p. 619, and Feng Tsŭ-chao, *op. cit.*, pp. 314–21.

[20] Resolution on the Draft Constitution, adopted by the Political Consultative Conference, January, 1946, *United States Relations with China*, pp. 619–21.

[21] Resolution on the Program for Peaceful National Reconstruction, *ibid.*, p. 613.

[22] Chap. viii, above.

and local governments.[23] Given the popular support enjoyed by the Chinese Communists, these provisions would not only have legitimized their *de facto* control over local governments in wide areas of China but would also have enabled them to extend their control into other regions.

In his testimony in the MacArthur hearings, General Marshall emphasized that he had taken no part in formulating the political program laid down by the Political Consultative Conference. He denied that he had personally suggested the formation of a coalition government to the Nationalist government.[24] But coming after Ambassador Gauss's suggestion in 1944 of a "united council of all Chinese parties,"[25] General Hurley's approval of the five-point draft agreement providing for a coalition government,[26] and President Truman's official statement of December 15, Marshall's mission to China gave a new impetus to the movement in China toward the establishment of a coalition government. While the Political Consultative Conference was in session, Generalissimo Chiang asked General Marshall to persuade the Communists to accept the proposals of the government. Marshall countered this request by offering Chiang a draft program which, in President Truman's words, "would convert the Central Government from an agency of the Kuomintang (which it legally was), to a coalition, basing its existence on the national sovereignty of all China."[27] There is scarcely any doubt that Marshall approved of the works of the Political Consultative Conference. In a statement issued on January 7, 1947, after his departure from China, he said that "the agreements reached by the Political Consultative Conference a year ago were a liberal and forward-looking charter which then offered China a basis

[23] *United States Relations with China*, p. 617.

[24] Senate Committee on Armed Services and Committee on Foreign Relations, *Hearing on the Military Situation in the Far East*, 82d Cong., 1st sess. (1951), p. 549 (hereafter cited as *Military Situation in the Far East*).

[25] See chap. v, above.

[26] See chap. viii, above.

[27] Truman, *op.cit.*, p. 74. This draft also contained a bill of rights. In his testimony in the MacArthur hearings, General Marshall referred to this episode in the following words: "Our government had represented [*sic*] its interests in the development of a two-party government, and beyond that I did not touch the matter at all, except to furnish the Generalissimo confidentially our Bill of Rights and *a possible interim set-up* while they were reaching formal constitutional status. I think that was prepared by Dr. Fairchild, I think he is from Yale, who was out there. But that did not enter into their political adjustments in this matter" (*Military Situation in the Far East*, p. 549). Emphasis added. If Truman's account is accurate, then this "possible interim set-up" took the form of a coalition government. The significance of this vague phrase eluded Marshall's questioner, Senator Knowland.

The draft under discussion was prepared by Professor Knight Biggerstaff, now of Cornell University, at the request of Marshall and in accordance with his general views. Marshall himself was an active participant in the final revision of the draft before it was handed over to Chiang (Letter from Professor Knight Biggerstaff, September 10, 1962).

for peace and reconstruction."[28] It is no exaggeration to assert that in reaching these agreements the Chinese delegates to the conference looked after their own interests with one eye and cast a glance at General Marshall with the other. In any case, when the settlement was crumbling after July, Marshall became directly involved in political discussions with the two sides in an effort to resolve the disputes over the implementation of the resolutions adopted by the Political Consultative Conference.[29]

c. *Marshall's program for integrating Communist forces into a national army.* — The cease-fire agreement of January 10 and the political program adopted by the Political Consultative Conference were the first two major parts of the settlement between the Kuomintang and the Communists. The third part was an agreement of February 25 on the reorganization and the integration of the Communist forces into a national army. General Marshall took an active part in the negotiations leading to this agreement which he also signed in his capacity of "adviser."

The agreement provided for an army of sixty divisions, with fifty Nationalist divisions and ten Communist divisions. All units other than those provided for in the agreement would be demobilized. This agreement thus preserved the five to one superiority of the Nationalist forces vis-à-vis the Communist forces, while envisaging a deployment of these divisions which would give a fourteen to one superiority to the Nationalist forces in Manchuria, sole Nationalist occupation of Northwest China, and a five to one Nationalist superiority in Central China. The heaviest concentration of Communist forces was in North China, where the ratio was eleven to seven in favor of the Nationalists. This projected deployment would have effectively blocked off any direct link between the Soviet Union and the Communist divisions. The Communist divisions in North China would have been surrounded with overwhelming forces from three sides. This military plan, highly favorable to the Nationalists, would be put into effect simultaneously with the processes of broadening the base of the government and of establishing a constitutional regime. The simultaneous implementation of the political and military agreements represented a compromise between the Nationalist demand that priority be given to the integration of Communist forces into a national army and the initial Communist proposal giving priority to the democratization of the regime. It was a compromise suggested first by Chou En-lai, in his press conference on December 18, 1945, which, according to him, the Communists had been trying for some time to persuade the Nationalist government to accept.[30]

This political and military settlement was enthusiastically received by

[28] *United States Relations with China*, p. 688.

[29] *Ibid.*, pp. 182–85, and *Military Situation in the Far East*, pp. 549–50.

[30] "The Press Conference of Communist Delegates, Chou En-lai and Yeh Chien-ying," *Hsin Chung-kuo ti shu-kuang*, p. 40.

the Chinese people. The Communists were jubilant.[31] The right-wing Nationalists were openly critical.[32] General Marshall was apparently satisfied with the results of his endeavors. On February 25, President Truman instructed the Secretary of State to conduct the necessary negotiations with the Nationalist government for establishing a United States military advisory group in China with a maximum of one thousand officers and men.[33] On March 11, General Marshall left China for the United States to arrange a loan of $500,000,000 from the Export–Import Bank to China and to secure other aid in the form of shipping and sale of surplus property.[34] With President Truman's backing, he succeeded quickly in gaining the agreement of the various agencies in these matters. In April, he made a report to the Foreign Relations Committee of the Senate on his mission to China. He had the impression that he "was supported" by the committee though there was no formal expression of opinion.[35] Meanwhile, in China, General Wedemeyer set up at the instruction of General Marshall a military mission, which was established under the war powers of the President.[36] Wedemeyer also took steps to withdraw American troops from China. On April 2, he announced that the United States Army in the China theater would be disbanded and the marines would revert to the command of the navy.[37]

After General Marshall returned to China on April 18, the policies set in motion by him moved forward in the United States on their own momentum. In June, bills to provide military advice and assistance to China were introduced in the Senate and the House to give a statutory basis to the military mission.[38] In a hearing before the House Committee on Foreign Affairs on June 19, it was made clear that one of the objectives in granting American assistance to Chinese ground forces was to help China

[31] The Communists held a mass meeting in Yenan to celebrate the successful conclusion of the conference. Addressing the meeting, General Chu Teh urged the Communists to make every effort to implement the resolutions (*Hsin Chung-kuo ti shu-kuang*, pp. 90–94). See also the two editorials of the Communist *Hsin-hua jih-pao* on February 1 and February 2, 1946, as reprinted in *ibid.*, pp. 99–104.

[32] *Central Daily News*, January 17, 1946, editorial; January 25, 1946, editorial (both as reprinted in Li Hsü, *op. cit.*, pp. 102–05, 114–16); Yeh Ch'ing, "A General Appraisal of the Five Principal Resolutions," *ibid.*, pp. 173–209.

[33] *United States Relations with China*, p. 339.

[34] Walter Millis suggested that Marshall hoped that he could bring pressure on the disputing factions in China by his trip to the United States (Walter Millis, with Harvey C. Mansfield and Harold Stein, *Arms and the State* [New York: Twentieth Century Fund, 1958], p. 196).

[35] *Military Situation in the Far East*, pp. 569–70.

[36] *Ibid.*, p. 558; *United States Relations with China*, p. 346. The group was established on March 19, 1946.

[37] *New York Times*, April 2, 1946, p. 19.

[38] *Congressional Record*, XCII, 79th Cong., 2d sess. (1946), 6773, 6979; *United States Relations With China*, p. 340; Norman Palmer, "Marshall's Mission to China," *Current History*, September, 1951, p. 146.

implement the program of integrating the Nationalist and Communist armies.[39] Undersecretary of State Dean Acheson told the committee that General Marshall granted a Communist request that the integration of Communist forces with the other forces "be preceded by a brief period of United States training and by the supply of minimum quantities of equipment."[40] On June 27, the committee reported favorably on the bill. However, no action was taken by the Seventy-ninth Congress. The American army mission continued to depend for its existence on the President's war powers. But events in China developed so quickly in another direction that they left American policies far behind. Even while Marshall was in the United States, the military-political settlement was fast disintegrating.

B. The Breakdown of the Settlement

1. Negotiation, Truce, and War in the Policies of the Kuomintang and the Chinese Communist Party

The process of the breakdown of the settlement and the negotiations after Marshall's return to China formed one of the most intricate chapters of American policy in China and of Chinese history. In Secretary Acheson's words:

> They [the negotiations] are incredibly complex, as complex as only Chinese negotiations can become. One side makes a proposal; the other side says that they will accept one of those proposals, but have four qualifications on each of the others. Then the one making the proposals comes back and will accept certain of the qualifications but has qualifications on those. And after a while it becomes impossible to follow.[41]

It would be unprofitable to recount the details of these negotiations. But if one grasps firmly the fundamentally irreconcilable nature of the conflict and the diametrically opposed positions and policies of the two sides, one can readily delineate the strategies and tactics of the two antagonists which made the breakdown of the settlement inevitable. One can also state the critical issues for which no new solution could be found in spite of Marshall's tremendous efforts. Such a discussion would not only throw light on the general problem of negotiations between two irreconcilable

---

[39] General Marshall's telegram to the committee, June 18, 1946, as reprinted in House Committee on Foreign Affairs, *Assist China To Modernize Her Armed Forces*, 79th Cong., 2d sess. (1946; House Report 2361, to accompany H.R. 6795), pp. 2–3; *Military Situation in the Far East*, p. 602.

[40] Excerpts from Undersecretary of State Acheson's testimony which were read into the *Congressional Record* on May 15, 1951, by Mrs. Edith Nourse Rogers (*Congressional Record*, XCVII, 82d Cong., 1st sess. [1951], 5386). This brief period of training by American officers was specified as 60 to 90 days (*ibid.*, p. 5387).

[41] *Military Situation in the Far East*, p. 1866.

forces, it would also demonstrate the futility of trying to resolve such conflicts by an elaborate structure of formal agreements publicly committing the two sides to detailed terms of concessions and co-operation.

In retrospect, it seems clear that, to say the least, both sides had serious reservations about the possibility of reaching a lasting settlement. The agreements worked out in January and February with the help of General Marshall represented only a deceptive façade behind which each side maneuvered for a better political and military position and hid its own strategies and tactics. Toward the end of his mission, General Marshall was convinced that, to use the words of the United States White Paper of 1949, "the Generalissimo was certainly following a definite policy of force under cover of the protracted negotiations."[42] "In the past [General Marshall] had often felt that the National Government had desired American mediation as a shield for its military campaign."[43] There is no positive evidence that Generalissimo Chiang did not negotiate in good faith in January and February. But subsequent events also suggest that, to state it mildly, he had never ruled out further use of force as one alternative. From available evidence, one cannot determine with certainty whether Chiang's objective was the total elimination of the Communist forces by all-out civil war or was limited to driving them out of the important regions and putting pressure on them to accept a settlement on his terms. But even if his objective was a limited one, his practice of raising his demands and stepping up military attacks after every temporary victory contributed to the expansion of the scope of the fighting and ultimately led to all-out war.

On their part, the Communists never failed to take actions in the field to occupy new territory, to expand their armies, and to increase their influence. These actions were taken when they were clamoring for peace and were justified by them as measures to prepare themselves for a breakdown of the negotiations or a collapse of the settlement. In an article written in 1951 to commemorate the thirtieth anniversary of the Chinese Communist party, General Chu Teh made this point quite clear. According to him, the Chinese Communist party was confronted in 1945 and 1946, on the one hand, with an intense desire for peace on the part of the Chinese people and, on the other, with the determination to wage a civil war on the part of the Generalissimo, who had the support of the United States. Chu wrote:

> Under these circumstances, the Chinese Communist Party, on the one hand, raised resolutely the banners for peace, democracy and unity, and endeavored with the utmost efforts to lead the Chinese people in seeking a way to avoid war and to realize

[42] *United States Relations with China*, p. 90.
[43] *Ibid.*, p. 217.

peace. On the other hand, it mobilized the Party, and all the people and armies in the liberated areas and the people of the whole nation to make full preparations so that it could be in readiness to defeat Chiang Kai-shek's anti-popular and anti-revolutionary military attacks when he resolutely destroyed the peace.[44]

By promoting 'peace, democracy, and unity," the Communists sought to avoid a civil war which they might have lost and to obtain a settlement which would have facilitated the rapid expansion of their influence. By advocating a moderate political program, they endeavored to isolate Generalissimo Chiang and to deprive him further of popular support when he persisted in his attempt to suppress or defeat them by military means.[45] All the while, they took actions to increase their military power and to prepare for a renewal of the civil war. Their dual tactics made peace impossible.

During the whole period of the Marshall mission, the Communists consistently followed this two-pronged policy. After the establishment of the truce in January, the Central Committee repeatedly instructed the Communist cadres in various areas to regard troop training, production, and land reform as their three central tasks. On May 4, it issued a directive changing its policy of reducing rent and interest to that of confiscating the

[44]Chu Teh, "Chung-kuo jên-min tsen-yang chi-pai liao Mei-ti-kuo-chu-i wu-chuang ti Chiang Kai-shek fan-tung-pai" [How the Chinese People Defeated the American Imperialist-armed, Reactionary Clique of Chiang Kai-shek,"] as reprinted in *Chung-kuo Kung-chan-tang chêng-li san-shih chou-nien chuan-chi* ["Special Compilation Commemorating the Thirtieth Anniversary of the Founding of the Chinese Communist Party"], I (Canton: Jên-min ch'u-pan-shê, 1951), 9–10.

[45]General Chu wrote gleefully: "Thus, when American imperialism and Chiang's reactionary faction of the Kuomintang felt that they had completed their preparations for their anti-popular, anti-revolutionary, large-scale civil war, they had been isolated politically and lost the sympathy of the people of the whole nation." Chu also said that by fighting vigorously for peace, democracy, and unity, the Chinese Communists exposed Chiang's plots to fight a civil war and helped the Chinese people to dissipate their illusions about Chiang through their own experience (*ibid.*, p. 10).

See also Hu Chiao-mu, *Chung-kuo Kung-ch'an-tang ti san-shih nien* ["Thirty Years of the Chinese Communist Party"] (Peking: Jên-min ch'u-pan-shê, 1951), pp. 52–56, and Yeh Hu-shêng, *Hsien-tai Chung-kuo kê-ming shih-hua* ["A History of the Revolution in Contemporary China"] (Peking: Kai-ming shu-tien, 1951), pp. 112–14. For an able contemporary report of the policies of the Communists, see Tillman Durdin's dispatch in the *New York Times*, March 17, 1946, Sec. 4, p. 5. Cf. Lord Lindsay of Birker, "1921 and After," as reprinted in Senate Committee on the Judiciary, *Hearings on the Institute of Pacific Relations*, 82d Cong., 1st and 2d sess. (1951–52), p. 5385 (hereafter cited as *Institute of Pacific Relations*).

It is interesting to note that the *Selected Works* of Mao contain nothing on China's internal situation between December 15, 1945, and July 20, 1946. There are no directives, speeches, or commentaries written by Mao on the negotiations, the truce, the Political Consultative Conference, the agreement on military reorganization, the fighting in Manchuria, and the breakdown of the truce. Available evidence does not permit us even to speculate on the reasons for this omission.

lands of the landlords and distributing them among the peasants.[46] The significance of this directive was that the Communists now abandoned the land policy which they had adopted in 1937 in order to bring about a united front with the Kuomintang and that they reverted to a slightly different version of the policy which they had followed during the first civil war with the Kuomintang. This change in land policy was obviously a measure to mobilize the peasants for the local fighting that was going on in various places despite the truce and for a possible outbreak of all-out war. As Mao pointed out some months later, "The peasants stood with our Party and our army against the attacks of the Kuomintang troops" after the truce had broken down in July wherever the new land policy was carried out firmly and speedily.[47]

Given the profound reservations of both sides about the possibility of a lasting settlement, the collapse of the delicately balanced structure of agreements was inevitable. Soon after the agreements were reached, both sides maneuvered to gain a better position than the settlement granted them. As a result of these maneuvers, the political and military situation was constantly changing; the changed conditions were made the basis of new demands and new negotiations.[48] As the political agreements militated against the interests of the Kuomintang, the Nationalists took actions which cast grave doubts whether they would sincerely honor these agreements. As the provisions in the February agreement regarding the integration of Communist forces into a national army militated against the interests of the Chinese Communist party, the Communists did not take the necessary steps to implement them. In spite of the cease-fire order, both sides took military actions in the field while they were negotiating on unresolved or new issues. Each hoped that certain important cities or areas might be brought under its control so that it would be in a stronger position when the coalition government or the constitutional regime was set up or, alternatively, in a better military posture when the settlement collapsed.[49] Actions on the part of the Kuomintang in the political realm were given as justification for actions on the part of the Communists in the military sphere. Then the actions on the part of the Chinese Communists were in turn cited as reasons why the Nationalist government was forced to take certain military actions against the Communists and to compel the Communists to accept its terms by military pressure. In taking military action against the Communists, the Nationalists relied on their immediate military superiority and sought a quick victory. In refusing to accept a new

[46] Mao Tse-tung, *Selected Works*, IV (Peking: Foreign Languages Press, 1961) 116, 118, n. 4, 124 (hereafter cited as Mao, *Selected Works*, IV [Peking]).
[47] *Ibid.*, p. 116.
[48] *United States Relations with China*, pp. 134–64.
[49] *Military Situation in the Far East*, p. 1866.

set of terms under military pressure, the Communists counted on their ability to avoid decisive engagements, to prolong the war, and eventually to counterattack. Thus, the fighting was gradually expanded in scope until it became an all-out civil war.

2. The Miscarriage of the Political Program

The process of the collapse of the settlement and the futile negotiations to arrive at a new accord went through three phases, each with its central issues and each leaving unsolved problems to the next. In each of these phases, Generalissimo Chiang moved a step away from the settlement of January and February and toward his own conception of how to deal with the Communists. Likewise, the Communists became increasingly uncompromising in their attitude. During the first phase, the political program laid down by the Political Consultative Conference miscarried. As soon as the PCC adjourned and the military agreement was reached, successful implementation of the agreements became doubtful. There were indications of strong resentments against the resolutions of the conference on the part of powerful groups within the Kuomintang and of opposition by a powerful group of Nationalist generals to any reorganization of the armies which would threaten their interests. Incidents occurred in Chungking and elsewhere which aroused fears that irreconcilable elements in the Kuomintang might sabotage the program worked out by the conference.[50]

At this crucial moment in Chinese politics, a discussion in the United States of the future disposition of former Japanese islands in the Pacific elicited a broadcast from Moscow stating its claim on the Kurile Islands and southern Sakhalin on the basis of a secret agreement made at Yalta.[51] The Yalta Agreement was simultaneously released, on February 12, in the

---

[50] The most notable instance was "an attack by alleged Kuomintang plainclothes men in a mass meeting held at Chungking to celebrate the success of the PCC." Other instances were also given in the *United States Relations with China*, pp. 143–144, 151. Commenting on these actions, General Marshall wrote in his personal statement issued on January 7, 1947: "They [the dyed-in-the-wool Communists] completely distrust the leaders of the Kuomintang and appeared convinced that every Government proposal is designed to crush the Chinese Communist Party. I must say that the quite evidently inspired mob actions of last February and March, some within a few blocks of where I was then engaged in completing negotiations, gave the Communists good excuse for such suspicions" (*ibid.*, p. 687).

[51] Following a public debate on the question of trusteeship for Pacific bases acquired by the United States, a reporter asked Undersecretary of State Acheson in a news conference about "a secret agreement" at Yalta which gave the Soviet Union possession of the Kuriles. Mr. Acheson replied that the Yalta decision on the subject had been concerned with Soviet occupation of the Kuriles and was not a final territorial decision (*New York Times*, January 23, 1946, p. 10). Acheson's interpretation was disputed by this broadcast from Moscow (*ibid.*, January 27, 1946, p. 19). In his news conference on January 29, Secretary of State Byrnes revealed that the Yalta Agreement had referred to Dairen and Port Arthur as well as the Kuriles and the southern half of Sakhalin. On January 31, President Truman told reporters that the Yalta Agreement would

United States, the Soviet Union, and Great Britain.[52] The publication of the agreement at this time had an unfortunate effect in China. It strengthened the hands of the Nationalist opponents of the Kuomintang-Communist accord, for they were now in a better position to charge that the United States had been sacrificing China's interests to appease the Soviet Union and her Chinese agents by signing the Yalta Agreement and by sponsoring the recent settlement with the Chinese Communists.[53] Their argument was further strengthened by the strained relations with the Soviet Union as a result of Soviet demands for a share of control over Manchurian industries and delay in withdrawing the Red Army from Manchuria after the agreed deadline of February 3. In late February, anti-Soviet student demonstrations, instigated by Ch'ên Li-fu, the leader of the right-wing C.C. clique, broke out in major cities in China.[54]

Against this background, the Central Executive Committee of the Kuomintang met from March 1 to March 17 to pass upon the PCC resolutions. In the meeting, members of the C.C. clique vigorously attacked those responsible for the conduct of Sino-Soviet negotiations in Manchuria.[55] The PCC resolution on the draft constitution was heatedly debated, with many speakers strongly advocating the presidential system and opposing the grant of a high degree of autonomy to the provinces.[56] The aim of these and other moves was to unseat or discredit the moderates of the Kuomintang who were attempting to work out an economic agreement with the Soviet Union in Manchuria and who, with Marshall's help, had negotiated the settlement with the Communists.[57] Although in the end the Central Executive Committee "ratified unanimously" all PCC agreements, it was clear that influential leaders in the Kuomintang wished to revise the PCC resolution on the draft constitution in order to make it conform with the concept of the "Quintuple-Power Constitution" and the Three Principles of the People of which the Kuomintang itself was the authorative interpreter.[58]

be made public if the Soviet Union and Great Britain had no objection (*Department of State Bulletin*, February 10, 1946, pp. 189–90).

[52] *New York Times*, February 12, 1946 p. 10; *Department of State Bulletin*, February 24, 1946, pp. 282–83.

[53] *New York Times*, February 15, 1946, p. 8.

[54] Chap. viii, above.

[55] Chang, *op. cit.*, p. 168; *New York Times*, February 23, 1946, p. 4.

[56] *United States Relations with China*, p. 634. The opposition to the grant of a high degree of autonomy to the provinces took the form of a demand that "provinces should not have their own constitutions," as provided by the PCC resolutions, and the "federalism should be discarded" (*ibid.*, and *China Handbook, 1937–1945* [New York: Macmillan Co., 1947], pp. 760–64).

[57] *New York Times*, March 16, 1946, p. 6.

[58] *United States Relations with China*, p. 144. See also the news release of the official Chinese News Service and the Manifesto of the Central Executive Committee of the Kuomintang, *ibid.*, pp. 634–39, and excerpts from Chiang's speech before the People's Political Council, *China Handbook, 1937–1945*, Supplement for 1946, pp. 760–64.

The Chinese Communist party and the Democratic League countered with the demand that any proposed revisions have the agreement of all parties and that the Kuomintang commit itself to the implementation of the revised PCC program. Meanwhile, they refused to nominate members to participate in a reorganized government. The Chinese Communist party postponed a March 31 meeting of its Central Committee which had been scheduled for the purpose of ratifying the PCC resolutions. The Communists also refused to submit a complete list of their military units as required by the military agreement of February 25. Toward the end of April, the discussions on political matters reached a complete deadlock.[59] It was also at this time that the fighting in Manchuria was moving toward a climax. So long as the issues in Manchuria remained unresolved, there was no prospect that any agreement on political matters could be reached.[60] Thus, the PCC plans to set up a transitional coalition government, to prepare a revised draft constitution, and to convoke the National Assembly on May 5 for the purpose of adopting a new constitution miscarried.[61]

3. The Crisis in Manchuria

The second phase of the breakdown of the settlement overlapped the first and its main issue was the crisis in Manchuria. The cease-fire agreement of January 10, 1946, granted the Nationalist government the right to move its troops into Manchuria for the purpose of restoring Chinese sovereignty as the Soviet troops left. There was a separate provision for the cessation of hostilities which, according to American interpretation, was applicable to Manchuria as well as to other regions of China.[62] On this basis, General Marshall urged the Nationalist government and the Communists to agree to the dispatch into Manchuria of tripartite field teams in order to supervise the truce and to prevent further conflicts. Marshall's proposal met with the approval of the Communists but was adamantly opposed by the government. In the words of the White Paper, "At this stage the National Government seemed determined to incur no restraints on its freedom of action in Manchuria and appeared bent on a policy of complete military occupation of the area and elimination of the Chinese Communist forces if they were encountered." [63] On March 11, the day of his departure for Washing-

[59] United States Relations with China, p. 148.

[60] Chang, op. cit., p. 156; Ch'ien, op. cit., pp. 379–80.

[61] According to the minor parties, it was agreed on April 24 by all sides concerned that the convocation of the National Assembly would be postponed and that a new date would be decided by discussion among all parties (United States Relations with China, p. 197).

[62] Ibid., p. 145.

[63] Ibid., p. 146. Testifying in the MacArthur hearings, Marshall stated that the Manchurian crisis was "precipitated largely by the manner in which the Nationalist troop commander proceeded in the case." He said in another context that "he [the com-

ton, General Marshall finally succeeded in persuading Generalissimo Chiang to agree to entry of the field teams into Manchuria. But the authority granted them was not sufficiently broad to bring about a cessation of hostilities. Their activities were also hampered by Nationalist obstructions.[64] Thus, fighting in Manchuria was never effectively stopped.

This already confused situation was further complicated by the withdrawal of Soviet troops which began on April 6. Soviet evacuation of Manchuria left a vacuum which both sides tried to fill. The Nationalist forces pushed forward, not only to take over cities and lines of communication from Soviet troops, but also to establish military control in rural areas occupied by the Communists. On their part, the Chinese Communist forces also rapidly expanded their control in Manchuria, for the Soviet troops were withdrawn in such a way as to facilitate their taking over the evacuated areas. On April 18, the Communist forces captured Changchun which had been garrisoned by the Nationalist forces for several months. The new confidence acquired by the Communists as a result of this development was evidenced by their demand for a revision of the ratio of military strength in Manchuria from the stipulated one Communist division to fourteen Nationalist divisions, to five Communist divisions for fourteen divisions of Nationalist forces.[65] Earlier, they had demanded joint control of Manchuria. They claimed to have 300,000 troops there.[66]

The Communist capture of Changchun was a flagrant violation of the cease-fire agreement.[67] It gave Generalissimo Chiang the needed justification to launch an all-out attack in Manchuria to defeat the Communists. After a month of hard fighting, the Nationalist forces with the American-trained New First and New Sixth Armies as their spearhead defeated the Communist troops and captured the strategic city of Ssŭpingchieh on May 19. Outflanked, outfought, and outnumbered, the Communists suddenly withdrew from Changchun.[68] Flushed with victory, the Nationalist forces disregarded all restraints and pushed toward Kirin and Harbin.

General Marshall made a valiant attempt to stop the fighting in Man-

mander of the Nationalist forces in Manchuria] had needlessly endangered his command and had conducted operations in the hinterland which were extermination, an effort to exterminate all Communists in that region, and they retaliated, of course, and very effectively" (*Military Situation in the Far East*, pp. 543, 544).

[64] *United States Relations with China*, p. 197.

[65] *Ibid.*, pp. 151–54.

[66] *New York Times*, February 16, 1946, p. 1.

[67] *United States Relations with China*, p. 159; Everett D. Hawkins, "War and Peace in Manchuria," *Far Eastern Survey*, January 29, 1947, pp. 18–20. General Marshall thought that this attack on Nationalist forces in Changchun was partly in retaliation for Nationalist assaults in Manchuria (*Military Situation in the Far East*, p. 543).

[68] It cannot be determined from available records whether Chou En-lai's acceptance of Marshall's proposal to evacuate Changchun played a part in the planned withdrawal by the Communists from that city. See pp. 420–21, below.

churia as soon as he came back to China from the United States on April 18, the day the Communists captured Changchun. He endeavored to persuade the Communists to evacuate Changchun voluntarily and to persuade Generalissimo Chiang to halt the advance of the Nationalist forces. His plan envisaged the establishment of an advance echelon of the Executive Headquarters at that city to stop the fighting and to enable the two sides to begin new negotiations. The city was to be turned over to the government within a maximum time of six months. After the Nationalist forces had captured Ssǔpingchieh, Generalissimo Chiang expressed agreement with Marshall's view that the government forces should not at this time occupy Changchun by force. He informed Marshall of his fear that his military commanders in Manchuria were advancing toward that city and said that he was leaving for Mukden to keep control of the situation. On the day he left Chungking, his forces entered Changchun. In spite of both his statements to Marshall and Marshall's new appeals by radio, Generalissimo Chiang took no action to stop the further advance of his troops, which were now pushing on to Harbin.[69] On the contrary, his presence in Mukden at the time of the capture of Changchun and his pronouncements issued in Mukden made it appear that his journey was timed to coincide with a previously planned military triumph. His use of Marshall's official plane for his flight to Manchuria conveyed the impression of Marshall's close connection with the trip.

Worst of all, Marshall, back in Chungking and taking Chiang's words at their face value, succeeded at precisely the same time in persuading Chou En-lai to agree to a halt in the fighting in Manchuria and to a voluntary evacuation of Changchun in return for a cessation of further advance of Nationalist forces.[70] Commenting on this series of events, the White Paper concluded:

> The fact that just as an agreement seemed to be on the verge of being reached the Generalissimo remained absent in Mukden and Peiping for a considerable period while his armies exploited their successful action south of Changchun aroused great suspicion against his good faith and particularly against the impartiality of General Marshall's attitude, since General Marshall had advanced proposals to the Chinese Communists for Communist evacuation

[69] In his memoirs, Chiang wrote: "General Tu [commander of the Nationalist forces] moved up from Ssupingkai to Changchun on May 23. Government troops *were ordered* to push on along the Chinese Changchun Railway with Harbin as their target. . ." (Chiang Kai-shek, *Soviet Russia in China* [New York: Farrar, Straus & Cudahy, 1957], p. 166. Emphasis added). Generalissimo Chiang apparently changed his mind after his arrival in Mukden and decided to push on to Harbin in an attempt to exploit his victory. All reports from the front which he received agreed that the Communists would not be able to fight after the recent defeat (*ibid.*, pp. 166–67).

[70] *United States Relations with China*, pp. 155, 159.

of Changchun and the cessation of further advances by National Government troops which the Communists had accepted.[71]

There began at this time violent Communist propaganda attacks against the alleged support given by General Marshall to the Nationalists in the fighting. The Manchurian crisis temporarily subsided when General Marshall finally succeeded in persuading Chiang and the Communists to issue, on June 6, an order halting advances, attacks, or pursuits by their troops in Manchuria for a period of fifteen days. This truce was later extended to June 30.[72]

4. The Process of Total Collapse

a. The impasse in the negotiations in June. — In the third phase of the breakdown of the settlement, fighting spread throughout China and the country drifted toward all-out civil war while negotiations undertaken with General Marshall as mediator ran into one impasse after another. This third phase began with the period of truce in Manchuria from June 7 to June 30. During this uneasy truce, Generalissimo Chiang presented the Chinese Communists with a series of stringent terms for a settlement with time limits varying from ten to seventy-five days attached to many of these demands.[73] These terms were presented to the Communists against the background of the smashing victory of the Nationalist armies in Manchuria in May. The truce in Manchuria was one of limited duration, and the original cease-fire agreement of January 10 was of doubtful effectiveness and validity. Sporadic but violent fighting took place in various localities, particularly in North China.[74] The freely expressed preference of some Nationalist leaders for a policy of force and their con-

[71] *Ibid.*, p. 159.

[72] Marshall's success in obtaining a truce was considered by Senator McCarthy as the second of Marshall's four interventions on the side of the Communists (*Congressional Record*, XLVII, 82d Cong., 1st sess. [1951], 6587).

Generalissimo Chiang also attributed immense significance to this cease-fire. He wrote in his memoirs: "The second cease-fire order turned out to be the beginning of the Government forces' debacle in Manchuria. If· at the time Government pursuit units near Shuangcheng, which is less than 100 kilometers from Harbin, had pressed on toward that city of strategic importance on the Chinese Changchun Railway, Communist remnants in northern Manchuria would have been liquidated and the situation throughout Manchuria stabilized. If the Chinese Communists were driven out of their foothold in northern Manchuria, Soviet Russia would have found no way to send them any more supplies and a fundamental solution to the problem of Manchuria would have been at hand. The subsequent defeat of Government troops in Manchuria in the winter of 1948 was largely due to the second cease-fire" (Chiang, *op. cit.*, p. 168).

Lt. Colonel Robert R. Rigg called the truce "the turning point not only of the Manchurian campaign but of the entire civil war" (*Red China's Fighting Hordes* [Harrisburg Pa.: Military Service Publishing Company, 1951], p. 254).

[73] *United States Relations with China*, pp. 160–61, 165.

[74] *Ibid.*, p. 159.

fidence in a quick victory [75] forcefully reminded the Communists of the possibility of Generalissimo Chiang's launching an all-out attack to enforce his demands.

Generally speaking, in the negotiations during this period the Communists gave the highest priority to the objective of obtaining a cessation of hostilities and an extension of the Manchurian truce, because the short-term military superiority rested with the Nationalists. Their desire to stop the sporadic fighting and to ward off Nationalist military pressure became stronger than their suspicion of American motives. They reversed their position and agreed to the Nationalist demand that the deciding vote be given to Americans on the field teams and in Executive Headquarters regarding matters pertaining to the procedures governing cessation of hostilities.[76] They demanded the issuance of a new order for the termination of hostilities in Manchuria and China proper prior to negotiation on other issues. They made proposals for strengthening the authority of the field teams. They agreed to a formal discussion of the central issue of redistribution of troops in North and Central China after the Generalissimo extended the truce in Manchuria to the end of June.[77]

On the substantive questions, they proposed at first the restoration of the status quo in China proper as of January 13, in accordance with the order for the cessation of hostilities of January 10, and the restoration of original positions in Manchuria as of June 7.[78] This proposal would have worked out to their advantage as they had been much less successful in their military operations than the Nationalists since the first truce had been declared. Later, with new attacks by the Nationalist forces looming on the horizon, they agreed to withdraw their troops under certain conditions from some of the areas claimed by the government and to reduce their forces in others. But they insisted that the Nationalist forces refrain from occupying the area which they would evacuate in accordance with agreements to be reached and during the period of army reorganization. They also demanded that the existing Communist local governments in evacuated areas be maintained.[79] Throughout the negotiations, they expressed concern over the fact that, while they made concessions on military matters, they did not know what the attitude of the government would be later in regard to political questions.[80]

[75] *Ibid.*, p. 161.
[76] *Ibid.* The proposal to give the American member of a field team the deciding vote was first made by the American branch of the Executive Headquarters. In May, the government adopted this proposal as one of its terms presented to the Communists (*ibid.*, pp. 154–55, 630).
[77] *Ibid.*, p. 164.
[78] *Ibid.*, p. 160.
[79] *Ibid.*, pp. 165–66.
[80] *Ibid.*, pp. 163–64.

To break this impasse, General Marshall prepared a draft proposal. Since he was anxious to prevent the renewal of large-scale fighting which would, he correctly predicted, lead to the collapse of the Nationalist government, Marshall's proposal accepted the basic position of the Communists while favoring the Nationalists in matters of detail. This document provided for the restoration of the status quo in China proper as of January 13 and in Manchuria as of June 7, except where specific exceptions were made.[81] It demanded that the Communists concentrate their forces in specified localities, but asked the Nationalist troops not to move into areas in China proper to be evacuated by the Communists. On their part, the Communists were asked not to station their troops in some of the areas which Generalissimo Chiang wanted the Communists to evacuate.[82] The existing local governments in the evacuated areas were to be maintained.[83]

The Generalissimo found fault with many points of Marshall's draft proposal. In particular he insisted on a change in the civil administration in northern Kiangsu.[84] The Communists were more amenable to Marshall's persuasion. After some discussions with Marshall, Chou En-lai said that he was prepared to consider any formula except that involving a change in the civil administration in northern Kiangsu.[85]

b. Marshall's failure to dissuade Chiang from his policy of force. — Thus the status of local governments, particularly those in northern Kiangsu, remained the only specific issue of any importance to cause a deadlock. But in sharp contrast to his remarkable success in working out a structure of sweeping agreements in January and February, General Marshall failed in June and July to produce a compromise acceptable to both sides. The reasons for this change in Marshall's effectiveness as a mediator are not hard to discover. At this time, Marshall's words carried little weight with Generalissimo Chiang and his advice was frequently rejected. For the Nationalists were now much less dependent on his help in fighting a civil war on a large scale. After the agreements in January and February had been completed, the United States had transported sizable Nationalist forces to Manchuria and North China.[86] This assistance had been rendered

[81] *Ibid.*, p. 167.

[82] *Ibid.*, pp. 166–67. An annex to Marshall's draft proposal provided that the Communist troops would not be garrisoned or concentrated within any of the following areas: all of Anhwei province; Kiangsu, south of the latitude of Hwaian (after an unspecified date) and south of the Lunghai railroad (after an unspecified date); specific points in Shantung province; Chahar, south of the latitude of Kalgan; Jehol south of the latitude of Chengte and Chengte itself; Hupeh-Hunan and all provinces in Manchuria except five northern ones (*ibid.*, p. 646).

[83] *Ibid.*, p. 167.

[84] *Ibid.*

[85] *Ibid.*

[86] In May, General Marshall explained to Chou En-lai that "when the United States had completed the movement of seven National Government armies into Manchuria

to the Nationalists in pursuance of the policy of supporting them to re-establish their authority as far as possible, particularly in Manchuria. Yet once the Nationalist military leaders felt strong enough in Manchuria and North China to defeat the Communists, they paid less heed to Marshall's advice. They were fully confident of an early victory over the Communists. If they had any apprehensions about fighting a long and losing war, these misgivings were offset by the evident belief, to use Marshall's words, that "they can drag along the United States while carrying out their campaign of force."[87] At this critical juncture, American policy seemed to be self-contradictory and vacillating. While General Marshall expressed to Generalissimo Chiang his opposition to the latter's plans, the American government extended lend-lease to China under the terms of the new military aid agreement of June 28, 1946.[88] A lend-lease "pipeline" credit from the United States of $51.7 million was provided for China while lend-lease to other countries was terminated on June 30.[89]

It is clear that sometime in the late spring or early summer Generalissimo Chiang decided to pursue a policy of force in dealing with the Communists, despite the opposition of General Marshall. The Generalissimo's mood at this time was vividly revealed in a passage in his memoirs. After having explained that he rejected "Stalin's second invitation" tendered to him on May 6 to visit Moscow because he was determined "not to follow the Russian Communists' consistent strategy toward China, i.e., cooperation between Kuomintang and the Chinese Communist Party, the joint establishment of a coalition government and complete dependence on Russia,"[90] he wrote:

> A hidden international current was already lashing at Sino-American relations, and China was already being isolated. It was no longer possible for China and the United States to work out a joint policy toward Soviet Russia on the basis of our common interests. Consequently the only thing we could do was to disregard what attitude and policy the Western nations might or might not adopt toward us, and to be prepared, in consonance with our own independent policy, to go it alone, if necessary, in combatting Soviet aggression to the bitter end.[91]

which it was committed to transport to that area, a total of 228,000 Government troops would have been moved by American facilities" (*ibid.*, pp. 151–52).

[87] *Ibid.*, p. 192.

[88] *Ibid.*, p. 969.

[89] *Ibid.*, pp. 363, 969.

[90] Chiang, *op. cit.*, p. 148. There is nothing in the records published by the American government to support Chiang's report of Stalin's invitations to him to visit Moscow.

[91] *Ibid.*, p. 149. When Chiang wrote of "combatting Soviet *aggression*," he was obviously referring to what many people would now call "indirect aggression" by the Soviet Union with the Chinese Communists as the instrument. When he spoke of a

Various items of information scattered here and there in the White Paper show beyond any doubt that by the end of June, Generalissimo Chiang had made up his mind to use force to drive the Chinese Communists from the strategic areas in China proper and to compel them by military pressure to accept his terms for a new settlement. A remark made by General Marshall to the Generalissimo on October 4 showed that Marshall had opposed at the end of June "the whole procedure in prospect for July and August" and that Chiang had assured Marshall that "there would be only local fighting in China proper and no fighting in Manchuria."[92] The Nationalist leader also said confidently to the American general: "Given time, the ripe apple will fall into our laps."[93] At this time, Nationalist military leaders expressed the view that Kiangsu province could be cleared of Communist forces within two months and that the Communists "could be brought to terms from a military standpoint within three months."[94] On June 30, General Marshall pointed out to the Generalissimo that statements issued by Nationalist military leaders indicated that "the Government was washing its hands of any democratic procedure and was pursuing a dictatorial policy of military force."[95] Marshall reminded Chiang of the possibility of violent military ruptures due to "the strong desire of Government military leaders to *settle matters by force for which the National Government plans were complete* and fairly well-known to the Communist Party."[96] In early July, Generalissimo Chiang told Marshall that "it was first necessary to deal harshly with the Communists, and later, after two or three months, to adopt a generous attitude."[97] He also said that "if General Marshall were patient, the Communists would appeal for a settlement and would be willing to make the compromises necessary for a settlement."[98]

"joint policy toward Soviet Russia," he was thinking of a joint policy toward Soviet Russia and the Chinese Communists whom he considered as nothing more than Soviet agents. At this time, Soviet troops had already completed their withdrawal from Manchuria, and there was no question of "Soviet aggression" in the literal sense. The controversy between the United States and China was not so much over the problem of a "joint policy toward Soviet Russia" as over a joint policy toward the Chinese Communists.

[92] *United States Relations with China*, p. 191. The quotations are taken from a paraphrase of a conversation between Marshall and Chiang as reproduced in the White Paper. Testifying in the MacArthur hearings, General Marshall said: "The general effort of the National Government to destroy the power of the Communist regime by military action had its beginnings in June [1946]" (*Military Situation in the Far East*, p. 659).

[93] *United States Relations with China*, p. 214. This statement by Chiang was given as a direct quotation in the White Paper.

[94] *Ibid.*, p. 216. This quotation is taken from the paraphrase of a talk between Marshall and Chiang on December 27, as given in the White Paper.

[95] *Ibid.*, p. 169. This and the following three quotations appeared in the White Paper as paraphrases of records of talks between Chiang and Marshall.

[96] *Ibid.* Emphasis added.

[97] *Ibid.*, p. 197.

[98] *Ibid.*, p. 176.

General Marshall's endeavors to find a new settlement were also frustrated by Communist policies and tactics. The Communists' expressed attitudes toward the United States at this time seemed at first glance to be contradictory but were complementary to each other. On the one hand, they continued to rely on Marshall's mediation to obtain an immediate cessation of hostilities, to ameliorate the Nationalist demands, and to put forth their own terms. These tasks were ably discharged by the suave, persuasive, and urbane Chou En-lai, who always appeared to be conciliatory, moderate, and reasonable. He always professed to trust Marshall. As late as October 10, he assured Marshall that "he did not cast any reflection on General Marshall's action throughout the entire period of mediation."[99] On the other hand, the pronouncements of other leaders and the Communist press castigated American policy with increasing vehemence in the hope of deterring the United States from giving further aid to the Nationalists. On June 26, Mao Tse-tung issued a statement in Yenan attacking the bill introduced in Congress, at the suggestion of the State Department, to provide for the establishment of an American military mission to train the integrated Chinese forces and for the sending of equipment and supplies to China, part of which, according to Undersecretary of State Acheson's testimony, would be given to the Communists.[100] Mao declared that the Chinese Communist party resolutely opposed the dispatch of the mission to China. He demanded that the United States stop all the "so-called military assistance" to China and withdraw all American troops from China.[101]

Interestingly enough, Mao's declaration coincided with a sudden intensification of interest in Chinese affairs on the part of the Soviet press. At this time, Soviet charges of American intervention in China became sharper than in previous months. The Soviet writers expressed greater confidence in the potentiality of the Chinese Communist movement than at any time since the 1920's.[102] On July 7, the Central Committee of the Chinese Communist party issued a statement demanding that the American government stop its "armed intervention in Chinese domestic affairs" and its "instigation of the Chinese civil war."[103] In mid-July, seven American

[99] *Ibid.*, p. 195.

[100] Pp. 411–12, above.

[101] *Wei tu-li ho-p'ing min-chu êrh tou-chêng* ["Struggle for Independence, Peace and Democracy!"], (Chin-ch'a-chi jih-pao-shê, 1946), p. 17. Naturally, General Marshall was aware of this Communist tactic. He complained to a Communist representative about the "Communist propaganda attacks directed against his personal integrity and honesty of purpose, which were paralleled by repeated private requests from the Communists that he continue his mediation efforts" (*United States Relations with China*, p. 187).

[102] Charles B. McLane, *Soviet Policy and the Chinese Communists, 1931–1946*, (New York: Columbia University Press, 1958), pp. 252–54, 256.

[103] *Wei tu-li ho-p'ing min-chu êrh tou-chêng*, p. 6.

marines were kidnapped and detained by the Communists for several days. On July 29, a marine convoy bound from Tientsin to Peiping was deliberately ambushed by the Communists.[104] The hostile Communist propaganda and the attack on the marines indicated to General Marshall that the Communists now followed a new policy toward the United States.[105]

c. The embargo and Marshall's renewed efforts. — In July, Generalissimo Chiang puts his plans into effect. Hostilities spread to various points in China proper. Efforts of the Executive Headquarters and its field teams to stop the fighting were futile. Without consulting the Communists and other parties, and thus violating an understanding with them, the Nationalist government announced on July 4 that the National Assembly would meet on November 12, 1946.[106] This move indicated an intention on the part of the Kuomintang to depart from the procedures provided by the PCC, according to which the Nationalist government would be reorganized into a multiparty government pending the convocation of the National Assembly. Consequently, a Communist spokesman declared that the Communists would participate in the assembly only if certain conditions were met and if the pending political problems were settled satisfactorily.[107] At a time when the truce was rapidly disintegrating, Generalissimo Chiang left Nanking on July 14 for Kuling, a summer resort far away from the capital. The *New York Times* reported that many well informed American and Chinese observers suggested that the Generalissimo left Nanking to give his generals leeway to carry out limited military objectives while he was away from sources of pressure for a peaceful settlement in Nanking.[108] Diplomatic and other qualified sources conceded privately the United States had failed in her prolonged effort to bring peace to China.[109]

On his part, Mao, in an inner-party directive dated July 20, called on the Chinese Communists to smash Chiang's "offensive by a war of self-defense." Mao told his comrades that they could defeat Chiang and should be fully confident of victory. He observed that, although Chiang had American aid, the feelings of the people were against him, the morale of his troops was low, and his economy was in difficulty. To win final victory, the Communists were told to make long-term plans, to abandon temporarily indefensible cities, and to engage in mobile warfare. They were to mobilize the masses by solving the land problem, by improving the livelihood of the people in the "liberated areas," and by meeting the needs of war and at the same time lightening the burden on the people. Mao concluded that

[104] *United States Relations with China*, p. 172.
[105] *Military Situation in the Far East*, p. 543.
[106] *United States Relations with China*, p. 197.
[107] *New York Times*, July 4, 1946, p. 7.
[108] *Ibid.*, July 20, 1946, p. 5.
[109] *Ibid.*, July 21, 1946, p. 1; editorial, Sec. 4, p. 8.

"we rely entirely on our own efforts, and our position is invincible; this is the very opposite of Chiang Kai-shek who depends entirely on foreign countries."[110]

To help him deal with the rapidly deteriorating situation, General Marshall secured the appointment of Dr. John Leighton Stuart, president of Yenching University at Peiping, as American ambassador to China, after the Chinese Communists had expressed their opposition to the appointment of General Wedemeyer who was Marshall's original choice for the position.[111] Then, in the latter part of July, General Marshall took an eventful step, which attracted little attention at the time. On July 22, the *New York Times* published a seven-line report by the Associated Press from Washington to the effect that top American officials had been considering a "shutdown on shipment of arms and ammunition to the Chinese government in the hope that such a move might assist their efforts to bring peace to China."[112] The prohibition on the export of arms and ammunition to China became effective in the United States on July 29 and in the Pacific in mid-August.[113] In explaining this action, the White Paper stated:

> With respect to United States military aid program General Marshall was being placed in the untenable position of mediating on the one hand between the two Chinese groups while on the other the United States Government was continuing to supply arms and ammunition to one of the two groups, namely, the National Government.[114]

Later, the critics of General Marshall were to charge that this embargo of ten months and the delay in shipping supplies to China after the lifting of the embargo led to a shortage of small-arm ammunition which, in their view, was the decisive factor in the military collapse of Nationalist China.[115]

This step had no appreciable effect on the policies of Generalissimo Chiang. He continued to refuse to issue an order for the termination of hostilities. To circumvent the deadlock, General Marshall and Ambassador Stuart proposed the organization of a five-man committee to be composed of Nationalist and Communist representatives under Stuart as chairman,

[110] Mao, *Selected Works*, IV (Peking), 89–92.

[111] General Wedemeyer's testimony, *Military Situation in the Far East*, pp. 2311–12; General Albert C. Wedemeyer, *Wedemeyer Reports!* (New York: Henry Holt & Co., 1958), pp. 364–67; John Leighton Stuart, *Fifty Years in China* (New York, Random House, 1954), pp. 165–66. Stuart's appointment was confirmed by the Senate on July 11.

[112] *New York Times*, July 22, 1946, p. 2.

[113] *United States Relations with China*, p. 356.

[114] *Ibid.*, p. 181.

[115] Utley, *op. cit.*, chaps. i, ii, and iii. Senator McCarthy listed the embargo as the third of the four actions in which General Marshall intervened on the side of the Communists (*Congressional Record*, XCVII, 82d Cong., 1st sess. [1951] 6587).

for the purpose of reaching an agreement for the reorganization of the State Council. They hoped that progress in political discussion would persuade the Generalissimo to agree to a cessation of hostilities.[116] But successes in the field had apparently emboldened the Generalissimo. On August 6, he demanded the fulfilment on the part of the Communists of five conditions within a month or six weeks as a prerequisite to starting discussion on political matters. These terms required the withdrawal of Communist forces from vital positions and lines of communication in Manchuria, North China, and East China. As the White Paper commented, "These terms were more exacting than those at the end of June when the stalemate had been reached."[117] Significantly, as the Communists were quick to point out, Chiang's proposal made no mention of the future disposition of the local governments in areas to be evacuated by the Communists. The Communists continued to adhere to their stand that the existing local governments in disputed areas should be maintained. They also made a demand for simultaneous discussion of political and military questions.

To break this new impasse, the American government took two steps. First, General Marshall and Ambassador Stuart issued on August 10 a joint statement, informing the Chinese public of the deadlock in the negotiations. It pointed out that certain of the unsettled questions related to the disposition of troops and that the most difficult and fundamental issue was the character of local governments to be maintained in the areas evacuated as a result of the military redisposition.[118] This was apparently a move to arouse public opinion in China to bring pressure on the two sides for a compromise. The second step was a personal message dated August 10 from President Truman to Generalissimo Chiang. In it, the President warned the Generalissimo that unless genuine progress was being made toward a peaceful settlement of internal Chinese problems, it would be necessary for the President to redefine and explain the position of the United States to the American people.[119] In conversations with the Generalissimo at this time, General Marshall told the Chinese leader that the policy of the government would probably lead to Communist control in China.[120] Whatever effect these warnings might have had on Generalissimo Chiang, they were weakened by other actions of the American government. On August 30, the American government signed an agreement with the Nationalist government on the sale to China of surplus property in the various Pacific

---

[116] *United States Relations with China*, pp. 174–75. It was a measure of the deep gulf separating the two sides that, in spite of the tremendous efforts made by Marshall and Stuart, the five-man committee never met. For the two sides made agreement on certain questions preconditions to the meeting of the committee.

[117] *Ibid.*, p. 175.

[118] *Ibid.*, p. 649.

[119] *Ibid.*, pp. 179, 652.

[120] *Ibid.*, p. 176.

islands.[121] At this time, the negotiations between the two governments on a treaty of friendship, commerce, and navigation were also entering their last stage. It was signed on November 4, 1946. It is quite true that, as the State Department emphasized, the treaty was not a move to strengthen the Nationalist government in its civil war with the Chinese Communists and that it had no political significance.[122] But occurring at this critical juncture both the negotiations and the signing of the treaty had unfortunate effects.

The Generalissimo's response to Marshall's and Truman's warnings was twofold. On August 13, he issued a public statement, holding the Communists solely responsible for the breakdown of the negotiations, demanding Communist withdrawal from areas "where they threatened peace and obstruct communications" and asking the Communists to give assurance and evidence that they would carry out the various agreements reached.[123] On August 28, Chiang sent a reply to President Truman's message. Chiang countered the President's demand for a peaceful settlement by arguing that the minimum requirement for the preservation of peace in China was the abandonment by the Communists of "their policy to seize political power through the use of armed force, to overthrow the government and to install a totalitarian regime such as those with which Eastern Europe is now being engulfed."[124] Meanwhile, the Nationalist government continued its offensive in northern Kiangsu, cleared the Communists from the Tsinan–Tsingtao Railway, and captured Chengte, capital of Jehol province, on August 29.[125]

On their part, the Chinese Communists seized upon the Marshall-Stuart statement of August 10 as an occasion to criticize American policy and impugn American motives. On August 11, the official Communist news agency reported that in the opinion of well-informed observers in Yenan the reason for the failure of Marshall's and Stuart's mediatory efforts was the erroneous American policy of supporting "Chiang Kai-shek's dictatorial government."[126] Two days later, the official Communist newspaper published an interesting commentary on the Marshall-Stuart statement. It asserted that the United States had two policies: "One is to assist Chiang in fighting the civil war — this is fundamental; the other is to persuade Chiang to stop the civil war — this is an adjunct or an ornament."[127] It said that Chiang realized the dual nature of American policy and that without hesi-

---

[121] *Ibid.*, p. 180. The procurement value of the surplus property was estimated at $900 million. The ultimate realization by the United States of this sale was $175 million (*ibid.*, p. 1043).

[122] *New York Times*, November 4, 1946, p. 1.

[123] *United States Relations with China*, pp. 177, 649–51.

[124] *Ibid.*, p. 653.

[125] *Ibid.*, p. 178.

[126] *Wei tu-li ho-p'ing min-chu êrh tou-chêng*, p. 23.

[127] *Ibid.*, p. 31.

tation he "accepted America's artillery and evaded the dove of peace."[128] It suggested that the United States had two choices before her. One was to cease her "one-sided assistance" to Chiang and withdraw her forces from China. The other was to continue her "deceptive" policy of "mediating with one hand and supporting Chiang with the other to oppose the Communists and the people."[129] The next day, a broadcast from Moscow went beyond the Yenan editorial in condemning the Marshall-Stuart statement which was said to mark the beginning of the second phase of American armed intervention in China.[130]

In an interview with Anna Louise Strong in August, Mao charged that "the United States reactionaries" were helping Chiang to fight a civil war. Some people seemed to feel, he said, that "United States imperialism" was terribly strong. The Chinese "reactionaries" were using the strength of the United States to frighten the Chinese people. But it would be proved that "the United States reactionaries," like all reactionaries in history, did not have much strength. Chiang and his supporters, "the United States reactionaries," were, Mao argued, "all paper tigers." Mao asserted: "The atom bomb is a paper tiger which the United States reactionaries use to scare people. It looks terrible, but in fact it isn't. Of course, the atom bomb is a weapon of mass slaughter, but the outcome of a war is decided by the people, not by one or two new types of weapon."[131] Soon after the conclusion on August 30 of an agreement between the American and Chinese governments for the sale of surplus property, the Chinese Communists issued a statement, denouncing the transaction and attributing to it every possible evil purpose. Meanwhile, the Communist forces launched an attack along the Lunghai Railway and began their siege of Tatung in early August. On August 19, shortly after the Nationalist planes bombed Yenan, the Chinese Communists ordered a general mobilization.[132]

In the fighting in July, August, and September, the Nationalist forces succeeded in taking over most of the localities and railways from which the Generalissimo had asked Communists to withdraw. The occupation of these localities by Nationalist forces was followed by the establishment of local governments under Nationalist control. Thus, by his military advances the Generalissimo transformed the five conditions into a *fait accompli*. Thus when Marshall and Chiang met, Marshall gained the impression that all the points covered by his demands would be automatically taken care of by his insistence on continued military occupation of places recent-

[128] *Ibid.*
[129] *Ibid.*, p. 33.
[130] Reprinted in *ibid.*, pp. 25–26. See also *New York Times*, August 11, 1946; Sec. 4, p. 8.
[131] Mao, *Selected Works*, IV (Peking), 97–101.
[132] *New York Times*, August 20, 1946, p. 4.

ly captured by Nationalist forces.[133] The question of local government in these areas was no longer an important issue. The Generalissimo now agreed that this question could be referred to the reorganized State Council.[134]

Having made his five conditions concerning military redisposition a *fait accompli*, in September the Generalissimo turned his attention to political questions. His policy was to compel the Communists by military pressure to accept his terms on political matters or, alternatively, to confront them with accomplished facts. His political program called for an early convocation of the National Assembly, denied the Communists and their allies a veto power in a reorganized State Council, and postponed the reorganization of the Executive Yüan. Despite Marshall's repeated advice, he refused to issue a cease-fire order before agreement on all issues was reached. He told General Marshall frankly that refusing to issue a cease-fire order was "his final trump card in forcing the Communist Party to name its delegates to the National Assembly."[135] Against the background of a series of Nationalist military advances and with the Nationalist government doing all the preparatory work, the National Assembly would meet, a constitution would be adopted, and a constitutional regime would be inaugurated under conditions entirely favorable to the perpetuation of one-party control.

As the Nationalist advance continued, the Communists became even more insistent upon an immediate cessation of hostilities. On the unsettled political issues, the position of the Communists was also diametrically opposed to that of the Generalissimo. They insisted on gaining fourteen seats for themselves and their allies in a State Council of forty members, which would give them the one-third vote necessary to veto any revision of the PCC resolutions. They maintained that the Executive Yüan should be reorganized prior to the convocation of the National Assembly. They resolutely refused to name their delegates to the National Assembly unless there was a cease-fire and the political questions were settled. Thus, no agreement was possible on any of these issues.

While Chou En-lai at Nanking was insisting on a cease-fire, Mao at Yenan issued an inner-party directive on September 16, instructing Communist cadres on the method of concentrating a superior force to destroy the Kuomintang's units one by one. Mao pointed out that this method was most useful when employed against an enemy lacking second-line troops. It was aimed at annihilating the Kuomintang's effective strength. Complete annihilation of the Kuomintang forces, Mao observed, was not only the main source of Communist arms and ammunition but also an important

---

[133] *United States Relations with China*, p. 183.
[134] *Ibid.*, pp. 183–85.
[135] *Ibid.*, p. 186.

source of Communist manpower through securing the surrender of Nationalist troops. Demonstrating his flexibility in military strategy, Mao told the Communists that during the war against Japan, the dispersal of forces for guerrilla warfare was primary, and the concentration of forces for mobile warfare was supplementary; but in the present civil war, the concentration of forces for mobile warfare should be primary, and the dispersal of forces for guerrilla warfare should be supplementary.[136] In an interview with A. T. Steele on September 29, Mao charged that American policy was "to use the so-called mediation as a smoke-screen for strengthening Chiang Kai-shek in every way."[137]

  d. The Nationalist attack on Kalgan, the convocation of the National Assembly, and the end of American mediation. — To enforce his demands, the Generalissimo continued his military advance. To check further Nationalist attacks and to gain acceptance of their minimum terms, the Communists played their last card — an open threat to fight a prolonged war. This critical stage in the negotiations was reached when the Nationalists announced on September 30 the start of their military operations against Kalgan, a center of Communist power in Inner Mongolia. On the same day, Chou En-lai informed General Marshall that, if the Nationalist government did not cease its advance toward Kalgan, the Communists would assume that the Government was giving public indication of a "total national split" and of its abandonment of a peaceful settlement.[138] The Nationalist drive against Kalgan led General Marshall to the belief that, to use the words of the White Paper, "the United States Government could not continue to be a third party to the existing procedure under which the Government had been proceeding with its 'local operations' for three months" and that the "campaign against Kalgan could be justified only on a basis of a policy of force."[139] Thus, on October 1, General Marshall sent a memorandum to Generalissimo Chiang warning him that "unless a basis for agreement is found to terminate the fighting without further delays of proposals and counterproposals, I will recommend to the President that I be recalled and the United States Government terminate its efforts of mediation."[140] After further talks with Chiang, Marshall became convinced, as he told the Generalissimo, that "a campaign of force was in progress and that negotiations could be described as a cover for this campaign."[141] He came to the conclusion that "the United States Government was being placed in a position where the integrity of

[136] Mao, *Selected Works*, IV (Peking), 103–6.
[137] *Ibid.*, pp. 109–10.
[138] *United States Relations with China*, p. 188.
[139] *Ibid.*, p. 189.
[140] *Ibid.*
[141] *Ibid.*, p. 191.

its actions could be successfully questioned and that he must, therefore, recommend to President Truman his recall."[142]

On learning through Ambassador Stuart that General Marshall had sent a message to Washington recommending his recall, Generalissimo Chiang agreed to declare a conditional truce of a few days in the Kalgan area.[143] General Marshall withdrew the recommendation for his recall.[144] But this hard-won proposal for a truce was rejected by the Communists on the ground that there should be no time limit to the truce and that they would not negotiate under military pressure.[145] Chou En-lai told Marshall that only a lasting truce would demonstrate that the government did not desire a "total split." As a counterproposal, he demanded that all troops resume the positions held in China proper as of January 13 and in Manchuria as of June 7. He also told Marshall that he would not negotiate under a limited agenda and with a deadline. Instead, he presented as a basis for negotiations a list of detailed points, making clear that the Communists would insist on the implementation of the PCC resolutions. The negotiations now reached a stage where the Communists took a firm and unyielding stand, refusing to make further concessions. The distance between the two sides was greater than ever.

Chou's firm stand reflected an appraisal of the military situation made by Mao in an inner-party directive dated October 1. After three months of fighting in July, August, and September, Mao was more confident of ultimate victory in a protracted war than in early July. He pointed out that a sharp contradiction had arisen between Chiang's overextended battle lines and his shortage of troops and that this contradiction would be the direct cause of Communist victory and Chiang's defeat. Mao explained that of Chiang's more than 190 brigades, nearly half had to perform garrison duties. When his field forces advanced into Communist territory, part or even a majority of them would have to switch over to garrison duty. His effective forces were bound to dwindle as the fighting went on. In the past three months, the Communist forces had destroyed twenty-five Nationalist brigades. He predicted that, after wiping out another twenty-five Nationalist brigades in the next three months or so, the Communist forces would certainly be able to halt Chiang's offensive, to recover part of the territory lost to him, to seize the strategic initiative, and to go over from the defensive to the offensive.[146]

The intransigence of the Communists led Marshall and Stuart to issue

---

[142] *Ibid.*, p. 192. General Marshall's action in recommending his recall was considered by Senator McCarthy as the last of his four interventions on the side of the Communists (*Congressional Record*, XCVII, 82d Cong., 1st sess. [1951], 6588–89).

[143] *United States Relations with China*, p. 192.

[144] *Ibid.*, pp. 190–93.

[145] *Ibid.*, p. 194.

[146] Mao, *Selected Works*, IV (Peking), 113–14.

a statement on October 8, which gave a factual account of the negotiations and the latest impasse.[147] It was also an implicit criticism of the Communist refusal to accept the Kalgan truce proposal. As no truce agreement was concluded, the Nationalist forces continued their operations against Kalgan. On October 10, Nationalist forces captured not only Kalgan but also Chihfeng, the last Communist stronghold in Jehol province. They were also continuing their advance in northern Kiangsu. The next day, the government announced that the National Assembly would be convened on November 12, as scheduled.[148] A set of eight conditions for cessation of hostilities was also presented to the Communists.[149]

It is a measure of the complexity of Chinese politics that negotiations continued even after these events and despite the Communist threat of a "total national split." In this last month of negotiation, the primary objective of the Communists was to influence the minor parties and groups, with the specific purpose of creating a united front in boycotting the National Assembly.[150]

Meanwhile, the Nationalist forces marched on without much opposition from the Communists. On October 16, Nationalist forces opened an attack on Antung and Chefoo. They occupied the last of the main stations on the Tsinan–Tsingtao Railway and were moving north along the Peiping–Hankow Railway in southern Hopei.[151] By late October, Generalissimo Chiang expressed to General Marshall the view that it was time to halt the fighting. On November 8, he issued an order for all Nationalist troops to cease fire. This unilateral declaration of a cease-fire served, to use his own words, "as a further evidence of the sincere desire of the Government to achieve a lasting peace and political stability."[152] Coming as it did after a series of sweeping military advances, it conveyed a sense of triumph as well as an impression of magnanimity. At the same time, it "still held, in effect, a threat of renewed battle to force a political decision,"[153] as the

[147] *United States Relations with China*, pp. 194, 665–67.

[148] *Ibid.*, pp. 196–97.

[149] *Ibid.*, p. 199. See Chang, *op. cit.*, for a more detailed account of the eight conditions.

[150] It is apparent that at this time the Communists did not expect the negotiations and American mediation to lead to a cease-fire. They reduced their personnel at the Executive Headquarters at Peiping to the point that the Communist branch was practically inoperative. They withdrew their members from all field teams in government-occupied areas in China except at four points. Communist party personnel was gradually withdrawn from Nanking, Shanghai, Chungking, and other cities.

[151] *United States Relations with China*, pp. 190, 200.

[152] *Ibid.*, p. 677.

[153] *Ibid.*, pp. 205–6. Chiang rejected a draft statement prepared by General Marshall, which would announce the cease-fire in such a way as to indicate a desire to reach an immediate agreement with the Communist party for the unconditional termination of hostilities and to agree to an immediate adjournment of the National Assembly after formal convocation so as to hold the door open for further negotiations (*ibid.*, pp. 676–77).

White Paper pointed out. The date set for the convocation of the National Assembly was then only three days away.

Confronted by the Generalissimo with a *fait accompli* in both the political realm and in the disputed territory, the Communists stood fast. Chou En-lai told Marshall that the unilateral action of the government in convening the National Assembly contrary to the PCC resolutions meant a definite "split" in China. The Communist party subsequently informed the government that it would not participate in the National Assembly. The impending meeting of the National Assembly also precipitated a crisis for the minor parties and groups. For the Nationalist government was pressing hard for the submission of a list of their delegates to the National Assembly and postponed its convocation for three days in order to give further time for them to do so.[154] At the same time, the Communists were urging them to take a common stand. The result was a definite split in their ranks. The Democratic League joined the Communist in boycotting the National Assembly, while the Youth party and a badly divided Democratic–Socialist party decided to co-operate with the government. The process of political polarization in a society in revolution had done its work.

The National Assembly was formally convened on November 15. Chou En-lai departed for Yenan on November 19, thus bringing to an end the long period of negotiations begun in January, 1946. Before Chou's departure, General Marshall asked the Communist negotiator to obtain a formal answer from the Communist leaders whether they wished Marshall to continue in his role as mediator.[155] On December 4, Chou sent a message to Marshall from Yenan. It set forth, for transmission to the Generalissimo, terms for reopening negotiations which the government could not be expected to accept. These were (1) dissolution of the National Assembly and (2) restoration of troop positions held as of January 13, in accordance with the first agreement on the cessation of hostilities. Furthermore, Chou's message did not contain a reply to Marshall's request for a definite answer from the Communist party on the question of the continuation of his mediation. The Communist party had, in effect, rejected American mediation.[156]

e. Chiang's miscalculations. — This review of the events from June to November shows that Generalissimo Chiang's actions bore all the marks of a carefully planned program. His policies would have worked out to the interests of his regime if his estimation of its military, economic, and political capabilities had been correct. He told General Marshall on December 1 that the Communist forces could be eliminated in eight to ten months

[154] *Ibid.*, p. 207; Chang, *op. cit.*, p. 184.
[155] It was an indication of the embarrassing position occupied by General Marshall that he had, on at least two occasions, told the Communists that if they doubted his impartiality as a mediator, he would withdraw (*United States Relations with China*, p. 195).
[156] *Ibid.*, p. 212.

and that there was no danger for a long time of an economic collapse.[157] It would seem that he also overestimated America's willingness to come to his assistance. At the very moment when the negotiations had completely broken down, two of his chief aides approached General Marshall for financial help.[158] Later, the requests for American economic and military assistance became increasingly insistent as the Nationalist military advances turned into disastrous defeats. Unfortunately for him, his judgments on both of these crucial points was far wide of the mark.

As General Marshall had frankly told the Generalissimo in August:

> The Government had much to lose and little to gain from hostilities at this time, which might end in the collapse of the Government and of the country's economy. The Generalissimo must remember that the long lines of communication and the terrain favored the employment of the Communist guerrilla tactics. . . . He [General Marshall] opposed the policy of the Generalissimo and his immediate advisers because he thought that the procedure of the National Government would probably lead to Communist control in China; the chaotic conditions then developing would not only weaken the Kuomintang but would also afford the Communists an excellent opportunity to undermine the Government.[159]

In a discussion with a high-ranking Nationalist official in July, Marshall had also emphasized that the United States would not underwrite a Chinese civil war.[160] Events in China in the next three years developed in the direction predicted by Marshall and he steadfastly adhered to his policy of refusing to intervene militarily in the Chinese struggle.

But Generalissimo Chiang apparently thought that, as long as he controlled the government of China, the United States would come to his aid sooner or later, notwithstanding his failure to co-operate with General Marshall and to reform his regime. For Chiang had an unbounded faith in his skill in manipulating the international situation to suit his own purposes.[161] His skill in extracting every possible temporary advantage served him well when he had the upper hand, but it tended to make his position untenable when he overestimated his own capabilities and his importance to his allies. In his internal program, he was also bound to fail. For he had never succeeded in providing his regime with a broad social base and in creating a common front of non-Communist forces to confront the Communists with an invincible alliance. He could manipulate individual poli-

[157] *Ibid.*
[158] *Ibid.*, p. 210.
[159] *Ibid.*, p. 176.
[160] *Ibid.*, p. 174.
[161] See chap. iv, above.

ticians, but the Chinese Communists were riding on a wave of popular support. He relied solely on his armed forces to crush a popular revolution. In this task, he could only fail, as General Marshall predicted at the time.

After the end of American mediation, General Marshall urged Nationalist leaders to adopt a constitution in consonance with the PCC resolutions. He still hoped that, if such a constitution were adopted and the State Council and the Executive Yüan were reorganized, it might be possible to bring the Communists into the National Assembly. His advice on the adoption of a forward-looking constitution was accepted and implemented by Generalissimo Chiang. On December 18, President Truman issued a statement, reaffirming the policy laid down in his press release of December 15, 1945. He characterized as still sound the plan for political and military settlement worked out in early 1946. He indicated that the United States continued to hope for a peaceful solution of China's internal problems and pledged the United States not to interfere in Chinese affairs and not to become involved in civil strife.[162] On January 6, Marshall's recall was announced by President Truman. Several months before, Marshall had been advised by Truman of the latter's intention to appoint him secretary of state. Shortly after his departure from China, the State Department made public his personal statement about his mission. He attributed his failure to "the complete, almost overwhelming suspicion with which the Chinese Communist Party and the Kuomintang regard each other."[163] For this mutual antagonism, he blamed, on the one hand, "a dominant group of reactionaries who have been opposed to almost every effort I have made to influence the formation of a genuine coalition government," and, on the other, the "dyed-in-the wool" Communists, "who do not hesitate at the most drastic measures to gain their ends."[164] A close reading of Marshall's statement shows that he placed the primary responsibility for the initial breakdown of the settlement on the Kuomintang. In Marshall's opinion, "Irreconcilable groups within the Kuomintang, interested in the preservation of their feudal control of China, evidently had no real intention" of implementing the agreements reached by the Political Consultative Conference in January, 1946.[165] In contrast, the Communists did not "appear last February" to be "irreconcilable."[166] However, in the last stage the Communists assumed, in Marshall's view, a heavy share of the responsibility because of their "unwillingness to make a fair compromise."[167] General Marshall saw the only hope in the "assumption of leadership by the liberals in the Government and in the minority parties, a splendid group of men

[162] *United States Relations with China*, pp. 218–19, 689–94.
[163] *Ibid.*, p. 686.
[164] *Ibid.*, p. 687.
[165] *Ibid.*, p. 688.
[166] *Ibid.*
[167] *Ibid.*

but who as yet lack the political power to exercise a controlling influence." He expressed the belief that "successful action on their part *under the leadership of Generalissimo Chiang Kai-shek* would . . . lead to unity through good government."[168] Thus, an honest effort to bring peace and unity in China ended in a forlorn hope.

The miscarriage of the political settlement, the progressive disintegration of the truce, the expansion of local fighting into nationwide civil war, and Marshall's abandonment of his effort to seek peace were publicly interpreted by Chou En-lai in a speech on January 10 as a process through which the true nature of the American policy was exposed. Even Marshall's statement of January 7 was cited as further proof that the American government had been helping Chiang to extend the civil war.[169] The intense hostility of the Chinese Communists toward the United States, their confidence in Soviet might, and their depreciations of American economic and political strength were made emphatically clear in an article which appeared in their official organ at Yenan under the by-line of Lu Ting-yi, chief of the Department of Information of the Chinese Communist party. Lu declared that after World War II, the "American imperialists" took the place of "Fascist Germany, Italy and Japan" and became the fortress of the world reactionary forces. The only difference which he saw between the policy of "American imperialism" and that of "Japanese Fascists" toward China was that "the venomous treachery of the means employed by American imperialism" surpassed that of Japanese imperialism. The "antidemocratic forces" would of necessity attack the "democratic forces." But the "democratic forces" would of necessity be victorious. "Capitalist encirclement" of the Soviet Union no longer existed. The world reactionary forces were outwardly strong but hollow inside. They were becoming daily more isolated. The American economic crisis would arrive "this year or next." "It may be forecast categorically," he asserted that "the face of China and the world will be vastly different after three to five years."[170] On February 1 the Central Committee of the Chinese Communist party formally declared that it would not recognize any foreign loans, treaties, agreements, and understandings concluded by the Kuomintang government after January 10, 1946.[171] This statement was aimed at the lend-lease "Pipeline" agreement of July 14, 1946, the surplus property agreement of August 30, 1946, and the Treaty of Friendship, Commerce and Navigation negotiated in 1946 between the United States and the Nationalist government.

These statements by Chou, Lu, and the Central Committee did not mark

[168] *Ibid.* Emphasis added.
[169] *Ibid.*, pp. 706–10.
[170] *Ibid.*, pp. 710–19.
[171] *Ibid.*, pp. 719–20.

a reversal of Communist policy, as the White Paper suggests. They marked the culmination of a process through which the Communist profession in 1944 of friendship for the United States was transmuted into outright hostility by the interaction between the deep-rooted suspicion of the Communists and the ambiguous American policies. The catalyst for this process was the shift of the balance of power in the Far East after 1944. The Chinese Communists must have come to the conclusion in 1947 that the time during which the United States could decisively influence their fortune had passed. The United States had completed her tasks of helping the Nationalist government to expatriate the Japanese and of transporting the Nationalist armies to Central China, North China, and Manchuria. She had terminated the Chinese theater and had reduced her forces in China from the peak strength of 113,000 men to 12,000. On January 29, the State Department had announced the withdrawal of the American personnel in the Executive Headquarters.[172] This action paved the way for the withdrawal of all marines from North China. At the same time, the Soviet Union was holding the ring for the Chinese Communists against possible American military intervention. Professions of friendship no longer served any political purpose. Overt hostility was in harmony with their ideological predisposition. It expressed their resentment against what they believed to be American partiality toward the Kuomintang in the mediation. It put them completely in step with the policy of the Soviet Union and the world-wide Communist movement.

The Chinese Communist leaders were equally optimistic about the military and political developments in China. In an inner-party directive dated February 1, Mao hailed the pending arrival of the new high tide of the Chinese revolution. He observed that the situation in China was about to enter a new stage of development in which "the country-wide struggle against imperialism and feudalism will develop into a great new people's revolution." He noted that, while Chiang's offensive continued, it had become much feebler than before because Chiang could no longer send, due to Nationalist losses and shortage of reserves, large combat-worthy reinforcements from his near areas to attack the Communist bases. As Mao saw it, the political development was equally favorable. The convening of the National Assembly by Chiang had, according to Mao, isolated the Nationalists instead of the Communists. Mao concluded that "our Party and the Chinese people have every assurance of final victory; there is not the slightest doubt about it."[173] Mao's growing confidence paralleled Marshall's pessimistic forecast that all-out civil war might very well lead to the collapse of the Nationalist Government. How did the United States assess the Chinese situation and what policy would she adopt?

[172] *Ibid.*, p. 695.
[173] Mao, *Selected Works*, IV (Peking), 119–25.

CHAPTER XI

PARTIAL WITHDRAWAL,

LIMITED ASSISTANCE,

AND

THE DECISION

TO ABANDON

CHINA

1947–1948

A. The Hypothetical Alternatives and the Middle Course

After the failure of his effort to achieve a political settlement between the Kuomintang and the Communists, Marshall returned to the United States to assume the post of secretary of state. On January 8, 1947, just before he left China, he asked Ambassador Stuart for his opinion on the future policy of the United States toward China. In his usual vague and restrained manner, Stuart outlined three possible courses of action: first, to give active assistance to the Nationalist government, conditioning American aid on Nationalist reform; second, to drift along with no strong program; and third, to withdraw entirely from any participation in Chinese affairs. He added that he was all for the first alternative but would much prefer the third to the second.[1] He realized that, if the United States followed the second course of action, she would antagonize every section of Chinese opinion. "The government leaders would charge us with desertion, the Communists with partisanship, and the intellectuals, speaking for the helpless masses, with imperialistic intrusion."[2] American action would merely prolong the civil war without preventing a Communist victory. The large reservoir of good will for the United States among the Chinese people would be destroyed by the belief that she was supporting a "rotten gov-

[1] John Leighton Stuart, *Fifty Years in China* (New York: Random House, 1954), pp. 178–79.
[2] *Ibid.*, pp. 181–82.

ernment."[3] Anti-American feeling would spread and deepen. Stuart recognized that "if nothing succeeds like success, nothing fails like failure."[4]

The principle underlying Stuart's remarks to Marshall was that either the United States should make an effort sufficient to stem the Communist tide in China or she should do nothing at all. In retrospect, Stuart seems to have been too optimistic about the effectiveness of American military aid and technical advice in changing the balance of forces in China. But the principle itself was sound. Indeed, it was indorsed by persons holding different views on what the China policy of the United States should be. Walter Robertson, chargé d'affaires of the American embassy in China during part of 1945 and 1946 and later one of the chief architects of the tough policy toward Communist China in the Eisenhower administration, told the House Committee on Foreign Affairs on March 4, 1948:

> I think we must face up to whether we, as Americans, are willing to undertake the job of doing what is necessary to be done in China, or if we are not willing to do that. . . . I would rather not do anything because I think you would be likely to lose what you did do.[5]

It was precisely on the basis of the same principle that Professor Nathaniel Peffer opposed the various proposals of giving additional aid to China in the winter of 1947–48. Writing in the *New York Times* on January 25, 1948, Peffer expressed the opinion that the real choice before the United States was between sending a large expeditionary force of 150,000 men to China and letting events run their course. In his view, the measures then proposed by American friends of Generalissimo Chiang to aid the Nationalists would drive the Communists into Russia's arms without enabling the government to defeat them.[6] General Marshall himself apparently subscribed to this conception insofar as it was applied to the European Recovery Program. Asking Congress for $6.8 billion as the cost of the program for the first fifteen months, he was reported to have said in January, 1948: "An inadequate program would involve a wastage of our resources with an ineffective result. . . . Either we undertake to meet the requirements of the program or don't undertake it at all."[7]

Whatever the basic views of General Marshall and the private wishes of other officials, American policy in the two years of 1947 and 1948 shifted erratically in the middle ground marked out by the two realistic alterna-

[3] *Ibid.*, pp. 188, 190.
[4] *Ibid.*, p. 188.
[5] House Committee on Foreign Affairs, *Hearings on United States Foreign Policy for a Post-war Recovery Program*, 80th Cong., 2d sess. (1948), p. 2082 (hereafter cited as *Foreign Policy for a Post-war Recovery Program*).
[6] *New York Times*, January 25, 1948, Sec. 6, pp. 8 ff.
[7] Robert Payne, *The Marshall Story* (New York: Prentice-Hall, Inc., 1951), p. 305.

tives, without following either of them. Starting out in early 1947 with a program of partial withdrawal, the United States adopted in October, 1947, a policy of limited assistance which culminated in the China Aid Act of April, 1948. This program of limited aid was enacted at a time when, according to Dean Acheson's subsequent testimony in the MacArthur hearings, the United States had the last chance to commit unlimited resources and her armed forces to the struggle in China, if she had wanted to do so, and when both the administration and Congress rejected that alternative.[8] The policy of limited assistance thus reached its climax at a juncture when it had even less chance of success than at any time since V-J Day and when its only political effect in China was to identify the United States further with an admittedly hopeless cause.

The program of limited assistance contained in the China Aid Act had scarcely been implemented when the Nationalists suffered disastrous defeats in three crucial battles in September, October, and November. By the end of 1948, Marshall had for all practical purposes written off both mainland China and Formosa. But economic assistance under the China Aid Act was never stopped. Nor was the shipment of arms under the $125 million special fund put at the disposal of the Nationalist government under the same act.[9] The United States thus continued to be entangled in China. Her immobilized position at the center not only deprived her of freedom of action but also incurred for her the liabilities of both a policy of active intervention and a program of prompt withdrawal. The American policy lent color to the Communists' distorted views of the United States, while failing to impress on them American strength and determination. It discarded the Nationalists while intensifying the hostilities of the Communists. The United States sought to avoid war by refraining from military commitments, but continued American entanglement in China intensified Communist hatred and prepared the ground for a military confrontation which was to take place after the neutralization of the Formosa Strait and the crossing of the 38th Parallel by the American forces. How did all this come about?

B. Marshall's Search for a Policy

In July, 1946, when the political-military settlement in China was rapidly disintegrating, General Marshall told Secretary of the Navy James Forrestal that, if the negotiations to preserve the settlement broke down, he would recommend a period of withdrawal so that the United States

[8] Senate Committee on Armed Services and Committee on Foreign Relations, *Hearings on the Military Situation in the Far East*, 82d Cong., 1st sess. (1951), p. 1869 (hereafter cited as *Military Situation in the Far East*).

[9] See chap. xii, below.

could take two or three months for reappraisal and re-evaluation of her policy toward China.[10] Shortly after he returned from China and assumed his new office of secretary of state on January 21, the policy of withdrawal was put into effect.[11] On January 29, the American government announced its decision to terminate its connection with the Committee of Three and the Executive Headquarters.[12] This decision made it possible to withdraw the American marines from Peiping, Tientsin, and Tangku where they had been stationed to guard the lines of communication.[13] A guard contingent remained at Tsingtao where the United States Naval Training Group was engaged in training Chinese naval personnel and kept a quiet watch on Russian activities at Port Arthur and Dairen.[14] In the first five months of 1947, the embargo continued in force.

Coming as it did after the failure of the United States and Nationalist China to work out a common policy had completely shattered Marshall's plans for a settlement, this policy of temporary withdrawal was sound. But in retrospect, it seems clear that maximum benefit would have flowed from this period of withdrawal only under two conditions. First, the American withdrawal would have had to be complete rather than partial, thus exerting overwhelming pressure on the Nationalist government to undertake the necessary reforms and to qualify itself for the renewal of American assistance and support. Second, the American government would have had to be able during this period to make a choice between two equally disagreeable alternatives in the light of the Nationalist response. If the pressure arising from America's withdrawal had led the Nationalist government to rejuvenate itself by a change in basic policies or in the top leadership, the indispensable condition for the effective use of large-scale American assistance would then have existed and a policy of holding part of China, by American armed intervention if necessary, might have had a fair chance of success. If the Nationalist government had failed to show the minimum stability and strength to stay in power with American support, the United States could then have promptly dissociated herself with a moribund regime and retained what was left of her freedom of action.

Unfortunately, neither of these two difficult steps was taken. The withdrawal was partial rather than complete. In some measure, this was the

[10] Walter Millis (ed.), *The Forrestal Diaries* (New York: Viking Press, 1951), p. 174.

[11] Department of State, *United States Relations with China* (Washington, D.C.: Government Printing Office, 1949), p. 219 (hereafter cited as *United States Relations with China*).

[12] *Ibid.*, p. 695.

[13] *Ibid.*, p. 219; *Military Situation in the Far East*, pp. 2235–36. In December, 1946, there was a total of less than 12,000 American soldiers, sailors, and marines in China (*United States Relations with China*, p. 694).

[14] In February, 1948, this guard contingent consisted of 2,600 men (Millis, *op. cit.*, p. 376).

result of the momentum of the ambiguous policies and actions of the past. In the first half of 1947, the Nationalist economy was bolstered by the final shipments of UNRRA supplies, totaling $235,108,000,[15] and by the matériel obtained through the surplus property agreement of August, 1946.[16] Both the United States Army Advisory Group and the Naval Advisory Group remained in China. The former was given permission to give advice concerning the organization and equipment of Nationalist units.[17] In April, the President instructed the secretary of the navy to transfer certain ships and floating dry docks to the Chinese government.[18] At a meeting of the Council of Foreign Ministers at Moscow in March, Secretary Marshall gave strong support to Nationalist opposition to the Soviet demand that problems relating to the settlement of the civil war in China be included in the agenda of the meeting.[19]

Furthermore, Marshall's search for a new policy did not lead, either during the period of partial withdrawal or later, to the adoption of one of the two realistic alternatives. Instead, he showed signs of being unable to make the difficult choice. His state of mind in early 1947 can be vividly seen in the following testimony in the MacArthur hearings:

> When I came back I was hard put to find a long-view conclusion in the matter because of the failing structure of the Kuomintang and the determination, organization, and discipline of the Communist group and their undoubted advice and possible support that would occur later from the Soviet government.[20]

[15] John C. Campbell, *The United States in World Affairs, 1947–1948* (New York: Harper & Bros., 1948), p. 190; *United States Relations with China*, p. 363.

[16] Royal Institute of International Affairs, *Survey of International Affairs, 1947–1948* (London: Oxford University Press, 1952), p. 278.

[17] *United States Relations with China*, pp. 346–47. The plan for the establishment of a military advisory group was drawn up under General Wedemeyer's direction shortly after V-J Day. It envisaged a group of 1,000 officers and 2,600 enlisted men from both the army and the navy for the first year or so (General Albert C. Wedemeyer, *Wedemeyer Reports!* [New York: Henry Holt & Co., 1958], pp. 400–401).

On March 31, 1947, Secretary Marshall informed the British and Russian foreign ministers in a note that, after the completion of the withdrawal of the American forces in China, there would remain in China some 6,180 members of the American armed forces connected with the advisory groups (*New York Times*, April 3, 1947, p. 2).

In the spring of 1948, there was a total of 572 officers and 921 enlisted men in China serving in the Army Advisory Group. See Senator Vandenberg's statement to the Senate on March 30, 1948 (*Congressional Record*, XCIV, 80th Cong., 2d sess. [1948], 3668).

[18] Campbell, *op. cit.*, p. 190.

[19] *United States Relations with China*, p. 235. Having recently returned from a trip to China, Representative Mike Mansfield of Montana suggested, in a speech on the floor of the House on February 3, that the United States take the initiative in calling a conference of interested powers to find a settlement of the Chinese civil war (*Congressional Record*, XCIII, 80th Cong., 1st sess. [1947], 767). Mansfield's suggestion elicited no positive response from the State Department. It seems clear that Secretary Marshall had ruled out international mediation as an alternative.

[20] *Military Situation in the Far East*, p. 397.

A year later in a meeting of the National Security Council on February 12, 1948, Marshall read two documents, the gist of which was that the problem of China was "practically insoluble."[21] When the Nationalist government was tottering on the brink of disaster, Marshall's puzzlement turned into despair. He was reported to have said on August 13, 1948: "I wash my hands of the problem which has passed altogether beyond my comprehension and my power to make judgments."[22]

Marshall's growing perplexity mirrored the fact that events in 1947 and 1948 sharpened the dilemma confronting him from the very beginning. The Nationalist setbacks on the battlefield after the summer of 1947 posed in an increasingly more acute form the question of giving large-scale military aid to China and eventual use of American armed forces. The mounting economic and political difficulties confronting the Nationalist government demanded immediate American assistance but at the same time multiplied the condition which in the past had rendered American aid ineffective. Marshall's dilemma was also sharpened by two developments outside of China. The first was the growing criticism of his policy by Republican leaders. The second was the rising tension between the United States and the Soviet Union and the revolutionary change in American policy which found concrete expression in the Truman Doctrine of March 12, 1947, and Marshall's European Recovery Program. Large-scale economic and military aid to Greece and Turkey furnished some Republican leaders with an additional reason to press for the adoption of a positive policy in China. Republican support for the Marshall Plan seemed to require some concession on the part of the administration to the views of Republican leaders on China policy. The lack of a bipartisan policy played into the hands of the Nationalist leaders, who quickly turned the checks and balances in American government to their advantage.[23] They were able to influence American policy through pressure exerted by Republican leaders in Congress.

The lack of a clear-cut policy on the part of the administration, the adoption of a policy of limited assistance under mounting congressional pressure, and the exploitation by the Nationalists of the division of American opinion constituted the main features in the development of American policy in 1947 and 1948. The developing partisan stalemate and the policy of limited assistance are paradoxical in terms of the realistic choices before the United States. But they are understandable as the products of the two inconsistent elements in the traditional pattern of American policy: the hope to preserve American influence and the incapacity to use force.

[21] Millis, *op. cit.*, p. 372.
[22] Payne, *op. cit.*, p. 311.
[23] Daniel S. Cheever and H. Field Haviland, Jr., *American Foreign Policy and the Separation of Powers* (Cambridge, Mass.: Harvard University Press, 1952), pp. 156–57.

C. The Gathering Storm of Republican Criticism

In order to put in historical context the rising Republican criticism of the administration's policy in 1947, it is necessary to recall that during the Marshall mission opposition to Marshall's policy was slight. Appearing in the Town Meeting of the Air on December 27, 1945, Representative Walter Judd gave his blessing to President Truman's statement of December 15, 1945, which formed the basis for Marshall's effort to promote a coalition government in China. Believing "completely in the sincerity of Chiang's desire to achieve a unified, democratic China without further warfare," he expressed the view that the administration's policy would expose the pretenses of the Communists that they supported political unity and democracy.[24] In April when Marshall made a personal report to the Foreign Relations Committee, he left with the impression that he had met with a general acceptance and approval of his policies, though there was no formal expression of opinion.[25] In May, sixty Americans interested in China issued a statement entitled "Manchurian Manifesto," sharply criticizing Soviet actions in Manchuria as a flagrant violation of the Sino-Soviet Treaty and the Yalta Agreement. It called on the American government to support "the demands of the Chinese people for a complete revision of the Yalta agreement."[26] But it made no direct attack on Marshall's policies and activities in China. In July, Senator Owen Brewster, Republican of Maine, was quoted as having said that "the Republican Party will go along with General Marshall in the Chinese situation."[27]

The first sign of dissent from Republican quarters came only on July 26, when Representative Clare Boothe Luce inserted into the *Congressional Record* a letter signed by thirty-eight Americans. This message was prompted by reports of a statement by Undersecretary of State Dean Acheson before the House Foreign Affairs Committee that, as part of Marshall's program to integrate the Communist and Nationalist armed forces, the American government was ready to supply and train Chinese Communist forces prior to their incorporation into a national army. It urged that no further aid or support be given to the Communists. It criticized Truman's statement of December 15 as "an invitation of the Communists to blackmail the Central Government."[28] After armed clashes began to spread in China,

[24] "What Should Be Our Policy in China?" inserted in the *Congressional Record* on January 16, 1946, by Representative Judd (*Congressional Record*, XCII, 79th Cong., 2d Sess. [1946], A107).

[25] Marshall's answer to Senator McMahon's question, in *Military Situation in the Far East*, pp. 569–70. The veracity of Marshall's statement has never been challenged by anyone.

[26] *Congressional Record*, XCII, 79th Cong., 2d sess. (1946), A2763.

[27] *New York Times*, July 8, 1946, p. 10.

[28] This letter was dated July 24, 1946. Among its signers were Alfred Kohlberg, Clarence Streit, Norman Thomas, Freda Utley, William Green, and Sidney Hook (*Congressional Record*, XCII, 79th Cong., 2d sess. [1946], A4494–96).

Life published on September 2 a lengthy editorial asking the United States to give "continuous, whole-hearted and plentiful aid" to the Nationalists, while inviting the Nationalists "to put their own house in order."[29]

Shortly before the Chinese Communists broke off further negotiations with the Kuomintang and rejected American mediation, the mid-term elections of 1946 resulted in a resounding Republican victory and a Republican-controlled Congress. The prestige of the Truman administration was at its lowest ebb, and there was widespread expectation of another Republican triumph in the presidential election of 1948. The division of control over the presidency and the Congress between the two parties intensified the struggle between the two branches of government for the privilege of directing American foreign policy. The likelihood of the Republican party's capturing the presidency in 1948 weakened credence in the Truman administration's capacity to control the long-term policy of the United States. Mr. John Foster Dulles, the principal foreign policy adviser to the Republican party, declared in late January, 1947, in a speech approved in advance by Senator Arthur Vandenberg, the Republican chairman of the Senate Foreign Relations Committee, and Governor Thomas Dewey, the titular head of the Republican party:

> A Democratic President and his Secretary of State can propose, but a Republican Congress can dispose. Foreign diplomats know that, and they suspect what we know — that two years from now, a Republican will be in the White House. So these foreign governments will not take very seriously American proposals which are backed only by the Democratic Party.[30]

There was no dearth of indications that the Republicans were advocating a different policy toward China. On January 11, Senator Vandenberg urged in a speech a shift of emphasis in America's policy toward China so as to encourage the Nationalists to develop a constitutional regime.[31] Advocating a tough policy toward Russia in a statement issued on January 31, Senator Styles Bridges, chairman of the Senate Appropriations Committee, said that the United States could not afford to push China into the Soviet orbit and that she must pledge her support to a nation which had just adopted a democratic constitution.[32] In a speech on February 10, Mr. Dulles called for continued support for the Nationalist government.[33]

[29] *Life*, September 2, 1946, p. 37.
[30] Quoted by Senator Claude Pepper, Democrat from Florida, from the *New York Herald Tribune*, January 26, 1947 (*Congressional Record*, XCIII, 80th Cong., 1st sess. [1947], 789).
[31] *New York Times*, January 12, 1947, p. 46. See also the speech by Senator Pepper, January 15, 1947, and the column by Joseph and Stewart Alsop quoted by Pepper (*Congressional Record*, XCIII, 80th Cong., 1st sess. [1947], 368).
[32] *Ibid.*, pp. 734–35.
[33] *New York Times*, February 11, 1947, p. 6.

The proclamation of the Truman Doctrine on March 12 and the President's request for $400 million in military and economic aid to Greece and Turkey quite naturally led some Republican leaders in Congress to challenge the administration's policy toward China. In a debate on the President's message in the House on the same day, Representative Judd took the occasion to criticize Marshall's effort to bring about a coalition government including the Chinese Communists. He asked Representative John W. McCormack, former majority leader:

> Does not the gentleman feel also that as we stand today at this crossroad we should add to our sense of grave responsibility a sense of regret that in some degree we have been assisting a Communist minority in China in its effort to overthrow the Chinese government, which with all its weaknesses has steadfastly refused to yield to such internal and external pressures as today threaten Greece and Turkey?[34]

The next day, Senator Brewster in a speech in New York called it an anomaly for the United States to help King George fight the Communists while urging Chiang to embrace them.[35]

In the hearings held on March 22 before the House Committee on Foreign Affairs on assistance to Greece and Turkey, Judd also asked Acting Secretary of State Dean Acheson to explain this "contradiction" in American policy. Acheson replied that the current American policy toward China as expressed in Marshall's statement of January 6, 1947, was "not directed toward including Communists in the Government, but making the Government more effective in carrying out the purposes of the Government." [36] He then explained:

> The Chinese Government is not in the position at the present time that the Greek Government is in. It is not approaching collapse. It is not threatened by defeat by the Communists. The war with the Communists is going on much as it has for the last 20 years.[37]

Several months later Acheson was severely criticized for his characterization of the situation of China as nothing serious in comparison to the conditions in Greece.[38] But at the time it seemed to be a reasonable appraisal

[34] *Congressional Record*, XCIII, 80th Cong., 1st sess. (1947), 734–35.

[35] *New York Times*, March 14, 1946, p. 4.

[36] House Committee on Foreign Affairs, *Hearings on Assistance to Greece and Turkey*, 80th Cong., 1st sess. (1947), p. 17 (hereafter cited as *Assistance to Greece and Turkey*).

[37] *Ibid.*

[38] House Committee on Foreign Affairs, *Hearings on Emergency Foreign Aid*, 80th Cong., 1st sess. (November, 1947), p. 24 (hereafter cited as *Emergency Foreign Aid*).

of the two situations. The alarming messages coming in from Greece had reached a climax with a report on February 20 by Ambassador Lincoln MacVeagh informing the State Department that Greece was in danger of complete collapse, economically, psychologically, and militarily, within a matter of weeks.[39] In contrast, the Nationalist forces were still launching large-scale attacks against Communist strong points with outward success, although by the end of February they were compelled to abandon their plans for attacking on all fronts, and the Communists had started a limited offensive in Manchuria.[40] On March 14, the Nationalists began their offensives against Yenan, the Communist capital, and captured it on March 19. The Nationalist chief of staff publicly claimed that the Communists would be defeated in three months.[41] Generalissimo Chiang told Ambassador Stuart that by the end of August or the beginning of September the Communists would either be annihilated or driven into the far hinterland.[42]

These Nationalist claims and the significance of the capture of Yenan were discounted by the American embassy. Its report at this time told of the failure of the Nationalist forces to score a decisive victory and the lowering of morale in Nationalist ranks. But there were no reports of serious Nationalist reverses. While the most serious economic crisis in decades broke out in early February, with prices doubled in a few days and the black market exchange rate tripled in three weeks,[43] the government was able to stabilize the situation by reimposing wartime wage and price controls and by prohibiting all strikes.[44] There were indications that during this period American officials expected a long war of attrition or a stalemate. Well-informed observers such as Nathaniel Peffer, who had recently returned from a trip to China to study "the cultural-relations program" of the State Department, expected a stalemate to ensue in six months or a year. He did not believe that the Communists would be able to conquer the whole of China.[45] In retrospect, it is clear that American officials and observers grossly underestimated the military capabilities of the Communists and, in spite of their severe criticisms of Nationalist failings, overestimated the military strength and political viability of the government. It would appear that this misjudgment with its consequent lack of a sense

[39] Joseph M. Jones, *The Fifteen Weeks* (New York: Viking Press, 1955), p. 131.
[40] *United States Relations with China*, p. 236; Liao Kai-lung, *From Yenan to Peking* (Peking: Foreign Language Press, 1954), pp. 51–53.
[41] *New York Times*, March 21, 1947, p. 17; *United States Relations with China*, p. 808.
[42] *Ibid.*, pp. 237–38.
[43] *New York Times*, February 12, 1947, p. 1.
[44] *Ibid.*
[45] *Ibid.*, May 4, 1947, Sec. 6, pp. 11 ff. Cf. Michael Lindsay, "Military Strength in China," *Far Eastern Survey*, April 9, 1947, pp. 80–82. Lindsay's perceptive analysis of the strength of the Communist forces and the weakness of the Nationalists was subsequently borne out by events.

of urgency was one of the explanations of the failure to adopt a clear-cut policy in the first three months of 1947. But, in extenuation, it should be pointed out that at this time and for more than a year afterward, the Communists themselves expected a long war.

D. The Administration in a Quandary

In April and May, conditions in China took a sharp turn for the worse. A new economic crisis broke out in the latter part of April. Despite controls, prices rose 50 to 100 per cent over a period of a few weeks, and the black market exchange rate made a new jump.[46] In Shantung, Communist forces counterattacked in the latter part of April and smashed another attack by the Nationalists in the middle of May. On May 13, they launched a powerful summer offensive in most of Manchuria and within a few weeks isolated the government units in Kirin, Changchun, and Ssŭpingchieh.[47] On May 30, the American consul general at Mukden warned of the possibility of a sudden debacle which would lay all Manchuria open to the Communists.[48] These Communist successes destroyed completely the Nationalists' hopes of an early victory.

Economic chaos and lack of military success led to political and social unrest. On May 5, a student demonstration in Shanghai started the "anti-hunger and anti-civil war" movement which soon spread to all other major cities in spite of a Nationalist order on May 18 prohibiting all demonstrations and strikes.[49] Ruthless repressive measures by the government succeeded in averting a nation-wide strike called for June 2. But they led to protests against police violence even among supporters of the government.[50] In May, twenty members of the Legislative Yüan presented a resolution calling for the resumption of peace talks with the Communists. On May 25, the People's Political Council, an advisory body set up in 1938 to give some degree of representation in the government to various non-Kuomintang groups, passed by a large majority a resolution inviting Communist representatives to come to Nanking for discussions on ways and means of bringing about the termination of the civil war.[51] It may very

[46] *New York Times*, April 30, 1947, p. 14; May 1, 1947, p. 16. See also Kia-ngau Chang, *The Inflationary Spiral* (New York: John Wiley & Sons, 1958), pp. 72–74.
[47] *United States Relations with China*, pp. 315–16; Liao, *op. cit.*, pp. 315–16.
[48] *United States Relations with China*, p. 316.
[49] *Ibid.*, p. 238; Dorothy Borg, "Students in Kuomintang China," *Far Eastern Survey*, July 23, 1947, pp. 4–7. For one aspect of the background of the student unrest, see James P. Speer II, "Liquidation of Chinese Liberals," *Far Eastern Survey*, July 23, 1947, pp. 160–62.
[50] A group of liberal legislators in the Legislative Yüan protested police actions. Dr. Hu Shih, president of Peking University, also expressed his disapproval of the high-handed methods of the government (*New York Times*, May 3, 1947, p. 6; June 4, 1947, p. 4).
[51] *United States Relations with China*, p. 240.

well be that these moves were purely political maneuvers designed to pin the sole responsibility for the continuation of the civil war on the Communists. But, even so, the very fact that the Nationalists found it necessary to take these measures indicated the extent to which anti-civil war sentiment had grown in the country.

The proclamation of the Truman Doctrine and the sharp turn of events in April and May in China provided the background for a series of Chinese requests for American aid. The Truman Doctrine had apparently raised the hope of the Nationalist government for obtaining large-scale assistance. The turn of events led it to rely even more heavily than before on renewed American aid for its salvation. From May to June, it made three different requests for large-scale economic aid.[52] To put pressure behind their last request, the Chinese leaders in several statements warned of the dangers of a Communist-dominated China.[53] Secretary of the Navy Forrestal noted in his diary on June 23 that Chinese officials in Washington were "apparently starting another drive around town to enlist further help for the Nationalist government, using particularly the danger of Communism as their chief argument."[54]

These requests confronted officials in the State Department with new complications in working out a policy toward China because they had to be weighed in the light of the administration's global program and Republican demands for a change in China policy. As early as March 5, American officials had begun to give serious thought to the question of granting large-scale economic aid to Western Europe.[55] In a speech in Cleveland, Mississippi, on May 8, Undersecretary of State Dean Acheson, with the advance approval of President Truman, floated a trial balloon for economic assistance to Europe at $5 billion a year for several years. To insure the adoption of such a program, the administration had to enlist the widest possible support. To do so, it had to conciliate Republican critics of its China policy. For the most serious obstacles to its European program were not the advocates of a change in its China policy but the combined force of economy-minded congressmen and unreconstructed isolationists. The Republican-controlled Congress had begun its session on a call made by Speaker Joseph Martin of Massachusetts for an across-the-board cut in income taxes by 20 per cent and sufficient reduction in government spending to make the cut possible.[56] Subsequently, Republican leaders in the House talked of reducing the President's budget of $37.5

[52] *Ibid.*, pp. 364–68.
[53] *New York Times*, June 8, 1947, p. 12; June 14, 1947, p. 8; June 21, 1947, p. 9; June 25, 1947, p. 2. See chap. ix, above.
[54] Millis, *op. cit.*, p. 285.
[55] Jones, *op. cit.*, pp. 199–206.
[56] *Ibid.*, p. 90.

billion by $6 billion. Although the bill authorizing $400 million to Greece and Turkey had sailed through Congress fairly smoothly, it was only with some difficulty that the administration had avoided a cut of $150 million in its request for $350 million post-UNRRA relief.[57]

Confronted with an economy-minded Congress and deeply preoccupied with the historic task of working out a costly recovery program for Europe, American officials feared that any large-scale assistance to China, which in their opinion would be largely wasted, would entail a decrease in funds available for Europe. The administration thus rejected the Chinese requests. But to conciliate the Republican critics of its China policy so as to win their support for its European program, it had to take some action to help the Nationalists which was subtle enough to avoid the appearance of open intervention in the Chinese civil war and inexpensive enough not to be a drain on American resources. When the American marines withdrew from North China between April and September, 1947, they "abandoned" over 6,500 tons of ammunition and other matériel to the Nationalists.[58] On May 26, 1947, the arms embargo was lifted after having been in effect for ten months.[59] With this action, the period of partial withdrawal came to an end. In June, 130 million rounds of surplus 7.92 rifle ammunition were sold to the Nationalist government at 10 per cent of the procurement cost.[60] On September 15, John Carter Vincent was succeeded by Walton Butterworth as director of the Office of Far Eastern Affairs. Like the lifting of the arms embargo, Vincent's transfer from that important office to serve as minister to Switzerland was a concession to the Republicans.[61] Still a third concession was the dispatch of General Wedemeyer on a "fact-finding" mission to China, announced on July 11.[62]

[57] H. Bradford Westerfield, *Foreign Policy and Party Politics* (New Haven, Conn.: Yale University Press, 1955), pp. 273–75; Jones, *op. cit.*, pp. 235–37.

[58] *United States Relations with China*, p. 970; *Military Situation in the Far East*, pp. 1950, 2235–36. Critics of the administration maintained that the ammunition abandoned would furnish only a six-day supply for the .30 caliber weapons of the Nationalists (*ibid.*, pp. 1952–53).

[59] *United States Relations with China*, p. 356.

[60] *Ibid.*, p. 975; *Military Situation in the Far East*, p. 1949. Colonel L. B. Moody, a United States Army Ordnance Corps officer and a critic of the administration's policy, calculated that in December, 1947, the total ammunition in the possession of the Nationalists was, at the normal rate of use, sufficient for only twenty-two days in the case of 7.92 millimeter weapons and for thirty-six days in the case of their .30 caliber United States rifles (*ibid.*, p. 1953; Freda Utley, *The China Story* [Chicago: Henry Regnery Co., 1951], p. 35). The validity of this calculation depends on the meaning given the phrase "the normal rate of use."

[61] Westerfield, *op. cit.*, pp. 259–60.

[62] In persuading Wedemeyer to go to China, Marshall admitted to Wedemeyer that, in the latter's words, "pressure in Congress (from Congressman Walter Judd, Senator Styles Bridges, and others) and from other sources accusing the Administration of pursuing a negative policy in China were compelling a reappraisal of United States policy" (Wedemeyer, *op. cit.*, p. 382).

This move was suggested by Representative Judd to Secretary Marshall[63] and came as a complete surprise to Ambassador Stuart.[64]

E. The Wedemeyer Mission

According to his retrospective account, Wedemeyer undertook his mission to China to perform a "double task: to convince the Chinese that they must produce proof that American aid would not be wasted; and to convince Washington that such aid must be given."[65] On the one hand, he endeavored to impress upon the Nationalist government that unless it instituted some essential reforms it would not be able to secure American aid. On the other, he sought to show that the security and interests of the United States could be protected only by granting large-scale, long-term assistance to "the presently corrupt, reactionary and inefficient Chinese National Government," to use the words of his subsequent report. He expected the signs of a Nationalist regeneration and his emphasis on the vital necessity of Nationalist reform and American supervision over use of its aid would help him persuade the administration to adopt a program of large-scale aid to China.

General Wedemeyer and the members of his mission arrived in Nanking on July 23, 1947, and spent a month in China visiting the major cities, interviewing Chinese and foreigners, and receiving written communications.[66] In strict conformity with his instructions and probably with a view to generating pressure for reform, Wedemeyer made it clear that he could not make any promise for assistance or indicate what his recommendations would be.[67] After he returned to Nanking at the end of his tour, Generalissimo Chiang asked him to address the high civilian and military officials and told him to give them frankly his observations, impressions, and advice. Urged on by Ambassador Stuart, he accepted the invitation and used the occasion to criticize the government severely and to stress the urgency of various reforms. He attributed the military reverses of the government to its political ineptitude. He took the government to task for its corruption, inefficiency, incompetence, nepotism, oppressive measures against political offenders, and failure to mobilize the foreign and domestic assets of the rich and powerful.[68] He asserted that the Communists could not be defeated by force, for "today China is being invaded by an idea instead of

---

[63] Wedemeyer's testimony, *Military Situation in the Far East*, pp. 2296, 2312. This is also Judd's view of the origin of the mission (Westerfield, *op. cit.*, p. 260, n. 35).

[64] Stuart, *op. cit.*, p. 185.

[65] Wedemeyer, *op. cit.*, p. 388.

[66] *United States Relations with China*, p. 824.

[67] *Ibid.*, p. 763.

[68] Wedemeyer pointed out to the Nationalist leaders that the Chinese could raise at least one billion United States dollars from their private investments abroad (*ibid.*, p. 761). See also *ibid.*, p. 770.

strong military force from outside."[69] He warned that the government could win the support of the people only by effecting immediate improvements in the political and economic situation and that whether the regime would stand or fall depended on the timeliness and effectiveness of these reforms. His speech was poorly received and the Generalissimo apparently took offense at his devastating criticisms.[70] Pursuing his campaign of urging sweeping reforms on the government, Wedemeyer restated his views in a public statement issued on August 24 at the time of his departure from China. In this, he criticized the apathy, lethargy, and abject defeatism in many quarters, which found expression in the time and effort spent in blaming outside influence and seeking outside help. He concluded with the admonition:

> To regain and maintain the confidence of the people, the Central Government will have to effect immediately drastic, far-reaching political and economic reforms. Promises will no longer suffice. Performance is absolutely necessary.[71]

If General Wedemeyer thought that verbal remonstrances backed by the power to grant or withhold aid could, at this juncture, induce a change of heart on the part of the Nationalist leaders and bring about needed reforms — and indications are that he did so believe — he was totally mistaken. Prior to his departure, General Wedemeyer was given a memorandum by the Chinese government in which it claimed that it had already undertaken most of the internal reforms recommended by the United States.[72] The Nationalist reaction to Wedemeyer's statement of August 24 was made clear in an interview given by Premier Chang Ch'ün to the United Press on September 2. Mr. Chang charged that General Wedemeyer had failed to understand the Chinese situation and had not sought his information impartially.[73] The Chinese official flatly declared that there would be no change in either the domestic or foreign policy of the Chinese government as a result of the Wedemeyer mission.[74]

One reason for this strong Chinese reaction was that General Wedemeyer failed to sweeten his criticism by any hint of the positive recommendations for large-scale aid which he had by that time decided to make. But a more fundamental reason is that sweeping reforms would have militated against

[69] *Ibid.*, p. 759.

[70] *Ibid.*, p. 257. See also Stuart, *op. cit.*, pp. 186–87. However, in his memoirs, Wedemeyer stated that at the end of the speech the Generalissimo and Madame Chiang and a few other officials shook his hand warmly and thanked him (Wedemeyer, *op. cit.*, p. 389).

[71] *United States Relations with China*, pp. 763–64.

[72] *Ibid.*, pp. 259–60.

[73] *Ibid.*, p. 258.

[74] *Ibid.*, p. 815.

the vested interests of the ruling group and probably would have destroyed
the whole foundation of its power. The basic fact in China was that there
could not have been any genuine reform without a change of leadership
at the very top. Such a change could have come about only if the pressure
exerted by military reverses and American withdrawal had so shaken the
confidence of the top leaders in their ability to remain in control that a
new group or combination of groups might have emerged to replace them.
But this was precisely the alternative which General Wedemeyer rejected.
For he feared that "such a policy would result at some point in the Generalissimo's seeking a compromise with the Chinese Communists" which
would give them a dominant position in the government; or that the long
period of disintegration might end in the emergence of the Communists
as the dominant group.[75] He thus rejected what he called a policy of "no
assistance" to China and a policy of "wait and see."[76] Furthermore, General Wedemeyer, like General Marshall, could not envisage a China without Generalissimo Chiang.[77] So he placed all his hope on the ruling group's
undertaking the necessary reforms. The hostile reaction on the part of the
Nationalist government to his criticism greatly surprised him and caused
him serious concern.[78]

Shortly after he left China, General Wedemeyer knew or should have
known that he had failed to achieve one of his two interdependent aims,
i.e., to convince the Nationalist government that it could not secure American aid without basic reforms. But in spite of the recalcitrance of the
Nationalist government, he proposed in his report long-term, large-scale
economic and military assistance to China. He apparently believed that
strict supervision of the use of American assistance, the presence of Ameri-
man advisers in the military and financial fields, and the continued use of
American aid as a lever to exert pressure could still bring about needed
reforms and rejuvenate the Nationalist government.[79] His retrospective
account of his mission also indicates that his strong criticisms of the Nationalist government and his emphasis on conditioning American aid on reforms were designed in part for domestic consumption. As he wrote in his
memoirs:

> My eyes were fixed on America, upon whom the fate of China
> depended. I hope that by honestly stating all that I found wrong

[75] Wedemeyer's report to the President, *ibid.*, p. 779.

[76] *Ibid.*, p. 778.

[77] *Ibid.*, pp. 768, 778, 779.

[78] *Ibid.*, pp. 258–59.

[79] For example, he wrote in his report: "The purpose of conditional American aid to
China should be to facilitate reorganization of her armed forces; to regain public confidence in the armed forces. . . . Such aid could be conditional to foster the emergence
of a regime which would develop along lines satisfactory to the United States . . ."
(*ibid.*, p. 810).

in China, my *bona fides* in nevertheless advocating aid to her
would be established.[80]

In any case, he considered China so important to the United States and
the menace of the Russian and Chinese Communists so immediate that he
was willing to take a much greater risk than the administration.

In his report of September 19, 1947,[81] General Wedemeyer pointed out
that the objectives of the traditional policy of the United States toward the
Far East and the principles of the United Nations Charter were jeopardized
by "forces as sinister as those operated in the past ten years leading to
World War II."[82] For the Soviet Union aimed at progressive expansion
of her sphere of control and dominant influence. In achieving this aim in
the Far East, she was actively assisted by the Chinese Communists.[83] "A
China dominated by Chinese Communists would be inimical to the interests of the United States in view of their openly expressed hostility and
active opposition to those principles which the United States regards as
vital to the peace of the world."[84] In time of war, an unfriendly China
would deny important air and naval bases to the United States and put
them in hostile hands to be used to neutralize American air and naval
bases in Japan, the Ryukyus, and the Philippines by relatively short-range
attacks.[85] A unified China friendly to the United States would not only
provide important air and naval bases but, because of its size and manpower, would be an important ally.

Wedemeyer advocated granting the Nationalist government "sufficient
and prompt military assistance under the supervision of American ad-
visors in specified military fields."[86] Under this program, the United States
would make arrangements for China to purchase military equipment, supplies, and ammunition from the United States. American advice and supervision of Nationalist operations would be extended to include field
forces, training centers, and particularly logistical agencies. Wedemeyer
rejected "active participation in operations by American personnel" as
contrary to current American policy.[87] To avoid involvement in any way
in actual combat against Chinese Communists and to prevent charges of

[80] Wedemeyer, *op. cit.*, p. 391.

[81] The report entitled "Report on China-Korea" is printed in *United States Relations
with China*, with the portion dealing with Korea omitted, pp. 764–814. For an excellent
summary of its content and an able survey of American policy in 1947 and 1948, see
Part V, "The Far East," by F. C. Jones in *Survey of International Affairs, 1947–
1948*, *op. cit.*, pp. 274–311.

[82] *United States Relations with China*, pp. 766, 775–76.

[83] *Ibid.*, pp. 813–14.

[84] *Ibid.*, p. 773.

[85] *Ibid.*, p. 809.

[86] *Ibid.*, p. 814.

[87] *Ibid.*, p. 811.

American military intervention, American advice should be carried on outside operational areas, although American personnel were to "provide advice *indirectly* to tactical forces."[88] In his estimation, approximately 10,000 officers and non-commissioned officers would be necessary to provide advice and supervision down to the regimental level of the Nationalist field forces.[89] The Army Advisory Group would continue to provide advice on the general staff level, and American advisers would be placed in the ministry of defense.[90]

Wedemeyer also advocated a program of economic assistance to China "over a period of at least five years."[91] This program, conditioned upon Chinese performance and continued progress, would assure an early undertaking of projects essential for China's economic reconstruction and eventually for stabilization of its currency system. Wedemeyer did not recommend any specific amount of financial aid. He left this to be determined by Congress acting on the recommendations of the appropriate agencies. To prepare a program of economic aid by the United States, he recommended the establishment by the Nationalist government of a "high-level planning and screening agency," with American advisers and a staff of qualified experts, to work out an over-all priority list of reconstruction projects. American advisers would also serve in the ministry of finance, particularly in the fields of budgeting and taxation.[92] Wedemeyer's program envisaged the assumption of vast responsibility by the United States for the military and economic affairs of China.

General Wedemeyer recognized the vital importance of Manchuria. But he also knew that it was not within the capabilities of the Nationalist government to defeat the Communists within a short time and eliminate Soviet influence in that region. He feared that the Chinese Communists might soon gain military control of Manchuria and announce the formation of a separatist government and that, following the pattern established for Outer Mongolia, the Soviet Union might conclude a "mutual support agreement with the Communist regime in Manchuria."[93] He reverted in his report to a recommendation which he had first made in November, 1945. This was to establish under the United Nations a five-power "guardianship" in Manchuria, with China, the Soviet Union, the United States, Great Britain, and France as the guardians. If the Soviet Union should refuse to participate in such a project, China might then request the General As-

---

[88] *Ibid.,* p. 813.
[89] Wedemeyer's testimony, *Military Situation in the Far East,* p. 2526. In Greece, American advice and supervision went down to the battalion level.
[90] *United States Relations with China,* pp. 802, 809.
[91] *Ibid.,* p. 806.
[92] *Ibid.,* pp. 801–2.
[93] *Ibid.,* p. 767.

sembly to establish a "trusteeship" for Manchuria.[94] He thought that the establishment of a "guardianship" or trusteeship for Manchuria would create a buffer zone between the Soviet Union and the areas to the south and thus confine Soviet influence.[95] This recommendation was subsequently characterized by him as "the most important element" of his report.[96]

Wedemeyer's recommendations to the administration fared no better than his efforts to convince the Nationalist government of the necessity of reforms. Secretary Marshall complimented Wedemeyer orally on his report but took no action on it. Wedemeyer was told not to disclose the contents of his report to anyone. Officials in the State Department did not discuss the report with him. It was soon apparent that his recommendations were rejected. Marshall rejected Wedemeyer's program for a complex of reasons. In the light of the American weakness in conventional forces and the global situation, both Marshall and the Chiefs of Staff felt that the United States could not commit 10,000 officers and non-commissioned officers to China.[97] In June, 1947, the effective strength of the army was 925,163.[98] Subsequently, Marshall never tired of repeating that there were only one-and-a-third divisions in the entire United States. Marshall also feared that Wedemeyer's program would lead to increasingly deeper commitments on the part of the United States. In the MacArthur hearings, Wedemeyer himself admitted under questioning that, as the situation developed, American personnel would have had "to go right into the area of combat and help these Chinese tactically."[99] Marshall was determined not to adopt any measure of military aid which would lead to American military intervention in China. Furthermore, by the time Wedemeyer submitted his report, it was clear that the Nationalist government had rejected his criticisms and would not launch the necessary reforms. The adoption of Wedemeyer's program would merely saddle the United States with serious responsibilities without having gained for the United States reciprocal commitments from the Nationalist government. These and other reasons are reflected in a statement in the White Paper, outlining the basic considerations in the formulation of American policy toward China in October 1947:

> It was recognized that in the main the solution of China's problems must largely be a task for the Chinese themselves. A United States program of aid to China should not be such as would place

[94] *Ibid.*
[95] *Military Situation in the Far East*, p. 2367.
[96] *Ibid.*
[97] *Ibid.*, pp. 465–66. The army chief of staff was General Dwight D. Eisenhower.
[98] John C. Sparrow, *History of Personnel Demobilization* (Washington, D.C.: Department of the Army, 1951), p. 360.
[99] *Military Situation in the Far East*, pp. 2418–19.

the United States in the position of direct responsibility for the conduct of the fighting in China or for the Chinese economy. The United States Government could not virtually take over the Chinese Government and administer its economic and military affairs. Any such undertakings would have involved the United States in a continuing commitment from which it would have been practically impossible to withdraw regardless of circumstances or of Chinese Government actions. Account also had to be taken of the heavy burden of foreign aid which the United States was assuming elsewhere and of the limitation on the extent to which American resources could be drawn upon for foreign aid under the peacetime organization of its economy.[100]

Secretary Marshall also found serious objections to the publication of Wedemeyer's report in its totality. Marshall sent Mr. Butterworth, the new director of the Office of Far Eastern Affairs, to ask Wedemeyer to delete the portions of his report dealing with the establishment of a guardianship or trusteeship for Manchuria. General Wedemeyer refused to comply, and his report was suppressed by Marshall personally.[101] The reason given for the suppression of the report was that Wedemeyer's recommendation of a guardianship or a trusteeship for Manchuria was an impractical one and that "any such recommendation, if made public at that time, would be highly offensive to Chinese susceptibilities as an infringement of Chinese sovereignty, and representing the Chinese Government as incapable of governing Chinese territory."[102]

The suppression of the Wedemeyer report was one of the most unnecessary as well as most unfortunate actions of the administration. Had the report been published, the public debate evoked would have clarified many of the basic issues. If the public had shown its unwillingness to assume the

[100] United States Relations with China, pp. 269–70.

[101] Testifying on September 19, 1950, before the Committee on Armed Services on his nomination as secretary of defense, Marshall said: "I did not join in the suppression of the report. I personally suppressed it. I sent General Wedemeyer over there as a last resort to find out what we might do, and when his report came back, a great deal that was happening elsewhere in the world, particularly that part of the world dominated by the Soviets, was not considered" (Senate Committee on Armed Services, Hearings on the Nomination of General George C. Marshall as Secretary of Defense, 81st Cong., 2d sess. [1950], p. 22 [hereafter cited as Nomination of Marshall]). See also Secretary Marshall's letter to President Truman dated September 25, 1947, as reproduced in Appendix III, in Wedemeyer, op. cit., p. 446.

[102] United States Relations with China, p. 260. Marshall said that this was "the major and really the sole reason" for suppressing the report (Nomination of Marshall, p. 22).

Senator Vandenberg was told the complete content of the Wedemeyer report by Marshall. He was persuaded that its publication would have been a serious blow to Sino-American relations (Vandenberg's confidential letter to Senator Knowland, December 11, 1948, Arthur H. Vandenberg, Jr. (ed.), The Private Papers of Senator Vandenberg (Boston: Houghton Mifflin Co., 1952), pp. 527–28).

costs of a positive policy in China and to risk eventual American participation in the Chinese civil war, the administration would have obtained some sort of indorsement of its passive policy. If the administration had lost the debate, it would not have been too late to inaugurate a new policy in China. In any event, the administration would not have been vulnerable to charges of concealing vital information from the Congress and the American people. Furthermore, the report was suppressed on the basis of an issue not central to the question confronting the United States, which was whether the United States should give large-scale, long-term assistance to China. The revelation of Wedemeyer's recommendations concerning Manchuria would not have strained Sino-American relations any more than the Yalta Agreement or Marshall's personal statement of January 7, 1947. By becoming suddenly oversolicitous of the susceptibilities of the Nationalist government, the administration committed an avoidable mistake.[103]

Many adverse consequences flowed from the Wedemeyer mission. The announcement of the dispatch of Wedemeyer to China had aroused hopes in the Nationalist government that large-scale American assistance would soon be forthcoming.[104] The subsequent disappointment of these hopes strengthened the right-wing C.C. clique and weakened the moderate Political Science group. In the Fourth Plenary Session of the Central Executive Committee of the Kuomintang meeting in September, 1947, the C.C. clique consolidated its position.[105] At its insistence and in the face of considerable opposition within the government, the Democratic League was outlawed.[106] This move played into the hands of the Communists, for it drove the non-Communist opposition groups into active collaboration with them.[107] Wedemeyer's public criticism of the Nationalist government in his farewell statement became grist for the Communists' propaganda mill.[108] The failure of the Wedemeyer mission to produce large-scale American aid precipitated many Nationalist hints and threats to seek a rapprochement with Russia.[109] After the suppression of his report, General

[103] It may very well be that the administration suppressed the report because, as some of its critics charged, it was not disposed to strengthen the hands of Republican leaders like Walter Judd (Westerfield, *op. cit.*, p. 260–61). But even taking the administration's explanation at its face value, the suppression of the report still seems to have been a mistake.

[104] Stuart, *op. cit.*, p. 185.

[105] *United States Relations with China*, pp. 826–30.

[106] *Ibid.*, pp. 834–40.

[107] According to the Communists, the outlawing of the Democratic League marked the end of all attempts to find a "third road" between the Kuomintang and the Communists and gave a great impetus toward the formation of a "revolutionary united front composed of the various democratic parties" (Liao, *op. cit.*, pp. 72–78).

[108] *United States Relations with China*, pp. 816–17.

[109] Chap. ix, above.

Wedemeyer began to feel that he "may have been sent to China to allay doubts in Congress and in the country and to provide justification for continuance of the old disastrous China policy."[110] If Wedemeyer was right in his judgment of Marshall's motives, it is obvious that the Secretary's maneuver boomeranged. The Republican critics of his China policy seized upon the suppression of the Wedemeyer report as a new issue in their campaign for larger aid to China.

The advocates of large-scale aid to China found a substitute for the suppressed document in Mr. William Bullitt's famous "Report on China" featured in the October 13, 1947, issue of *Life*. Recently returned from a trip to the Far East, Bullitt offered a three-year plan to save China at a cost of $1,350 million for both military and economic assistance. He urged the immediate delivery of certain stocks of munitions by the United States to China, particularly Manchuria, the placing of American advisers in the training and operation of Nationalist forces, American management of the Chinese services of supply in Manchuria, the building up of thirty new Chinese divisions, and the dispatch of General MacArthur to China as the personal representative of the President. Like Wedemeyer, Bullitt did not feel that Americans should command Chinese units in the field.[111] He was, however, willing to accept even greater responsibility in advising the Nationalists and controlling military affairs. Coincidentally, members of the House Military Affairs Committee called on Generalissimo Chiang on October 11. The Nationalist leader repeated his request for greater American aid, warning that if the Chinese government were finally defeated, it would be the result not of Soviet or Chinese Communist efforts but of American failure to give "promised assistance at a time of desperate need."[112]

F. The Policy of Limited Assistance

In the face of mounting Republican demands, the administration found it necessary to prepare a program for China which would, on the one hand, ward off the rising pressure for large-scale military assistance and, on the other, strictly limit American commitments. What apparently forced the hand of the administration was the necessity of enlisting Republican co-operation to meet the growing economic crisis in Europe. To pass legislation for emergency aid to Europe pending the preparation of the full European Recovery Program, the administration summoned a special session of Congress to meet in November. On September 30, President Truman asked Senator Vandenberg to begin hearings on the ad-

[110] Wedemeyer, *op. cit.*, p. 383.
[111] *Life*, October 13, 1947, pp. 35 ff.
[112] *United States Relations with China*, p. 264.

ministration's proposal to grant interim aid to France, Italy, and Austria. In the latter part of October, the State Department began the formulation of a program of aid to China in what the White Paper called a "redefinition of American policy."[113] It was preparing a proposal for economic aid to China for submission to Congress.[114] On October 27, the American government concluded an agreement with the Nationalist government granting $27.7 million of economic aid to China, earmarked by Congress in the previous spring for post-UNRRA relief.[115] In the same month, the State Department agreed to the participation of the Army Advisory Group in the training activities of a training center in Taiwan.[116] In November, Major General David G. Barr was sent to China to head the Army Advisory Group and was authorized to give operational advice to Generalissimo Chiang on an informal and confidential basis but not to accept responsibility for Chinese strategic plans and operations.[117] The policy of limited assistance was thus launched. It followed a period of five months of indecision after the arms embargo was lifted in May.

This policy of granting limited assistance to China was entirely necessary to guarantee the acceptance by Congress of the administration's programs for Europe. But it did not represent a realistic program for China. In the second half of 1947, Communist forces went on the offensive on a nationwide scale. In July, August, and September, three Communist columns crossed the Yellow River in their southward advance. In the last four months of 1947, they strongly intrenched themselves in the large region south of the Yellow River and north of the Yangtze, east of the Han River and west of the sea. This bold movement of troops was undertaken when the main Nationalist forces were attacking Communist forces in Shantung and northern Shensi, leaving inadequate garrisons in the central plain. By the close of 1947, Communist units lay in strength along the railroad from North China to Manchuria, constantly interrupting traffic on these lines.[118]

Mao knew that he was winning the war. In a report to the Central Committee of the Communist party on December 25, he declared that China stood at "a turning point in history," "the turning point from growth to extinction for Chiang Kai-shek's twenty-year counter-revolutionary rule." He was so confident of future success that he proclaimed, for the world to ponder, the military principles which had guided the Communist forces to victory and would continue to serve as their guide. He was certain that the Nationalists could neither adopt his strategy nor design effective

[113] *Ibid.*, p. 269.
[114] Senate Committee on Foreign Relations, *Hearings on Interim Aid for Europe*, 80th Cong., 1st sess. (1947), pp. 2–10 (hereafter cited as *Interim Aid for Europe*).
[115] *United States Relations with China*, p. 367.
[116] *Ibid.*, p. 348.
[117] *Ibid.*, p. 324.
[118] *Ibid.*, p. 317.

countermeasures against it. He was sure that American advice and military aid alone would not save the government forces from defeat. He pointed out that his strategy and tactics were built upon the political foundation of the widespread popular support which he enjoyed and which Generalissimo Chiang had lost. He explained:

> [Our] strategy and tactics are founded on a people's war. No anti-popular army can utilize our strategy and tactics. A vital factor in conquering the enemy is the establishment of strong and powerful political work by the People's Liberation Army based on a people's war and on the solidarity of army and people, the solidarity of commanders and fighters, and the disintegration of the enemy.[119]

Mao was also reported to have said that besides its political and economic weaknesses the Nationalist government suffered from five basic contradictions or defects in the military field which doomed its military efforts to failure. These were, first, the contradiction between the strategic objective of occupying large areas of China and the insufficient number of troops and reserves; second, the contradiction between the same strategic objective and the tactical necessity of concentrating its forces to take the initiative; third, the frictions between the armies commanded by Chiang's personal following and the armies commanded by other Nationalist generals; fourth, the contradiction between the preference for war on the part of a few Nationalist commanders and the anti-war sentiments of the rank and file; fifth, the many defects in the tactical field such as lack of unity of command and failure to utilize American equipment effectively.[120] As will be shown, three months later Marshall also came to the conclusion that the United States must face the possibility of an early collapse of the Nationalist regime.

G. Interim Aid for China and the Intensifying Debate on China

On November 10, the Senate Committee on Foreign Relations and the House met jointly to begin hearings on the administration's proposal to grant interim aid to France, Italy, and Austria. A day before the hearings began, the Republican position on aid to China was once more under-

[119] "The Present Situation and Our Tasks," a report made by Mao Tse-tung to the Central Committee of the Communist party of China, on December 25, 1947. It was published in the United States under the title *Turning Point in China* (New York: New Century Publishers, 1948), p. 9. See Mao Tse-tung, *Selected Works*, IV (Peking: Foreign Language Press, 1961), 157–73 (hereafter cited as *Selected Works*, IV [Peking]).

[120] Sun Han-p'ing, *Chung-kuo hsien-tai kê-ming shih chiao-hsüeh ts'an-kao ti-k'ang* ["A Reference Outline for the Teaching of the History of Revolution in Contemporary China"] (Tientsin: T'ung-shu ch'u-pan-shê, 1955), p. 187.

scored by Speaker Joseph Martin. Martin urged that the proposed program for aid to Europe be expanded to fight communism everywhere in the world, not just in Europe. He said that Congress probably would wish to provide China as well as Western Europe with assistance.[121] In his opening statement, Secretary Marshall asked for $597 million for interim aid to France, Italy, and Austria. He also informed the committees that the Department of the Army would soon present requests for approximately $500 million of supplementary funds for occupied areas during the current year, of which $300 million would be used in Western Germany. As to the full European Recovery Program, Marshall put the tentative estimate at about $1.5 billion for the last three months of the fiscal year 1948 and $6 billion for the fiscal year ending June 30, 1949.[122]

In proposing a series of programs involving huge expenditure in Europe, the State Department found it necessary to make some positive response to Republican demands for aid to China. Thus in his opening statement Marshall also told the committees that a definite proposal for economic aid to China was under preparation in the State Department for early submission.[123] In response to a question by Senator Vandenberg, Marshall said that the administration would ask for $300 million for economic aid to China over a period of 15 months, beginning in April, 1948. This figure, arrived at on the basis of $20 million a month, came very close to the Bullitt estimate of $250 million a year of economic aid needed by China. At this time, the administration did not plan to provide any American funds which could be used by the Nationalist government to purchase military supplies. Furthermore, the administration's program was one of short duration and it was to begin at the same time as the European Recovery Program. This recommendation for economic aid to China was apparently the price which the administration was willing to pay to insure the adoption of the interim aid and the full recovery program for Europe.

The administration's caution was justified by the initial reactions of the Republican leaders to the administration's request for interim aid to Europe as a preliminary to the full Marshall Plan. At one extreme stood Senator Robert Taft whose views at this time reflected the basic attitudes of the isolationist and economy-minded leaders in the Republican party. On November 10, Taft declared that provision for further aid to China had to be considered. The next day, after Secretary Marshall completed his testimony before the congressional committees, Taft said that he was "absolutely opposed" to extending the $2,657 million in additional foreign aid

[121] *New York Times,* November 10, 1947, p. 1.
[122] *Interim Aid for Europe,* pp. 2–10.
[123] *Ibid.,* p. 7. It is perhaps not without significance that the State Department began to work on a program of further aid to China in October after Truman asked Senator Vandenberg on September 30 to hold hearings on interim aid to Europe.

which, according to Marshall, was needed for the remainder of fiscal year 1948. In his view, granting aid to Europe would only furnish the Communists with further arguments against the "imperialist" policy of the United States.[124] Later, when the Senate was considering the Marshall Plan, Taft made an unsuccessful attempt to cut more than one billion dollars from the program. He was won over to support full authorization for the European Recovery Program only shortly before the Republican convention.[125]

The hearings on the interim aid program elicited from Representative Judd a systematic statement of his views, many of which were widely shared by the pro-Chiang critics of the administration's China policy — a group of persons whom Westerfield designated the "China bloc."[126] In principle, Judd supported the administration's program for Europe but he conditioned this support on the adoption by the administration of a similar program for China. He informed his colleagues that American assistance and actions had helped turn the tide against communism in Greece, France, and Italy. In his view, however, full European recovery depended on the return to something like the prewar pattern of trade between Europe and Asia. He declared: "[W]e have got to win in Asia, too, or we will ultimately lose in Europe. I cannot myself vote to put some $20,000,000,000 into holding the line on one front and then ignore another front equally vital to our future."[127] To Judd, China was the key to Asia. If China were to be taken by Communists, "how long," he asked, "can India, Malaysia, the East Indies, even the Philippines, resist the pressures?"[128] Judd did not place Asia above Europe in priority, but he believed that a non-Communist Western Europe could not long survive without a non-Communist China.

Judd reported that the Chinese Communists were making rapid progress in destroying the Nationalist government at home while Communist-inspired propaganda since 1944 had succeeded in discrediting it abroad. In the United States, this campaign, Judd charged, "was largely led by about 20 or 30 writers and lecturers and commentators, and by some men who became Far Eastern advisers to our State Department," including some in "what has become widely known as the 'Red cell' in the State Department, the Far Eastern office."[129] These men "have consistently followed the party line with respect to the Chinese Communists."[130] Thus, the Far Eastern experts' accurate appraisal of Chiang's weaknesses, their moral revulsion against aiding a corrupt, oppressive regime, and their underesti-

---

[124] *New York Times*, November 12, 1947, pp. 1, 7.
[125] Westerfield, *op. cit.*, pp. 289–90.
[126] *Ibid.*, pp. 344, 347.
[127] House Committee on Foreign Affairs, *Hearings on Emergency Foreign Aid*, 80th Cong., 1st sess. (1947), p. 239 (hereafter cited as *Emergency Foreign Aid*).
[128] *Ibid.*
[129] *Ibid.*, pp. 243–44.
[130] *Ibid.*, p. 244.

mation of the Chinese Communist threat were turned into a partisan issue. This partisan attack further complicated the task of policy-making. It rendered the advocacy on realistic grounds of prompt and complete withdrawal a hazardous undertaking merely because the Communists and their fellow-travelers were demanding American withdrawal for reasons of their own.

Judd based his condemnation of the administration's program on the traditional policy of the United States. His task was facilitated by the ambiguities of the traditional policy and by the lack of a commonly accepted understanding of this policy. According to his version of history, a "handful of Communists, fellow-travellers, and misguided liberals" [131] caused "one of the most amazing reversals of history": [132] the abandonment of America's traditional Far Eastern policy at the very moment of its success. As defined by Judd, this policy was to support an independent, sovereign government of China against the encroachment of other powers, even if that government was completely undemocratic, inefficient, and corrupt. [133] It was reversed when President Truman's press release of December 15, 1945, announcing the Marshall mission, declared that American aid would be conditional on the achievement of peace and unity in China. According to Judd, this one sentence, written by an unknown official, informed the Chinese Communists that by blocking peace and unity, they could cut off American assistance to China.

"For us not to help China," Judd declared, "because her government is portrayed as unworthy of support is not only being victims of distorted propaganda; it is ignoring our own history and our own interests." [134] Without naming General MacArthur, Judd reported:

> A great American out in the Far East said to me: "For the first time in our relations with Asia, we have endangered the paramount interests of the United States by confusing them with an internal purification problem in China. It may prove to be the greatest single blunder in the history of the United States." [135]

At this time, the aftermath of the Wedemeyer mission had already shown that no sweeping reforms would be undertaken by the Nationalists. By de-emphasizing the need for reform and by stressing America's historic interests in China, Judd endeavored to justify his program of aid to China. Four months later, MacArthur himself was to state his own ideas in a cable to the chairman of the Committee on Foreign Affairs:

[131] *Ibid.*, p. 246.
[132] *Ibid.*, p. 251.
[133] *Ibid.*, pp. 250–51.
[134] *Ibid.*, p. 250.
[135] *Ibid.*

The international aspect of the Chinese problem unfortunately
has become somewhat clouded by demands for internal reform.
Desirable as such reform may be, its importance is but secondary
to the issue of civil strife now engulfing the land, and the two
issues are as impossible of synchronization as it would be to alter
the structural design of a house while the same was being con-
sumed by flame.[136]

Judd urged a return to "our basic policy for 100 years" of "standing for
the sovereignty, the independence, the territorial and administrative integrity of China." [137] He recommended the adoption of a program of military
and economic assistance to enable the Nationalists to eliminate the Communists south of the Great Wall and, at least, to hold their present position
in Manchuria. His proposals for military assistance consisted of sending
to China "surplus munitions — at little or no cost to us" and an "expanded
program of training and advising Chinese forces at all levels." [138] Neither
then nor later did he suggest the use of American troops for combat duties
in China.

Governor Dewey followed a similar line. In a speech on November 24
which was reported to have been written in consultation with leading
Republican members of Congress, Dewey declared that if China fell, all
Asia would fall. He compared the free world to a patient with gangrene
in two legs, Europe and Asia, and asserted that the patient could not be
saved by treating the gangrene in one leg only.[139] The position taken by
Representative John M. Vorys, an influential member of the Committee
on Foreign Affairs, is of particular interest because he was the outstanding
example of a prewar isolationist who became a strong advocate of a program of aid to China and who conditioned his support for the administration's program for Europe on the administration's concessions to his views
on China. In 1939, Vorys introduced an amendment to a bill sponsored by
the Roosevelt administration to revise neutrality legislation. This amendment provided for an embargo on the shipment of "arms and ammunition"
and thus cut the heart out of the bill.[140] Now he stated in the committee that
China should be included in the proposal for emergency aid for "all the
reasons that apply to Europe." Commenting on the long-term plan for
European recovery, he warned that "we must be aware of not only doing
too little too late but doing too much too soon in one limited part of the

[136] Foreign Policy for a Post-war Recovery Program, p. 2044.
[137] Emergency Foreign Aid, p. 250.
[138] Ibid., p. 255.
[139] New York Times, November 25, 1947, p. 18.
[140] William L. Langer and S. Everett Gleason, The Challenge to Isolation (New
York: Harper & Bros., 1952), p. 142.

world, and thus crippling ourselves in the world-wide long pull."[141] He referred with pride to the position he took in 1939 to the effect that it was a great mistake to try to determine America's possible conduct in a future war in Europe before determining her present conduct in the Sino-Japanese struggle in Asia.[142] Thus, Vorys stood somewhere between Taft and Judd in his orientation toward foreign policy.

Some three months later, MacArthur was to make the following ringing declaration of his views on the relation of the United States to Europe and Asia:

> America's past lies deeply rooted in the areas across the Atlantic but the hope of American generations of the future to keep pace with the progress of those of the past lies no less in the happenings and events across the Pacific. While fully availing ourselves of the potential to the east, to our western horizon we must look both for hope of a better life through yet untapped opportunities for trade and commerce in the advance of Asiatic races, and [for] threat against the life with which we are even now endowed.[143]

During the Pacific war, MacArthur had declared:

> Europe is a dying system. It is worn out and run down, and will become an economic and industrial hegemony of Soviet Russia. . . . The lands touching the Pacific with their billions of inhabitants will determine the course of history in the next ten thousand years.[144]

The basic attitude of MacArthur, whose views inspired many of the actions of the China bloc, was thus as "isolationist" toward Europe and "interventionist" toward Asia as Taft's.

Even Senator Vandenberg, upon whose help depended the success of pushing the Marshall Plan through Congress, dissociated himself from the administration's China policy. When he was presenting to the Senate on November 24 the bill for interim aid to France, Italy, and Austria, he expressed regret that the bill did not include interim aid for China and welcomed Marshall's assurance that China would be included in subsequent plans.[145] He again made it clear, just as he had in April, 1947,[146] that he had not been consulted "in any substantial degree regarding Asiatic

---

[141] *Emergency Foreign Aid*, p. 295.

[142] *Ibid.* Vorys also discussed the link between his own views in 1939 and in the late 1940's in a speech on the floor of the House on April 4, 1949, when the House debated the extension of the China Aid Act of 1948 (*Congressional Record*, XCV, 81st Cong., 1st sess. [1949,] 3826–27).

[143] *Foreign Policy for a Post-war Recovery Program*, p. 2042.

[144] Millis, *op. cit.*, p. 18.

[145] *Congressional Record*, XCIII, 80th Cong., 1st sess. (1947), 10704.

[146] *Ibid.*, p. 3474.

policy." [147] In a debate on December 15 he declared that he had "for some time been out of harmony with our official attitude toward China," and that he had "repeatedly urged a different attitude." [148]

A number of influential Republican leaders were thus united in demanding aid to China. This unity made it necessary for the State Department to propose a program for aid to China which would at least satisfy Vandenberg and conciliate the China bloc. For the greatest danger confronting the global policy of the administration, of which the Marshall Plan was the key, came not so much from the China bloc in Congress, of which Judd and Vorys in the House and Bridges in the Senate were the leading figures, as from the combined forces of the economy bloc and the unreconstructed isolationists, of which Representative John Taber in the House and Taft in the Senate were the spokesmen. Subsequent events show that by making limited concessions to the China bloc, the administration succeeded in averting serious opposition from that quarter to its European program. Indeed, Vorys, Judd, and Bridges all were to lend their support to the Marshall Plan in Congress, while continuing to push their program for China. In the final authorization bill on interim aid, China was named along with France, Italy, and Austria as one of the recipient countries of a total of $597 million in emergency aid. But there was no specific allocation to China or any other country. In appropriating money for interim aid, Congress adopted Vandenberg's suggestion that it appropriate to China $18 million under the post-UNRRA relief act.[149] The amount of money granted China was small but it was a sign that the United States was moving toward a larger program of aid to China.

H. The China Aid Act and the Traditional Dilemma

In the hearings on interim aid and the public debate at that time, much attention was given to Marshall's prospective program of aid to China. The debate clearly showed that the State Department was on the defensive. As noted above, one basic theme of the critics of the administration was that it confused the paramount interests of the United States with an internal purification problem in China.[150] In contrast, the premise of the administration's policy was that without sweeping internal reforms in Nationalist China, American assistance would be wasted and would not save China. As Marshall stated, "Only the Government and the people of China can solve

[147] *Ibid.*, p. 10708.
[148] *Ibid.*, p. 11351.
[149] For some of the high points in the debate and actions taken by Congress, see *ibid.*, 10701–4, 11037, 11296–97, 11344–47, 11679. See also *United States Relations with China*, p. 367; Holbert Carroll, *The House of Representatives and Foreign Affairs* (Pittsburgh, Pa.: University of Pittsburgh Press, 1958), pp. 116–17; Westerfield *op. cit.*, pp. 262–64.
[150] *Emergency Foreign Aid*, p. 250.

their fundamental problems,"[151] and the State Department had been hard put to find a means to help China which would "get about a 70 per cent return in effectiveness of use."[152] Governor Dewey countered this thesis with the assertion that "I do not know whether it [aid to China] would be 50 per cent or 80 per cent effective, and I doubt if anyone knows. Of one thing I am sure, it would be immensely more effective than nothing."[153]

The purely economic nature of the administration's prospective program was another target of Republican criticism. Marshall disclosed that the State Department was working on a program of economic assistance to China which would bring about "a stay of execution in the deterioriation of their [the Chinese] monetary situation. . . ."[154] Judd took Marshall to task by pointing out that economic and financial measures could not arrest further deterioration as long as the military situation continued to go from bad to worse.[155] When Marshall made it clear that his program would not contain any measures to deal with the military situation, Judd asked: "Are we justified in appropriating the tax payers' money as a palliative if we are not prepared to attack the real causes?"[156]

Judd's last question brought out the real dilemma confronting the United States. For the program of military and economic assistance proposed by such persons as Bullitt was precisely nothing more than a palliative. Such a program, particularly American advice and supervision of Nationalist logistical services, might have been the necessary first step. But in itself it would not have been sufficient to stabilize the critical situation. As Marshall was to point out three months later, there was little evidence that the weakness of the government and the deteriorating military structure could be basically changed by foreign aid and "any large-scale effort to oppose the Communists would most probably degenerate into a direct United States undertaking and responsibility, involving the commitment of sizeable forces and resources over an indefinite period."[157] The two realistic alternatives open to the United States were, first, to prepare to intervene with her own armed forces if military assistance and American supervision of Nationalist operations and logistics could not be expected to turn the tide; and, second, to withdraw completely from China as soon as possible. From the beginning, the administration ruled out the first alternative and even the strongest advocates of aid to China refrained from suggesting American military participation.[158] There remained the second alternative. This

[151] *Ibid.*, p. 7.
[152] *Ibid.*, pp. 14, 23.
[153] *New York Times*, November 25, 1947, p. 18.
[154] *Emergency Foreign Aid*, p. 23.
[155] *Ibid.*
[156] *Ibid.*, p. 24.
[157] *United States Relations with China*, p. 384.
[158] Chapter ix, above.

could have been justified on the ground that it would avoid further identification with an admittedly moribund government, minimize American defeat, hinder Communist efforts to stir up anti-American sentiments, and, above all, lessen the chance of an eventual war with the Chinese Communists. But the administration either did not choose it or dared not advocate it openly. Instead, Marshall repeatedly assured Congress that "we have been searching . . . with almost complete unanimity for some way to help [China]."[159] Senator Tom Connally, a staunch defender of the administration's China policy, found it necessary to deny any "disposition on the part of the State Department . . . to close the door on China."[160] Once this basic point was conceded, there was no effective argument to resist Republican and Chinese pressure for granting aid to China. The Chinese government shrewdly timed its demands for large-scale assistance to take advantage of the pressure generated by Congress. On December 22, 1947, it asked for a four-year program of aid at a cost of one-and-one-half billion dollars. Of this amount, $500 million of economic aid and another $100 million for military supplies were requested for the first year.[161]

By the time the administration was ready to submit its proposals, it was compelled to move toward a program of economic assistance to China which cost almost twice as much as its original plan in November, 1947. It insisted merely on avoiding any implications of underwriting the Chinese economy and the Nationalist military efforts. On February 18, President Truman asked Congress for a grant to China of $570 million over a period of fifteen months.[162] The total amount requested exceeded slightly Bullitt's estimate of $450 million a year needed by the Nationalists to purchase both civilian and military supplies.[163] Although the administration's new program did not include any provision for military aid, it did not ignore the military needs of the Nationalist government. The increase of $270 million equaled almost exactly the $274 million of China's reserves of gold and foreign exchange, as of January 1, 1948. It freed China's own resources for "purchasing things for their military effort if they wish to do so," as Marshall testified.[164] Thus, aside from the duration of the program, the major difference between the administration's program and Bullitt's or Wedemeyer's proposals was the absence in the former of any provision committing the United States to supervise Nationalist military operations and logistics.

Both President Truman in his message of February 17 and Marshall in

[159] *Emergency Foreign Aid*, p. 24.
[160] *Congressional Record*, XCIII, 80th Cong., 1st sess. (1947), 11351.
[161] *United States Relations with China*, p. 377.
[162] *Ibid.*, pp. 379–80.
[163] Bullitt himself recognized this. See his testimony in *Foreign Policy for Post-war Recovery Program*, p. 1910.
[164] *Ibid.*, p. 1596. See also *ibid.*, pp. 1546–47; Westerfield, *op. cit.*, p. 264.

his testimony in the public hearings told Congress that the proposed program would not be adequate to solve the problems of China and that it would at most "retard" the current economic deterioration and provide a "breathing space" for the Chinese government.[165] In a statement read to a joint meeting of the Senate Foreign Relations Committee and the House Foreign Affairs Committee, Marshall frankly admitted "the possibility that the present Chinese Government may not be successful in maintaining itself against the Communist forces." [166] He argued that in order to enable the Nationalist government to reduce the Chinese Communists to a completely negligible factor in China, the United States "would have to be prepared virtually to take over the Chinese Government and administer its economic, military, and governmental affairs."[167] This alternative was rejected for all the reasons given in chapter ix. Marshall thus gave up what Acheson subsequently called the last chance for the United States to intervene with her armed forces in China. According to Acheson, "This matter was laid before the Congress," and "the Congress understood it perfectly" and had the "sound judgment not to choose armed intervention."[168] At this time, the actual strength of the army and air force was only 898,000 men with 140,000 deployed in the Far East.[169]

Marshall realized that his program would not be effective in checking the advance of communism in China. But withholding assistance and complete withdrawal were equally impossible. As Marshall explained, "We are already committed by past actions and by popular sentiments among our people to continue to do what we can to alleviate suffering in China and to give the Chinese Government and people the possibility of working out China's problems in their own way."[170] The traditional attachment to

[165] Truman's message, *Congressional Record*, XCIV, 80th Cong., 2d sess. (1948), 1396. Marshall's testimony, *Foreign Policy for a Post-war Recovery Program*, p. 1545.
[166] *United States Relations with China*, p. 382.
[167] *Ibid.*
[168] *Military Situation in the Far East*, p. 1869.
[169] Millis, *op. cit.*, p. 375. Nowhere in published records can one find an official estimate of the magnitude of American military efforts necessary to stabilize the situation in China. But writing in the *New York Times* in January, 1948, Professor Nathaniel Peffer asserted that only a large American expeditionary force of 150,000 men could do the job (*New York Times*, January 25, 1948, Sec. 6, p. 8 ff). In the hearings on the European Recovery Program and the bill to give aid to China, Wedemeyer expressed the view, contrary to Acheson's retrospective judgment, that military participation by the United States was not necessary "at this time" (*Foreign Policy for a Post-war Program*, p. 2070). But Joseph C. Harsch reported in October, 1958, that the administration rejected a proposal made by Wedemeyer sometime in 1948 to send ten American divisions to hold a line along the Yellow River (*Christian Science Monitor*, October 8, 1958, p. 1). Professor Stefan T. Possony estimates that it would have taken seven American divisions in Manchuria and fifteen divisions in other parts of China to pacify and reorganize China (Stefan T. Possony, *A Century of Conflict* [Chicago: Henry Regnery Co., 1953], p. 323).
[170] *United States Relations with China*, p. 383.

China, now reinforced by a perception of the Communist threat to the United States, found its most vociferous spokesmen in the Republican critics of the administration. To the traditional sentiments and objectives, and thus to the China bloc, some concession had to be made.

It is not accidental that the events accompanying the enactment of a program of renewed assistance to the Nationalist government coincided with official statements proclaiming the burial of the policy of seeking to establish a coalition government in China including the Communists. In the hearings on the foreign aid program before the House Committee on Foreign Affairs, Representative Fulton charged that there had never been a disavowal of the American policy of favoring a coalition government in China and that this was still the official policy. On March 10, Secretary Marshall was asked in a news conference whether this was so. Marshall answered that President Truman's statement of December 15, 1945, urging the Chinese government to broaden its base, was still the American policy. Then, the specific question was raised whether broadening of the base of the Chinese government meant the inclusion of the Chinese Communists. Marshall replied that the Communists were now in open rebellion against the government and that it was for the Chinese government to decide, and not for the American government to dictate, whether or not to include the Chinese Communists.[171] Marshall's answer to the first question was easily misconstrued, for the phrase "broadening the base" in Truman's statement of 1945 clearly meant the inclusion of the Chinese Communists in a coalition government. It was in this light that the press interpreted his reply that the Truman statement of 1945 was still the official policy.[172] Marshall's clarification of his first answer by his somewhat contradictory remark was neglected. The next day, President Truman sought to correct this impression by expressing his hope that the Chinese liberals would be taken into the government and by stating at the same time that "we did not want any Communists in the Government of China or anywhere else if we could help it."[173] These words marked the interment of the policy of a coalition government. But the President did not help to clarify the record when he said that his statement of December 15, 1945, still stood.

The program of limited assistance as embodied in the China Aid Act of April, 1948, and the accompanying appropriations in June were even more inadequate to deal with the turbulent situation in China than the proposal submitted by the administration in February. With the help of Senator Vandenberg and his committee, the administration defeated the attempts of the House to force on the administration a program of military

[171] *Ibid.*, pp. 271–72.
[172] *The New York Times*, March 11, 1948, p. 6.
[173] *United States Relations with China*, p. 273.

assistance to China similar to that carried out in Greece under which, as the report of the Committee on Foreign Affairs significantly noted, American military personnel had been engaged, since December, 1947, in providing strategic and tactical advice to the Greek army units down to the divisional level.[174] As a compromise between the House and the China bloc on the one hand and the Senate and the administration on the other, Congress set aside a special fund of $125 million to be "used at China's option for military purposes and in the purchase of urgently needed military supplies."[175] A stipulation put into the appropriation bill by Chairman Taber, under which the special fund must be administered "consistent with the general objectives and the requirements of supervision provided for in the Act for Assistance to Greece and Turkey,"[176] went through the House but lost in the conference committee.[177] As a result of Taber's attempt to cut 30 per cent of the funds asked by the administration, the final appropriation of $400 million (including the $125 million special fund) for a period of twelve months represented a 13 per cent reduction. The lofty purposes of the China Aid Act were, as the preamble put them, to encourage China and her people "to maintain the genuine independence and administrative integrity of China and to sustain and strengthen the principles of individual liberty and free institutions in China." Once again, a verbal affirmation of sweeping principles was juxtaposed with an incapacity to use force in a program of half measures which had no chance of success.

In sum, the China Aid Act represented a compromise between two conflicting views which reflected the inconsistent elements of the traditional policy. Marshall came to be the embodiment of the traditional view that American interests in China were not worth a war, while his Republican critics held to their conception of America's traditional purposes in China. Marshall relied on the principle of non-intervention while his Republican critics appealed to the principle of upholding China's integrity against the encroachment of other powers. Like Theodore Roosevelt and Elihu Root, Marshall was intensely conscious of the limits of American power and China's inability to help herself, while his critics, following William Taft, Charles Evans Hughes, and Henry Stimson, clung tenaciously to the hope that somehow American interests and purposes could be promoted

[174] House Committee on Foreign Affairs, *Report on Foreign Assistance Act of 1948*, House Report No. 1585, 80th Cong., 2d sess. (1948), p. 51. Later, American advisers were sent down to the battalion level.
[175] Senator Vandenberg's speech, *Congressional Record*, XCIV, 80th Cong., 2d sess. (1948), 3668.
[176] House Committee on Appropriations, *Report on Appropriations on Foreign Aid*, House Report No. 2173, 80th Cong., 2d sess. (1948), p. 9.
[177] *Conference report*, *Congressional Record*, XCIV, 80th Cong., 2d sess. (1948), 9292–93.

without the use of American forces. The lack of a bipartisan policy was thus the expression of the inconsistencies and ambiguities of the traditional policy. Meanwhile the pre-1939 active, "interventionist" policy in the Far East, as contrasted with the passive, "isolationist" policy toward Europe, found an echo in the Republican demands that China be included in the administration's policy of containment and economic assistance which was first applied in Europe. The China bloc's demands for concessions to its views as a condition to its support for Marshall's European policies were the growing pains of a nation in the process of making a basic reorientation of her policies and assuming world leadership.

Yet none of Marshall's critics advocated the use of American ground forces in China; nor were there readily available troops for that purpose. Their program was to give large-scale, long-term military and economic assistance to China and to place American advisers with Nationalist units. Some of them such as General MacArthur dismissed the importance of Nationalist reforms in a Sino-American program to defeat the Chinese Communists. Others like Wedemeyer and Bullitt hoped to improve the effectiveness of the Nationalist government by conditioning American aid on Chinese reforms and by American supervision and advice. Marshall, however, was convinced that sufficient personnel to carry out the proposed program was not available. He feared that provision of large-scale military aid and advice would lead to military involvement. He realized that reforms in China were a prerequisite for effective use of American aid. At the same time he came to believe that American pressure and advice would not bring about the desired results and that reforms were not possible under Chiang but that there was no other Chinese leader to replace the Generalissimo. Neither Marshall nor his critics favored active intervention in Nationalist politics to bring about a change in the top leadership.

Thus, a wide gap existed between the critics' objectives and Marshall's estimation of available means. The critics urged making a greater effort in China while Marshall was more ready to abandon the objective of sustaining the Nationalist government. The compromise program of limited aid was necessitated by Marshall's need for the China bloc's support for his European Recovery Program and by the China bloc's inability to impose its views on the administration. In this official program, the discrepancy between end and means was wider than in any policy which the administration or its critics would have followed if either had had a free hand. It was adopted at a less auspicious moment than at any time since the end of the Pacific war. It delayed but did not obviate the necessity of making a clear-cut choice between the China bloc's objective of sustaining the Nationalist government and withdrawal from China. The first choice would have entailed the eventual use of American military power in China

and the second choice would have meant the abandonment of the traditional purposes. The long tradition of American policy thus ruled out the
timely adoption of a policy of prompt and complete withdrawal as well as
a policy of armed intervention.

I. The Effects of the China Aid Act

1. Military Developments and the Anti-American Movement in China

The passage of the China Aid Act marked the culmination of the
gradual return to the policy of limited assistance. Such a shift may have
been entirely necessary to insure the adoption of the full European Recovery Program and, in this sense, may be said to have served the over-all
national interest of the United States. But it did not help to promote the
cause of the United States in China. For the military situation in China
deteriorated so rapidly in the first half of 1948 that the program could not
even delay the outcome of the civil war. It succeeded only in stirring up
the most widespread anti-American movement up to that time.

During the debate in the United States over the administration's program
of aid to China, the Chinese Communists launched, from mid-December,
1947, to mid-March, 1948, their largest offensive in Manchuria up to that
time. This carefully planned attack isolated huge Nationalist forces in
three strongholds: Changchun, Mukden, and Chinchow. While Chiang
was trying hard to supply his armies in Manchuria, the Communist forces
in the northwest scored, in late February and early March, their first great
victory. In March, the Communists began placing under the direction of
a single government and military command the area between the Lunghai
Railway in the south and the Peiping-Suiyüan Railway in the north, between the Tatung-Puchow Railway in the west and the Tientsin-Pukow
Railway in the east. They were contemplating the establishment of a
Central People's government in 1949.[178]

In Shantung, Communist forces overwhelmed the strategic city of
Weihsien on April 29 in a campaign which became a subject of controversy
in subsequent congressional hearings. It was cited by the critics of the
administration as a prime example of the defeat of the Nationalist forces
due to a lack of ammunition which the United States could have supplied to them. To a spokesman of the administration, it symbolized
the futility of sending supplies to the central government.[179] In Honan,
the Communist forces occupied Loyang in March and Kaifeng in June,
two of the key points in the central plains. These Communist victories

[178] Mao, *Selected Works*, IV (Peking), pp. 211–15.
[179] *Military Situation in the Far East*, pp. 2998, 2999.

pointed to a most significant military development in China in the first half of 1948. The Communists for the first time demonstrated their ability to breach the defenses of well-fortified points held by the Nationalists. This in turn showed that they mastered the use of artillery and the techniques of demolition and that they could wage positional warfare as well as guerrilla and mobile warfare. Amidst charges in the United States that the Nationalists lost the battle primarily because of lack of ammunition, the Communist forces claimed to have captured in the twelve months between July, 1947, and June, 1948, more than 82 million rounds of ammunition,[180] a figure not far from the 110 million rounds in the hands of the Japanese army in China proper and Formosa when they surrendered in 1945. In summing up the results of the first two years of the civil war since July 1, 1946, the Communists declared on July 30, 1948, that the demise of the Nationalist regime was "not too far away," although they still envisaged "three or four years of hard struggle" before they could unify China.[181]

The China Aid Act, which reinforced the tie between the United States and the increasingly unpopular and apparently moribund government of Chiang Kai-shek, brought about the most widespread and outspoken anti-American movement up to that time. This anti-American sentiment originated in the commonly held belief that Chiang was leading the country to ruin and that he could not do so without American support.[182] The China Aid Act was condemned by a large segment of Chinese opinion as a factor in prolonging the civil war and strengthening a detested regime. As the government prohibited anti-government and anti-war propaganda, the anti-American groups chose an issue on which to attack the United States which was not related at first glance to internal Chinese politics. This was the alleged policy of the United States to rearm and rebuild Japan. As the embassy reported, "The condemnation of our aid is sublimated and transformed into an attack on our policies in Japan by student groups and other elements."[183] In May and June, anti-American demonstrations swept the country. Ambassador Stuart expressed to the State Department his deep concern that many normally pro-American Chinese had become receptive to anti-American propaganda.[184]

[180] This figure was taken from a Communist communiqué summarizing the military developments between July, 1947, and June, 1948, as reprinted in *Ti-san-tz'ŭ kuo-nei kê-ming chan-chêng kai-k'uang* [A Survey of the Third Revolutionary War in China] (Peking: Jên-min ch'u-pan-shê, 1954), p. 55.

[181] *Mu-ch'ien hsing-hsi yü wo-mên ti jên-wu* ["The Present Situation and Our Task"] (Shanghai: Hsin-hua shu-tien, 1949), pp. 151–52.

[182] *United States Relations with China*, p. 906.

[183] *Ibid.*, p. 913.

[184] *Ibid.*, pp. 276–77.

2. American Officials in China Belatedly Adopt a New Approach

American officials began to implement the China Aid Act when the Chinese civil war entered its decisive phase in the second half of 1948. At the outset Washington reaffirmed its policy of avoiding further military commitment. In a meeting on June 4, attended by Secretary Marshall, Secretary of the Army Kenneth C. Royall, General Omar N. Bradley, chief of staff of the army, and General Wedemeyer, director of plans and operations, it was again decided that the United States should not place American advisers with Chinese units in combat areas.[185]

Congress had indicated that the $125 million special grant was to be used as the Nationalist government saw fit. But in China, American officials inaugurated a more positive and aggressive policy in the use of the special fund. In the summer of 1948, Admiral Oscar C. Badger, the commander of naval forces in the western Pacific, Ambassador Stuart, and Mr. Roger D. Lapham, the newly appointed chief of the Economic Cooperation Administration Mission to China, made a tour of North China which was then under the military command of General Fu Tso-yi.[186] Fu was a tested general who had distinguished himself in many battles against the Japanese and the Communists. He was popular with the people and with the troops under his control. But he was not a member of the Whampoa clique, and Generalissimo Chiang's policy of discriminating against military commanders outside of his personal following deprived him of sufficient equipment. He had under his command eleven armies of which four were unequipped and three were poorly equipped. In July, Admiral Badger submitted a list of supplies estimated at a total cost of $16 million which were urgently needed by General Fu and recommended that these be sent to him on a first priority basis. Within a few days the Joint Chiefs approved the sending of these supplies to Fu when they were available. Ambassador Stuart also pushed this project of supplying General Fu. In a conference at Stuart's residence on August 30, attended by Stuart himself, General Barr, and General Ho Ying-ch'in, the minister of national defense, it was agreed that 60 per cent of the total equipment to be sent by the United States under the special grant would be delivered to Shanghai for the defense of East China, 30 per cent would go to Tientsin for the

[185] Acheson's testimony, *Military Situation in the Far East*, p. 1854; *United States Relations with China*, p. 284.

[186] This account of this interesting and highly important episode is based on the testimonies of Admiral Badger and General Barr in the MacArthur hearings (*Military Situation in the Far East*, pp. 2745–749, 2964, 2987, 2990–991, 3083). Admiral Badger's testimony was vague about dates and details and was encumbered with obvious errors of fact. General Barr's testimony conflicted at various points with that of Admiral Badger. But a composite picture can be reconstructed by a careful reading of their accounts and the documents, tables, and reports printed in the White Paper. Cf. Possony, *op. cit.*, pp. 347–49.

defense of North China under General Fu's command, and 10 per cent would be shipped to Tsingtao for the defense of Shantung Peninsula.[187] For the first time, there was an attempt to bypass the Generalissimo and to give part of the American supplies directly to Nationalist commanders who had distinguished themselves in battle.

But the project of shipping arms and ammunition to China under the $125 million special grant had to find its way slowly through the labyrinth of American and Chinese bureaucracy and the conflicting purposes of American and Chinese officials. The first request of the Chinese government for new shipments of arms under the $125 million program was made only on July 23. This first list gave highest priority to small arms and ammunition. But another request chiefly contained items such as raw materials for the Chinese arsenal program which could not be delivered until the fall of 1949 and would not have any immediate effects on the battlefield.[188] On receipt of the first Chinese request, the Department of the Army initiated availability studies and the computation of prices to be charged the Chinese government. The availability studies and the computation of prices by American officials and the attempts on the part of the Chinese to get a bargain resulted in a delay of a month.[189] Further confusion was occasioned by the submission on September 20 of a revised list of requirements by the Chinese ambassador which superseded all previous Chinese requests. Probably reflecting the rapidly deteriorating military situation in China, the list included weapons and ammunition primarily. It nullified most of the work previously done by the Department of the Army. New availability studies and computations of prices were initiated, and the Chinese government was asked to show the requirements in the order of the most urgent priority. It was partly in response to this request that the Chinese government sent to the Department of the Army on October 4 a list which specified the destinations and the approximate percentage of the supplies to be delivered to different parts of China in accordance with the understanding reached between Ambassador Stuart and General Ho on August 30. Having received this list, the Department of the Army took steps on October 5 to implement Admiral Badger's July

[187] *Military Situation in the Far East,* pp. 2990–91.

[188] Statement submitted by Brigadier General T. S. Timberman to the House Committee on Foreign Affairs, June 21, 1949 (*United States Relations with China,* pp. 976–77).

[189] The administration spokesman endeavored to put all the blame for this delay on the Chinese. See for example General Barr's testimony in the MacArthur hearings (*Military Situation in the Far East,* p. 3038). The statement submitted by Brigadier General T. S. Timberman to the House Committee on Foreign Affairs on June 21, 1949, was slanted to give that impression (*United States Relations with China,* p. 976).

On the other hand, the critics of the administration either blamed the delay on some mysterious, unknown cause or attributed it to bureaucratic bungling on the part of the United States. The views of both sides were biased in different degrees.

recommendation to support General Fu in North China and to send supplies to him on a first priority basis. It transmitted the entire list of Chinese requirements to General MacArthur and on October 27 ordered the Far Eastern commander to send to North China all available items on the Chinese list. These supplies, amounting to approximately 1,200 tons of small arms and ammunition with a total value of a little over $2 million, reached Tientsin on November 16.[190] This shipment of supplies, which arrived at its destination four months after Admiral Badger's recommendation, constituted only one-eighth of the supplies which he had urged be sent on a first-priority basis. The only other large shipment of small arms and ammunition, procured through the Department of the Army and sent to mainland China in the remaining days of 1948, was one consignment at a value of $16 million which reached Shanghai on December 1, 1948. Subsequent shipments were diverted at Generalissimo Chiang's request to Taiwan.[191] Of the $125 million special fund, $60.9 million was disbursed during 1948, and $55 million was spent during 1949, leaving a balance of $9 million on January 1, 1950, and $1 million as of February, 1951.[192] None of these expenditures played any significant part in the defense of mainland China.

What evidence we have suggests that a conflict of political purposes between American officials in China and the Nationalist government may have been an important cause for the delay in the shipment of arms to China under the China Aid Act. For some time, Ambassador Stuart had been trying to use the prospect of American aid as a lever to exert pressure on Generalissimo Chiang to select the right men for key posts and to implement a program of reforms. The Generalissimo had outmaneuvered Ambassador Stuart by appealing to his supporters in Congress, who had generated sufficient pressure on the administration to force it to redefine its policy and submit a program of economic assistance to Chiang. As Stuart sadly commented in a dispatch to Secretary Marshall on May 10, 1948, "Any broad or powerful bargaining position vis-à-vis the Chinese Government disappeared on the date Congress passed the China Aid Act of 1948."[193] But Ambassador Stuart was not without hope that in the process of implementing the act he could still exert a certain amount of pressure on Chiang. According to its terms, the use of American economic aid was to be governed by an agreement to be concluded by the two governments. Thus Stuart told Marshall in the same dispatch that the

[190] Ibid., pp. 954, 978; Admiral Badger's testimony, Military Situation in the Far East, p. 2747; General Barr's testimony, ibid., p. 2964.
[191] United States Relations with China, pp. 953–55; Military Situation in the Far East, p. 1930.
[192] Ibid., p. 1929–30.
[193] United States Relations with China, p. 993.

United States should use the period of negotiating the bilateral aid agreement to press the Chinese government to undertake measures of self-help and reform. Stuart recommended that the American government display no haste in the negotiations so as to learn at least the identity of the individuals to be appointed to the ministries directly concerned with the aid program, and to extend the period in which American pressure could be applied.[194]

It appears possible that Ambassador Stuart also employed the same tactics of pressure in his endeavor to influence Generalissimo Chiang in the latter's use of the special grant. This seems to be indicated by his initiative in working out a scheme for the distribution of American military supplies between North China and Central China in a conference with Nationalist officials in his residence on August 30, as already recounted.[195] It is probably significant as an indication of Chinese resistance to his suggestion that the scheme of distribution apparently agreed on in August was not sent by the Chinese government to the Department of the Army until October 4.[196] While Ambassador Stuart could use diplomatic influence, the Chinese government had legality on its side. For the legislative history of the China Aid Act had made it clear that the special fund was to be used at the option of the Chinese government. According to the implementing directives, the process of spending the money could be initiated only by specific requests of the Chinese government.[197] Admiral Badger and Ambassador Stuart could advise, suggest, and even use their considerable political influence to push their policy. They had no final authority to use the special fund under the China Aid Act as they saw fit. Admiral Badger's recommendation in July to the Joint Chiefs was merely a suggestion made by an American officer to his superiors and not an official request made by the Chinese government through diplomatic channels in accordance with the procedures laid down by the implementing directives. This conflict of purpose between American and Chinese officials was not conducive to speed.

But even if the shipments of arms had arrived in China several months earlier, they could hardly have averted the four major defeats which the Nationalist forces suffered in the seven months following the inauguration of the China aid program in June. For it was not due to the lack of arms and ammunition that the Nationalist forces lost the first three battles: the battle of Tsinan, the battle of Manchuria, and the battle of Huai-Hai. These three battles brought out, each in its own way, some of the causes of the Nationalist defeat. The Nationalists lost the strongly fortified city

[194] Ibid., pp. 993–94.
[195] Pp. 479–80, above.
[196] United States Relations with China, pp. 993–94.
[197] Ibid., pp. 949–50.

of Tsinan on September 23 after the defection of an entire division helped the Communists breach the defenses at a critical point.[198] This outright defection, as well as the immediate surrender of other forces and their failure to stand and fight, had a basic political cause. As the consul general at Tsingtao reported, "Nationalist soldiers and population [in] Shangtung in general no longer consider [that the] Nationalist Government merits continued support in the civil war." [199] The Nationalist forces in Manchuria and the troops sent to reinforce them were totally destroyed in October because they were accustomed to holding fixed points, failed to launch a co-ordinated attack with all their armies, and thus enabled Mao to concentrate his forces to annihilate them one after another. The Nationalist defeat in the battle of Huai-Hai in November and December underlined still another factor contributing to the military debacle. Against the repeated admonitions of Vice-President Li Tsung-jên and General Pai Ch'ung-hsi, the leaders of the Kwangsi group, Chiang decided to meet the all-out attack of half a million Communists at the exposed salient of Hsüchou instead of holding the more easily defensible line of the Huai River. He passed over General Pai and selected two incompetents as commanders for this fateful battle. The Huai-Hai campaign was planned, directed, fought, and lost almost exclusively by generals of the Whampoa clique. Chiang's power interests thus hastened the collapse of the Nationalist regime.

In each of these three battles, the Nationalist forces were vastly better equipped and supplied than the Communist troops, and a large amount of matériel was captured by the latter. General Barr reported on November 16, 1948, that "no battle has been lost since my arrival due to lack of ammunition or equipment. Their [the Nationalists'] military debacles in my opinion can all be attributed to the world's worst leadership and many other morale destroying factors that lead to a complete loss of will to fight."[200] It is possible that, as Admiral Badger charged, the lack of a sufficient reserve of matériel prevented the Nationalists from making plans for offensive actions.[201] Even if this was one of the reasons for the collapse of the Nationalist government, it was a relatively minor factor in one of the most profound social and political revolutions in world history. When asked in the MacArthur hearings for his opinion on the cause of the military defeat of the Chinese Nationalists by the Communists, General Wedemeyer replied: "My military opinion on that, sir, is lack of spirit, primarily lack of spirit; it was not lack of equipment."[202] How could the Nationalist

[198] *Ibid.*, pp. 319, 331.
[199] *Ibid.*, p. 319.
[200] *Ibid.*, p. 358.
[201] *Military Situation in the Far East*, pp. 2762, 2763.
[202] *Ibid.*, p. 2329.

forces have the spirit to fight when the political foundation of the regime had already been eroded?

The early arrival of supplies might have helped General Fu in North China. But after the first three defeats, the Peiping-Tientsin-Kalgan area was surrounded by superior forces on three sides. General Fu could not possibly have held out against overwhelming odds for any length of time. As Dean Acheson testified in the MacArthur hearings:

> By the end of 1948, the struggle in North China had virtually ended with the complete collapse of the Nationalist armies. Eighty percent of all the matériel which we had furnished, both during the war and after, to the Nationalist government, was lost; and seventy-five percent of that is estimated to have been captured by the Communists.[203]

General Fu surrendered Peiping on January 22 under a negotiated agreement with the Communists.

The destruction of the core of the Nationalist forces made it impossible to defend the Yangtze River. General Barr reported on December 28:

> Marked by the stigma of defeat and the loss of face resulting from the forced evacuation of China, north of the Yangtze, it is extremely doubtful if the National Government could muster the necessary popular support to mobilize manpower in this area (South China) with which to rebuild its forces even if time permitted. . . . The complete defeat of the Nationalist Army . . . is inevitable.[204]

3. American Economic Aid and the Chinese Currency Reform

In contrast to the poor handling of the special grant, the economic program of the China Aid Act was effectively implemented. As a result of the lessons learned from the misuse of the UNRRA funds provided to China, the American government insisted on the inclusion in the Economic Aid Agreement, signed on July 3, of provisions for joint supervision of the distribution of United States aid goods within China. Under these provisions, the Chinese government agreed that all United States aid goods should be processed and distributed according to terms, conditions, and prices agreed upon between the two governments. The Chinese government also undertook to achieve a fair and equitable distribution of United States aid food and similar commodities, insofar as possible through rationing and price-control systems in urban centers of China. From the beginning, the E.C.A. mission to China exercised tight control over the

[203] *Ibid.,* p. 1856.
[204] *United States Relations with China,* p. 336.

program of aid. It set out to help the Chinese people and their economy by importing four urgently needed commodities: food, cotton, petroleum, and fertilizer. This program of commodity imports under joint supervision was a major factor in alleviating unrest in China's main urban centers and it succeeded in delivering food and other commodities to the people who were its intended beneficiaries.

But the economic program of the China Aid Act, no matter how effectively implemented, could only have a marginal effect on the Chinese economy, because it was not designed to attack the most pressing economic problem in China, runaway inflation. The inflation in China resulted from two factors directly related to the civil war: the size of the government's budget deficit and the loss of public confidence in the viability of the government. The budget deficit was running at the rate of $50 million a month while economic aid to China amounted only to about $20 million a month. Moreover, the loss of public confidence in the government as a consequence of military defeats sharply affected the value of Nationalist currency. Thus, no purely economic program could stop the inflation.[205] Furthermore, in making an over-all evaluation of the economic program of the China Aid Act, one must ponder the following appraisal by Ambassador Stuart. Stuart, a lifelong missionary, wrote in his memoirs:

> While it [the E.C.A. grant of $275 million] brought some humanitarian relief, yet from the standpoint of American national interests this had to be estimated against the political ill will it helped to aggravate. . . . Perhaps a somewhat cynical moral might be drawn about the futility of mixing philanthropy with politics.[206]

The Chinese government did on its own initiative attempt to check the inflation by a program of currency reform and price and wage control which was proclaimed on August 19. It was enforced by stringent police measures in Shanghai by Chiang Ching-kuo, the Generalissimo's son. But this program could not change the two basic realities in China: increasingly serious military defeats and mounting budgetary deficits. Early in October, a rush away from the new currency started even in Shanghai while price control resulted in a shortage of food and other commodities. The abandonment of price and wage controls on October 31 and the resignation of Chiang Ching-kuo on November 1 meant the total failure of the

[205] Harlan Cleveland, "Economic Aid to China," *Far Eastern Survey*, January 12, 1949, pp. 2–6; Dorothy Borg, "Economic Cooperation Administration and United States Policy in China," *Far Eastern Survey*, August 24, 1949, pp. 197–99; *Economic Aid to China* (Washington, D. C.: Economic Cooperation Administration, 1949).

[206] Stuart, *op. cit.*, p. 245. Stuart also observed that the $400 million had achieved nothing and might better not have been spent (*ibid.*, p. 190).

program.[207] The net effect of this ill-fated attempt was to alienate further the middle classes. For under the currency reform program, all persons holding gold, silver, and foreign exchange were required, under threat of severe punishment, to surrender them to the government in exchange for the new currency, the Gold Yüan, at the rate of one United States dollar to four Gold Yüans. The value of the Gold Yüan collapsed so quickly that by late April and early May, 1949, one United States dollar was worth five million to ten million Gold Yüans. The middle class was, in effect, expropriated. They asked: "Could the Communists be any worse than the Kuomintang?"

J. Mainland China and Formosa Written-off

The disastrous military, economic, and political developments in China during and after the enactment of the China Aid Act brought about two contrasting reactions. On the one hand, the Nationalist government increased its efforts to obtain additional aid from the United States, not only through the normal diplomatic channels, "but also through publicity," as the White Paper put it.[208] On the other hand, the Department of State became even more reluctant than before to throw good money after bad. It adopted a "hands-off" and "wait-and-see" policy. This was shown in Secretary Marshall's rejection of three separate recommendations of Ambassador Stuart in August and October to follow a more positive policy in China.

By August the military defeats suffered by the Nationalist forces and the economic chaos in the big cities had already created powerful public sentiment both within and outside the government in favor of a termination of the civil war through negotiations with the Communists. In view of this development, Ambassador Stuart made three specific recommendations on August 10. First, he suggested that the United States should give continued or increased support to the Nationalist government as the best means to prevent the formation of a "coalition government" including the Communists. Second, if some kind of accommodation between the Nationalists and the Communists could not be prevented, he suggested that:

> [American] influence should be used to arrange a cessation of
> hostilities on a basis of very loose federation with territorial di-

[207] *United States Relations with China*, pp. 278, 400–401, 877–79; *Report by Consultant William C. Bullitt to the Joint Committee on Economic Cooperation Administration Concerning China*, 80th Cong., 2d sess. (December 24, 1948), pp. 1–13. For an interesting sidelight on Chiang Ching-kuo's honest efforts to enforce the program and his conflicts with vested interests, see K. M. Panikkar, *In Two Chinas* (London: Allen and Unwin, 1955), pp. 32–33; *New York Times*, November 1, 1948, p. 1. For the account of an economist, see Chang, *op. cit.*, pp. 82–85.

[208] *United States Relations with China*, p. 279.

vision which would leave as large an area of China as possible
with a government or governments free of Communist participation. Third, in the event of a return to regionalism, American
economic aid be given to strengthen regional governments.[209]

Stuart's recommendations showed that American officials had learned from
bitter experience the fallacy of seeking a genuine coalition government
including the Communists. They had also begun belatedly to realize that
accommodation with the Communists on a basis of territorial division was
the only realistic alternative to fighting a civil war which, without American military intervention, the Nationalist would lose. They also saw at
last that the regional leaders furnished an alternative to the moribund
central government under Chiang Kai-shek. Stuart's recommendations
were in complete accord with his attempts to divert American military
supplies to regional commanders.[210] Had it been adopted two or three
years earlier, such a policy as Stuart envisaged might conceivably have
preserved a part of China under non-Communist control.

But in August, 1948, its chances of success were slim. Thus, it was rejected by Secretary Marshall, who now did not want to take any step
which would implicitly place political and moral responsibility on the
United States. In an instruction sent to Stuart on August 12, Marshall
ruled out any "overt United States opposition to Chinese Government
compromise with the Chinese Communists or even secretly expressed
opposition, which would become known," while, somewhat inconsistently,
he told the ambassador "to overlook no suitable opportunity to emphasize
the pattern of engulfment which has resulted from coalition governments
in eastern Europe.[211] He dismissed the second suggestion by informing
the ambassador that "the United States Government has no intention of
again offering its good offices as mediator in China."[212] The next day, the
secretary told the ambassador:

> It is not likely that the situation will make it possible for us at
> this juncture to formulate any rigid plans for our future policy
> in China. Developments in China are obviously entering into a
> period of extreme flux and confusion in which it will be impos-
> sible with surety to perceive clearly in advance the pattern of
> things to come and in which this Government plainly must pre-
> serve a maximum freedom of action.[213]

[209] *Ibid.*, p. 279.
[210] Pp. 479–82, above.
[211] *United States Relations with China*, p. 280.
[212] *Ibid.*, p. 279.
[213] *Ibid.*, p. 280.

Thus, the policy of "waiting for the dust to settle" for which Dean Acheson was later severely criticized was launched at this time.

The military debacles of Tsinan, Chinchow, and Changchun led to an extensive policy review in late October in the State Department. A series of decisions were reached which mark it as one of the three most significant events in the development of American policy in 1947 and 1948, next only to the rejection of Wedemeyer's recommendations and the decision in early 1948 not to take the last chance to intervene in the Chinese civil war. The policy review seems to have been prompted by a series of cables from Ambassador Stuart asking whether there was any change in American policy. He seems to have suggested the adoption of a more positive program for China under which the American government would press Chiang to remove incompetent leaders, step up aid to China, and expand the function and authority of the Army Advisory Group after prior agreement by Chiang on the acceptance and implementation of American advice.[214] In dismissing these recommendations, Secretary Marshall was able to cite Stuart's numerous dispatches to show how American advice had been ignored in the past and why the policy of granting conditional aid to Chiang would be impossible to implement. Marshall again reminded Stuart forcefully that "direct armed intervention in the internal affairs of China runs counter to traditional American policy toward China."[215] Once more the Secretary of State informed the ambassador:

> To achieve the objective of reducing the Chinese Communists to a completely negligible factor in China in the immediate future, it would be necessary for the United States virtually to take over the Chinese government and administer its economic, military and government affairs. Strong Chinese sensibilities regarding infringement of China's sovereignty, the intense feeling of nationalism among all Chinese, and the unavailability of qualified American personnel in large numbers required argues strongly against attempting such a solution.[216]

Still trying to persuade Marshall to adopt a positive policy, Stuart asked the State Department on October 23, among other things, whether the American government "would advise the retirement of the Generalissimo in favor of Li Tsung-jen or some other national political leader with better prospects of forming a republican non-Communist government and of more effective prosecution of the war against the Communist rebels."[217]

[214] *Ibid.*, p. 284. Stuart's telegram is not printed, but his suggestions can be inferred from Marshall's reply.
[215] *Ibid.*, p. 280.
[216] *Ibid.*, p. 281.
[217] *Ibid.*, p. 285.

Here is another alternative which might have been successfully implemented if the American government had skilfully promoted it over a period of time. But the hour was late and Secretary Marshall did not want to offer any advice which would imply a commitment to support the succeeding regime.[218]

It was also at this time that the State Department ruled out the use of American forces to defend Formosa. This decision was in harmony with Marshall's policy not to intervene militarily in the Chinese internal strife. Once more it revealed the unwillingness of the United States to use her military power to defend her interests in China. It assumed that the United States had a strategic interest in preventing Formosa from falling into the hands of a hostile power, but American occupation or use of Formosa as a base would give her little advantage. It also rested on the belief that the existing condition and strength of American armed forces precluded the possibility of committing any American forces whatever to the defense of Formosa. The American policy was to try by diplomatic and economic means to keep Formosa from falling into hostile hands. According to Acheson's subsequent testimony, this policy was "unanimously recommended to the President by all the departments concerned, and was approved by him."[219] It is apparent that the policy review in the State Department resulted in the conclusion that the United States should not use her armed forces to prevent any part of China from falling into Communist hands.

Ambassador Stuart was certainly disappointed but probably not surprised at the rejections of his recommendations. Nor did the Nationalists place much hope on a drastic change of policy under the Truman administration. While the American government hoped that the China Aid Act would give the Nationalists a breathing space to undertake sweeping reforms and measures of self-help, the Chinese government saw in it nothing but a prelude to increased American assistance under another Republican-controlled Congress and under a new Republican administration.[220] There was much in the developments in American politics to justify this hope. Soon after he was overwhelmingly nominated by the Republican party as its presidential candidate, Governor Dewey stated on June 25 that one of the cardinal principles of his administration, if elected, would be to help China combat Communist influence within its borders and that the United States should provide military advisers, the kind of matériel needed by the Chinese, and far greater financial assistance.[221] His subsequent references to China were less specific. But the repeated pledges

[218] *Ibid.*, chap. ix, above.
[219] *Military Situation in the Far East*, p. 1671.
[220] *United States Relations with China*, p. 877; Stuart, *op. cit.*, p. 219.
[221] *New York Times*, June 26, 1948, p. 1

to bring an end to the "tragic neglect" of China certainly gave the Nationalist government reasons for new hope.[222] At the height of Dewey's campaign and amidst universal expectations of a sweeping Republican victory, Mr. Ch'ên Li-fu, the leader of the extreme right-wing C.C. clique and vice-president of the Legislative Yüan, visited Dewey with a letter of introduction from Generalissimo Chiang. On returning to China he was reported to have said that, if elected, Governor Dewey would take extraordinary measures toward giving military aid to China.[223] Two days before the election Generalissimo Chiang released, on October 31, a lengthy statement in answer to questions submitted by a noted American correspondent. It concluded with the remark: "The center of endeavor in the salvation of Asia must be China. This is the great task unprecedented in human history. I hope that the American people and their statesmen will dedicate their lives to this task."[224]

But the unpredictable American voters confounded the calculations of even the shrewdest politicians. President Truman was re-elected in a great electoral upset on the very same day the Nationalists surrendered Mukden. Truman's electoral victory compelled the Chinese government to appeal once more to the Democratic administration for aid. On November 6, during a meeting of the General Assembly of the United Nations at Paris, Dr. T. F. Tsiang, head of the Chinese delegation, handed Secretary Marshall a message from the Chinese foreign minister. This inquired about the possibility of appointing American army officers to actual command of Chinese army units under the guise of advisers, and the appointment of an officer of high rank to head a special mission to China.[225] Secretary Marshall rejected this oblique request. He emphasized to the Chinese government the inherent difficulties involved in an attempt on the part of a newly appointed foreign official to advise the Chinese government regarding its course of action. Probably having in mind his own experience as well as Stilwell's, he said it would be "a very serious matter for the United States to send an officer to almost certain failure."[226] Dr. Tsiang's initial inquiry was followed by a letter from Generalissimo Chiang to President Truman making the same requests. In addition, the Chinese leader also asked for a firm statement of American policy in support of the Nationalist cause.[227] In response, President Truman called Generalissimo Chiang's attention to Secretary Marshall's recent reply to the Chinese foreign minister. As for

[222] See Dewey's speeches in Salt Lake City, on September 30; in St. Paul, on October 15; and in Cleveland, on October 27, 1948; in *ibid.*, October 1, 1948, p. 17; October, 16, 1948, p. 7; October 28, 1948, p. 24.
[223] Charles Wertenbaker, "The China Lobby," *Reporter*, April 15, 1952, pp. 18–19.
[224] *United States Relations with China*, p. 894.
[225] *Ibid.*, pp. 287, 887.
[226] *Ibid.*, pp. 287, 887–88.
[227] *Ibid.*, pp. 888–89.

Chiang's suggestion for a declaration of American policy, Truman said that his statement of March 11, 1948, expressing the American desire not to have Communists in the Chinese government, and the China Aid Act, extending assistance to China, had made the position of the American government clear.[228]

Coincidental to the Nationalist appeal for additional aid, Senator Styles Bridges, chairman of the Senate Appropriations Committee and of the watchdog committee on foreign aid, denounced the administration's China policy and urged President Truman to call a special session of the Eightieth Congress to consider further aid to China. This demand elicited no positive response from the administration which had just received a new mandate from the people. Not long afterward, two of Senator Bridges' consultants returned from a trip to China and submitted their reports. These clearly indicated the tremendous responsibility and cost which had to be assumed by the United States in any program to save the Nationalist government. Mr. D. Worth Clark, a former Democratic senator who went to China as the consultant to the Senate Appropriations Committee, reported on November 20 that a program to stop the Communists had to include immediate shipment of large supplies of arms and ammunition, combat advice on both the strategic and tactical levels, the assumption by the United States of a major share of the Nationalist government's budget, a minimum loan of $200 million to stabilize the currency, and strict American supervision of expenditure. Clark asserted that nothing less would do the job and anything less would be wasted.[229] The report of Mr. William C. Bullitt, consultant to the Joint Committee on Foreign Economic Cooperation concerning China, emphasized the need for "American direction and control, exercised by a fighting general of the highest qualities, with an adequate staff of able officers." [230] In his judgment, "There is not a single Government general who has the military training and technical skill to handle the over-all problems of logistics involved in meeting the attack of a Communist army of more than 2,000,000 men." [231]

The Nationalist campaign for further aid reached a climax with the arrival of Madame Chiang in Washington on December 1.[232] At his press conference the next day, President Truman declined to comment on the question of sending new aid to China. But he gave a negative answer with

[228] *Ibid.*, p. 889.

[229] *New York Times*, November 21, 1948, p. 1.

[230] *Report by Consultant William C. Bullitt to the Joint Committee on Foreign Economic Cooperation Concerning China*, 80th Cong., 2d sess. (December 24, 1948), p. 12.

[231] *Ibid.*

[232] The advisability of allowing Madame Chiang to come was discussed at a cabinet meeting on November 26. The question was raised by Secretary Marshall and President Truman ruled in favor of it (Millis, *op. cit.*, p. 533).

curt finality when asked about the rumor that the United States was considering sending General MacArthur to China.[233] In her pleas for aid,
Madame Chiang asked for three billion dollars over a period of three years.
In addition, she renewed the already rejected request for a military mission
to China headed by a high-ranking officer and for a forthright declaration
of the determination of the United States to halt the expansion of communism in Asia.[234]

In December, the Berlin blockade entered its sixth month and the
Western powers were engaged in a costly airlift to supply the city. Europe
was more than ever the center of attention. American officials received
Madame Chiang with personal courtesy but held firmly to their policy.
On December 16, the administration released a statement recapitulating
American aid to China to date, putting the total amount at more than $3,884
million. Instead of sending a high-ranking officer to China, the administra-
tion not long afterward ordered the Joint United States Military Advisory
Group to withdraw from China.[235] In taking these steps, Secretary Marshall
did not go as far as some officials in the State Department had recommended. In a cabinet meeting on December 26, Marshall had read a paper,
originating in the State Department, which advocated explaining to the
American public the inadequacies of the government of Chiang Kai-shek.
With the approval of the President, Marshall rejected this recommendation
on the ground that such a public statement would administer the final coup
de grâce to the Nationalist government.[236]

With the inauguration of the second Truman administration, Marshall
was replaced by Dean Acheson as secretary of state. This change marked
the end of one tragic phase of the China policy of the United States. From
the beginning of his mission to China to the end of his tenure as secretary
of state, Marshall adhered consistently to the postulate that the United
States should not intervene in the Chinese civil war with her armed forces.
His realistic estimate of the relative military and political strength of the
Nationalists and the Communists led him to the accurate conclusion that
the government could not win the civil war without American participation.
Unwilling to abandon his basic postulate, he saw no solution to the problem of China after he failed in his endeavors to seek a political settlement
through the establishment of a coalition government. In effect, he aban-

[233] *New York Times*, December 3, 1948, p. 3. It was reported that General Mac-
Arthur did not think that much could be done to arrest the sweep of communism in
China (*ibid.*, December 12, 1949, under the by-line of Hanson Baldwin).

[234] *Ibid.*, December 10, 1948, p. 1.

[235] The Joint United States Military Advisory Group was formally established only
two months previously, on November 1, 1948, by merging the Army Advisory Group,
the Naval Advisory Group, and other American units (*United States Relations with
China*, p. 340).

[236] Millis, *op. cit.*, p. 534.

doned China in order to concentrate American resources and efforts in Europe. Yet he certainly could not and perhaps would not have followed a policy of total and prompt disengagement. To conciliate the Republican opponents of his China policy and to insure the full authorization of his European Recovery Program, he returned to a policy of granting China limited assistance after a period of partial withdrawal. The program of economic and military assistance contained in the China Aid Act was too little and too late to give the Nationalist government much of a breathing space, while it was large enough to elicit the most widespread anti-American movement up to that time. But the course of action followed by the United States was merely a new manifestation of the traditional pattern of American policy. Since the nation was unable either to use the necessary means to achieve her purpose or to define her objectives in the light of available means, her policy necessarily ended in failure. The partisan debate simply dramatized the dilemma between ends and means. The resultant compromises led to an erratic shift in policy without changing its basic course, until events forced the nation to make a choice between the abandonment of China and the use of her armed forces.

CHAPTER XII

DISENGAGEMENT

AND

CONTAINMENT

JANUARY, 1949–

JUNE, 1950

A. The Moral Issues and the Practical Considerations

General Marshall left the thankless and perplexing task of disengagement from China to Dean G. Acheson, who became secretary of state on January 21, 1949. Acheson had served as undersecretary of state from August, 1945, to June, 1947, first under Byrnes and then under Marshall himself. He had been one of the chief contributors to the instructions given Marshall before the latter's departure to China.[1] During Marshall's mission to China, he had been, by prearrangement between Truman and the General, the latter's representative, or to use Marshall's own words, "rear echelon," in Washington.[2] To the hazardous task of disentanglement, Acheson brought his conviction of the correctness of Marshall's policy, his personal courage, and his diplomatic skill. But admitting the defeat of a policy would have been difficult for a nation under any circumstance. It was still more difficult when the policy had been surrounded by a cluster of myths[3] and had remained the object of sentimental attachment, at least for a vociferous group of politicians. The difficulties were multiplied when many of the actions and omissions of the past could easily be distorted to serve a partisan purpose. It was difficult to see that for fifty years a nation had pursued a policy which was doomed to eventual failure by its inherent contradictions. But it was easy to attribute the responsibility for failure to individual officials. While it was embarrassing for critics of the administration to admit that at one time they shared the erroneous judgments of these

[1] Herbert Feis, *The China Tangle* (Princeton, N.J.: Princeton University Press, 1953), pp. 413–20.
[2] Dean Acheson, *Sketches From Life* (New York: Harper & Bros., 1959), pp. 149–54.
[3] See chap. i, above.

officials, it was normal human frailty to cast the first stone. Politically risky to advocate openly the use of American forces in China, it was safe to condemn inaction. Acheson was particularly vulnerable to partisan attacks because he lacked an independent base of political power and had to rely almost entirely on the support of the President. His past role in shaping China policy and his loyalty to his subordinates made him a symbol of everything that had gone wrong with American policy toward China. Moreover, his intellectual pre-eminence in official circles eventually made him a target of assaults which can be characterized as nihilistic. Hemmed in by partisan and demagogic attacks, he never had the freedom of action necessary to effect a prompt disengagement and his policy retained some of the ambiguities of the traditional policy.

As noted in the last chapter, the State Department in October, 1948, had, in effect, written off China, including Formosa. From that time to January 21, when Acheson assumed office, the Chinese Communists had completed the conquest of Manchuria, scored another smashing victory in the Huai-Hai campaign, and practically won the battle for North China. The alternatives before the United States were either to defend the Yangtze with American armed forces or to withdraw from China. The Yangtze was a formidable barrier against the advance of the Communists, who had neither a navy nor an air force and lacked experience in amphibious warfare. As General Wedemeyer puts it, the Nationalists "could have defended the Yangtze River with broomsticks if they had the will to do so."[4] Events show that it took the Communists three months to regroup and train their armies for the crossing of the river.

But to adopt the alternative of defending the Yangtze with American forces would have implied a drastic reversal of Marshall's policy at a time when its assumptions were being underscored by developments both outside and inside China. With the cold war more intense and the Berlin crisis unresolved, the use of American forces in China seemed more reckless than ever. President Truman's call for rearmament on March 17, 1948, was followed by little action.[5] The administration's proposal for universal military training was not acceptable to Congress. While selective service was finally re-enacted by Congress, the Joint Chiefs envisaged an increase of the active strength by only 411,000 men to an aggregate of 1,795,000. President Tru-

[4] Senate Committee on Armed Services and Committee on Foreign Relations, *Hearings on the Military Situation in the Far East*, 82d Cong., 1st sess. (1951), p. 2329 (hereafter cited as *Military Situation in the Far East*). American military and naval attachés in China believed that the river could be held for several months if the Nationalist ground, naval, and air forces could be co-ordinated under a unified command and if the soldiers were paid in silver (John Leighton Stuart, *Fifty Years in China* [New York: Random House, 1954], p. 235).

[5] Walter Millis, with Harvey C. Mansfield and Harold Stein, *Arms and the State* (New York: Twentieth Century Fund, 1958), pp. 214–28.

man put the upper limit of the annual expenditure for defense permanently at $15 billion, which was said to be what the American economy could bear. Military strategy was based primarily on America's monopoly of the atomic bomb.

America's subsequent entry into the Korean War shows that a sudden reversal of American policy is possible when a clear-cut moral issue is combined with a perception of the serious consequences of inaction and when a sense of shock overcomes the unwillingness to use force. In the case of China in 1949, however, the moral issue seemed to be ambiguous. As the American consul general at Tientsin reported in March, 1949, Americans in that key port in North China felt that "our global policy of opposition to Communism should not oblige us to support a hopelessly inefficient and corrupt government which has lost the support of its people."[6] The recognition that Chinese communism was genuine communism merely intensified America's dilemma. As Professor John K. Fairbank put it, "China has been going through a social revolution on which the Chinese Communists have capitalized and of which they have taken the leadership."[7] Similarly, awareness of the ties between Moscow and the Chinese Communists did not resolve the moral issue. To quote Fairbank again, "On balance, I am afraid we must put the Communist victory in China down as a case of self-determination, not of outside aggression."[8] Moreover, a Communist-dominated China did not appear to be a serious threat to American interests. As noted in chapter ix, Marshall did not believe that China would soon become a strong power. Some people believed, to use the words of a report indorsed by the International Committee of the National Planning Association, that "the national interests of China in Asia run parallel rather than counter to the interests of the United States."[9] This traditional view underlying the Open Door policy survived the Chinese Communists' vociferous denunciation of "American imperialism." The expectation of a Chinese Titoism on the part of some officials in the early months of 1949 increased American complacency.[10] The Gallup Poll found in several surveys that only a minority favored strong measures to resist Communist expansion in China.[11]

It is possible, though not likely, that if the administration had proposed a strong China policy, public support would have been forthcoming. But

[6] Department of State, *United States Relations with China* (Washington, D.C.: Government Printing Office, 1949), p. 300 (hereafter cited as *United States Relations with China*).

[7] John K. Fairbank *et al.*, *Next Step in Asia* (Cambridge, Mass.: Harvard University Press, 1949), p. 4.

[8] *Ibid.*, p. 18.

[9] Luther Gulick, *A New American Policy in China* (Washington, D.C.: National Planning Association, 1949), p. 22.

[10] See chap. ix, above.

[11] Gabriel A. Almond, *The American People and Foreign Policy* (New York: Harcourt, Brace & Co., 1950), p. 105.

after the breakdown of the Marshall mission, American officials felt that conditions necessary for the efficient use of American aid and effective Sino-American co-operation did not obtain in China. Did the conditions now exist? At first glance, it would seem that the "retirement" of Chiang on January 21, 1949, and the elevation of General Li Tsung-jên as acting president, had removed the major obstacle to the success of an active American policy in China. But a closer look at Chinese political developments shows that this was not the case.

Before Chiang announced his retirement, he had transferred the gold and silver bullion and foreign exchange of the government from Nanking to Formosa.[12] He had requested the American government to ship to Formosa after December, 1948, all the remaining military supplies under the $125 million special grant. He had tightened his political control over that island. After his "retirement," he still controlled the party machinery of the Kuomintang in his capacity as its director general. He interfered with governmental affairs and political policies by behind-the-scene maneuvers and through his personal followers. He retained actual control over the navy and the air force and two major army groups on the mainland, whose active co-operation and effective employment were indispensable for a successful defense of the Yangtze.

Chiang and Li entertained different plans for military operation. Li

[12] *New York Times*, February 15, 1949, p. 1. Chiang's shipment of the gold and silver holdings to Formosa and his refusal to turn them over to Acting President Li were subsequently the subject of a heated debate in September, 1949, between Senator Connally and Senator Knowland on the Senate floor in connection with an amendment to the mutual defense assistance legislation offered by Knowland to give $150 million to the Nationalist government.

Opposing Knowland's amendment, Senator Connally declared on September 7: "I do not think it is fair for the Senator [Knowland] to be making speeches on the floor of the Senate for popular consumption, in an effort to stir up the ragged battalions of those who would throw $2,000,000,000 or $3,000,000,000 more into the rat hole in China in order to resuscitate and bring to life Chiang Kai-shek, who has deserted his people and has gone to Formosa with $138,000,000 in gold in his pocket, money which does not belong to him. It did belong to the government, but he has absconded with it. Why do not they spend that $138,000,000 before they call on us for another handout?"

Two days later Senator Knowland let it be known that he was going to address some remarks to Connally on the Senate floor and asked Connally to be on hand. Toward the end of a lengthy speech on China policy, Knowland challenged Connally's statement that Chiang had "absconded" with the $138 million.

Immediately after Knowland had finished his speech, Connally replied: "I want to apologize. I made an error in my statement. . . . I said that Chiang Kai-shek had taken $138,000,000 in gold. I was absolutely in error. He took more than $300,000,000 in gold to Formosa. I did not say he took it to spend for himself. I said it belonged to the Nationalist Government of China. He resigned his position in the Nationalist Government. He is supposed to be a private citizen, and yet he takes the gold that belongs to the treasury of the Nationalist Government" (*Congressional Record*, XCV, 81st Cong., 1st sess. [1949], 12640 and 12758). For a vivid description of this episode, see William S. White, *Citadel* (New York: Harper & Bros., 1956), pp. 5–6.

hoped to defend the Yangtze and, failing that, to defend several provinces
in the southwest which were the base of his power. Chiang apparently
planned only to fight a delaying action on the mainland so as to gain time
to prepare against a Communist assault on Formosa which was under his
tight control. While Chiang as president had been vulnerable to the political maneuvers of the Kwangsi leaders, General Li as the acting president
was now subject to all the political machinations of Chiang. Li lacked
money even to pay his troops, not to mention the necessary financial resources to fight a successful war. He could not obtain American military
supplies, which were diverted to Formosa. His orders to the military units
commanded by Chiang's followers were not obeyed.[13] All these facts were
known to the American government. Defending the Yangtze was a hopeless task. The passive American policy and the program of limited assistance had helped Chiang to stay in power for so long that he had destroyed
whatever chances other political leaders might have had for salvaging a
part of China.

B. The Perplexing Tasks of Withdrawal

If last-minute armed intervention was not a practical alternative,
prompt and complete withdrawal would have been the logical course to
follow. But prompt withdrawal was rendered difficult by the same considerations which had made it necessary for Marshall to return to a policy
of limited assistance after a brief period of partial withdrawal. It was also
hindered by insufficient awareness of the possibility that continued entanglement might increase the chance of an eventual armed clash with the
Chinese Communists. The resulting absence of a sense of urgency in withdrawing from China was rooted in the basic assumption behind Marshall's
refusal to undertake armed intervention, *i.e.*, that China could not soon be
a serious threat to American security.

There was little doubt that State Department officials were advocating
and implementing a policy of withdrawal. On January 26, the American
government officially terminated its participation in the training of Nationalist forces and recalled General Barr. The next day, the withdrawal of
the United States Joint Military Advisory Group was announced.[14] The

[13] *United States Relations with China*, pp. 250, 290–91, 292–304, 403, 901, 921; Yin
Shih, *Chiang Li kuan-shih yü Chung-kuo* ["The Chiang-Li Relationship and China"]
(Hong Kong: Freedom Press, 1954), pp. 103–28; Liang Shêng-chün, *Chiang Li tou-
chêng nei-mo* ["The Inside Story of the Struggle between Chiang and Li"] (Hong
Kong: Union Asia Press, 1954), chaps. ii, iii, and iv; F. F. Liu, *A Military History of
Modern China* (Princeton, N.J.: Princeton University Press, 1956), pp. 264–67; *Mili-
tary Situation in the Far East*, p. 1930.
[14] Senate Committee on Foreign Relations, *Hearings on the Nomination of Philip C.
Jessup To Be United States Representative to the Sixth General Assembly of the United
Nations*, 82d Cong., 1st sess. (1951), pp. 820–21 (hereafter cited as *Nomination of
Jessup*).

National Security Council recommended that the American government halt shipment of $60 million in military supplies which remained out of the $125 million special grant.[15] American officials feared that these supplies would simply fall into the hands of the Chinese Communists. In an off-the-record conference on February 5, Senator Vandenberg strongly opposed the recommended action on moral and sentimental grounds. In his opinion, such an action would substantiate the charge that "we are the ones who gave poor China the final push into disaster." He urged that "this blood must not be on *our* hands."[16] President Truman and Vice-President Alben W. Barkley supported Vandenberg. Shipments of arms to Formosa continued. The unexpended balance of the $125 million special fund for arms shipment was never cut off, not even after President Truman's statement on January 5, 1950, announcing the "hands-off-Formosa" policy.[17]

Moralism and sentimentality constituted only one of the factors making it difficult to implement a policy of withdrawal. There were demands for a re-examination of the administration's policy and clamors for a positive program of aid to China. On February 7, fifty-one Republican representatives addressed a letter to Truman, demanding the appointment of a commission to make an immediate re-examination of the situation in China.[18] On February 24, Secretary Acheson explained to thirty signers of the letter in an off-the-record meeting that he could not foresee clearly the outcome in China "until the dust settled."[19] He thus sidestepped their demand.

The following day, Senator Pat McCarran, anti-administration Democrat from Nevada, introduced a bill to provide $1.5 billion in loans for the Nationalist government and to authorize American officers to direct Chi-

---

[15] The published records do not show whether this recommendation originated in the State Department or the Defense Department. Senator Vandenberg, who recorded this episode in his diary, was silent on this point. Westerfield stated that the proposed action "most probably originated from the State Department" and "was certainly approved by Acheson" (H. Bradford Westerfield, *Foreign Policy and Party Politics* [New Haven, Conn.: Yale University Press, 1955], p. 346).

For Harold Stassen's charge that Dr. Philip Jessup made the recommendation of stopping all supplies to China, see Senate Committee on the Judiciary, *Hearings on the Institute of Pacific Relations*, 82d Cong., 1st and 2d sess. (1951–52), pp. 1068–69 (hereafter cited as *Institute of Pacific Relations*); see also *Nomination of Jessup*, pp. 805–7, 890–98.

[16] Arthur H. Vandenberg, Jr. (ed.), *The Private Papers of Senator Vandenberg* (Boston: Houghton Mifflin Co., 1952), pp. 530–31. See also Harold Stassen's testimony, in *Institute of Pacific Relations*, p. 1068.

[17] See p. 531, below.

[18] *Congressional Record*, XCV, 81st Cong., 1st sess. (1949), 1950–51.

[19] Westerfield, *op. cit.*, p. 347. See also two speeches by Representative Robert Hale, Republican of Maine, in *Congressional Record*, XCV, 81st Cong., 1st sess. (1949), 1950–53; *ibid.*, p. 6137.

The *New York Times* reported the meeting on February 25, 1949, p. 1. Secretary Acheson explained in the MacArthur hearings that this phrase was not meant to denote the administration's policy and that it simply described "my own inability to see very far in this situation" (*Military Situation in the Far East*, pp. 1765–66).

nese troops in the field.[20] On March 10, fifty senators, of whom twenty-four were Democrats, sent and released a letter to Chairman Connally, asking his committee to give the McCarran bill full consideration and hearings.[21] Of the fifty signers, only two were members of the Committee on Foreign Relations. That Senate committee was, broadly speaking, sympathetic toward the State Department's desire to withdraw from China. In the MacArthur hearings, Senator McMahon stated without contradiction that, after a thorough review of the Chinese situation in March, there was complete agreement in the committee that "we had best get out of China as fast as we could" and that "the only point upon which there was some difference of opinion was as to the rate of withdrawal." [22] On March 15, some five weeks before the Communists crossed the Yangtze virtually unopposed, Acheson flatly rejected McCarran's proposal.[23] The 1948 elections and the developments in China had strengthened the hand of the administration. In contrast to its success in 1947 and 1948, the China bloc now failed to force on the administration a program of additional aid to China.

In rejecting the McCarran proposal, however, Acheson found it necessary to make a conciliatory gesture toward the China bloc. Furthermore, Vandenberg's opposition to the halting of arms shipment to Formosa had made it clear that the administration could not suspend economic assistance to China without courting violent reaction from Republican leaders. Acheson thus expressed his willingness to permit the unobligated appropriations under the China Aid Act of 1948 to be spent in a limited period beyond the expiration date of April 2.[24] On the same day, the administration sent Congress a bill to effect this change. In this bill, the administration sought full discretion for the use of the $54 million unexpended fund. It also separated its proposed legislation for China from the bill extending the European Recovery Program. Both of these features were opposed by the China bloc. As finally enacted by Congress on April 14, the bill to extend the European Recovery Program included in substance an amendment proposed by Senator Knowland which qualified the discretion granted the President by limiting the use of the balance appropriated under the China Aid Act to

[20] Congressional Record, XCV, 81st Cong., 1st sess. (1949), 1530, 1532–33; New York Times, March 11, 1949, p. 13; April 15, 1949, p. 10; United States Relations with China, pp. 1053–54.
[21] New York Times, March 11, 1949, p. 13. It was the understanding of Senator George D. Aiken, Republican of Vermont, that the letter merely asked the committee to consider the McCarran bill. It was not his intention to ask for aid to China in signing the letter. Senator Connally interpreted the letter to mean that the signers were merely asking his committee "to give attention to the Chinese situation." He asserted that "we have done so, and are continuing to do so" (Statements by Aiken and Connally on March 24, Congressional Record, XCV, 81st Cong., 1st sess. [1949], 3085).
[22] Military Situation in the Far East, p. 1909.
[23] United States Relations with China, pp. 1053–54.
[24] Ibid.

non-Communist areas of China.[25] The United States thus continued to be bound to the Nationalists by a program of economic assistance as well as shipment of arms.

The China bloc was hardly satisfied with this meager result. Since it could not force its views on the administration, it intensified its attacks on State Department officials, obviously hoping that these attacks would modify the administration's program of withdrawal, or that a change in personnel would bring about a reversal of policy. These countervailing pressures constituted another obstacle to rapid disengagement. On the same day that Congress adopted the bill to provide the $54 million unexpended fund to China, Acheson's letter of March 15 to Senator Connally commenting on the McCarran bill was made public.[26] The next day, Senator Bridges called for a "full-dress investigation by Congress of the State Department's position toward China." He accused Acheson of "what might be called sabotage of the valiant attempt of the Chinese Nationalists to keep at least part of China free."[27] His attack was strongly supported by McCarran and Knowland.[28] On April 21, the day on which the Communists crossed the Yangtze, Knowland submitted a concurrent resolution providing for an investigation of America's foreign policy in the Far East by a joint bipartisan committee of five senators and five members of the House of Representatives.[29] Such a setup would have given the pro-Chiang congressmen on the House Committee on Foreign Affairs a voice in the investigation.[30] The Senate Foreign Relations Committee pigeonholed Knowland's resolution.

C. The Communist Sweep across the Yangtze River

The conflict over China policy and the immobilized position of the administration created a paradox: only Communist successes could strengthen the hand of the administration over its critics and enable it to carry out its program. As a result, the United States could withdraw only a step ahead of the Communist advance, thus strengthening the impression of her impotence and lack of foresight. The spectacular sweep on April 21 of the Communist forces across the Yangtze confirmed the official view of

[25] For the high points in the legislative history of this bill, see *Congressional Record*, XCV, 81st Cong., 1st sess. (1949), 3237, 3765, 3771, 3823, 3828, 3829; House Committee on Foreign Affairs, *Report on Amending the China Aid Act of 1948*, House Report No. 329, 81st Cong., 1st sess. (1949), p. 5; and *Report on Extension of European Recovery Program*, House Report No. 323, 81st Cong., 1st sess. (1949), Part 2, p. 5; Westerfield, *op. cit.*, pp. 347–50.

[26] *New York Times*, April 15, 1949, p. 10.

[27] *Ibid.*, April 16, 1949, p. 3.

[28] *Ibid.*, April 16, 1949, p. 3; April 17, 1949, p. 25.

[29] *Congressional Record*, XCV, 81st Cong., 1st sess. (1949), 4862.

[30] Westerfield, *op. cit.*, p. 350.

the hopelessness of the Chinese situation. The administration pushed forward its program of disentanglement. Ambassador Stuart, together with the ambassadors of other nations except the Soviet Union, remained in Nanking even after the Communist forces occupied it on April 24. The Soviet Union was the only major power which sent her ambassador to Canton, the new capital of Nationalist China. Throughout May, the Russians continued to negotiate with the Nationalist government with a view to concluding commercial agreements regarding Sinkiang.[31] As a step to justify the administration's policy and to cut the ties to the Nationalist government, Acheson revived a proposal which Marshall and Truman had rejected in November, 1948. He now secured President Truman's approval for the preparation and publication of what was subsequently called the White Paper on China. In the spring, a large number of officials were engaged in this task, with the director of the Office of Far Eastern Affairs, Walton Butterworth, in charge.[32] In June, Philip Jessup, who had successfully negotiated a settlement of the Berlin blockade earlier in the year, was assigned to work on Far Eastern problems. The first task given him was to edit the materials collected and written by subordinate officials.[33]

The smashing military success of the Communists and a private conference with President Truman and Acheson on April 28 had a temporarily sobering effect on Senators Bridges and Wherry.[34] There was a brief lull in the debate over China policy. Only the indomitable Knowland continued his crusade for additional aid to China with undiminished vigor. At his suggestion, General Chennault was brought home to testify before the Armed Services Committee on May 3. Chennault advocated a program at a cost of $700 million a year to support the local and provincial regimes along the peripheral areas in Southwest and Northwest China.[35]

This suggestion was dismissed by Acheson the next day in a flat declaration that American policy remained unchanged. In May, the State Depart-

[31] Allen S. Whiting and General Sheng Shih-ts'ai, Sinkiang: Pawn or Pivot? (East Lansing, Mich.: Michigan State University Press, 1958), pp. 116–18; Max Beloff, Soviet Policy in the Far East, (London: Oxford University Press, 1953), pp. 63–65, 97–101; Henry Wei, China and Soviet Russia (Princeton, N. J.: Van Nostrand Co., 1956), pp. 230–32.

[32] Acheson's testimony, Military Situation in the Far East, p. 1769; Dean Rusk's testimony before a subcommittee of the Foreign Relations Committee on October 9, 1951, as reprinted in Nomination of Jessup, p. 813.

Arthur Krock reported that eighty persons were involved in the preparation of the White Paper. See Krock's column, New York Times, August 12, 1949, as reprinted in Congressional Record, XCV, 81st Cong., 1st sess. (1949), A5391–92.

[33] Acheson's testimony, Military Situation in the Far East, p. 1769; Rusk's testimony, as reprinted in Nomination of Jessup, pp. 810–11; Jessup's testimony, ibid., p. 603.

[34] Westerfield, op. cit., p. 350.

[35] Congressional Record, XCV, 81st Cong., 1st sess. (1949), 5480–84. In a speech delivered on April 1, Harold Stassen also advocated a similar program (ibid., A2325). See also Institute of Pacific Relations, p. 1037.

ment made public its tentative program for granting military assistance to Europe to implement the North Atlantic Pact. On May 17, Knowland served notice on the Senate floor that he would offer an amendment to provide aid to non-Communist forces in China.[36]

D. The Controversy over the Confirmation of Butterworth

Past failures repeatedly came back to haunt the administration. A divisive post-mortem occurred on almost every issue, even if it was only remotely connected with the current policy of the United States. In June, the partisan controversy was rekindled with new intensity by the question of confirming the nomination of Butterworth to the newly created post of assistant secretary for Far Eastern affairs. This debate revealed a widening cleavage along party lines.

It found even Senator Vandenberg openly and severely criticizing the State Department. In the Senate Committee on Foreign Relations, Vandenberg voted "present" on confirmation in spite of the otherwise unanimous approval given by the committee. On June 24, he explained that in his opinion it was a "great mistake," in appointing a new assistant secretary, not "to bring a fresh point of view in the assignment" and "simply to continue the regime which, for one reason or the other, is connected with a very tragic failure of our policy in the Far East."[37] But given the discrepancy between ends and means, and within the limits imposed by the traditional pattern of policy, there could not have been any obvious alternative to the policy that had failed. Vandenberg thus admitted judiciously: "It is a very easy, simple matter to dissociate one's self from a policy. It is not easy to assert what an alternative policy might have been. I concede that it is far easier to be critical than to be correct."[38]

This same dilemma was revealed in the attack by the China bloc and the defense made by the administration's spokesmen. Bridges characterized Butterworth as "the symbol of failure and of a tragic era in our relations with China."[39] Brewster launched into a general attack on the administration's policy.[40] Senator Connally countered with the question "whether there is any member of the Senate who would have voted to send a United States Army to try to settle the controversy between the Chinese factions . . . ."[41] Another bitter debate took place on September 26 and 27 with Senator Knowland playing a prominent part.[42] Senator Fulbright

[36] *Congressional Record*, XCV, 81st Cong., 1st sess. (1949), 6306.
[37] *Ibid.*, p. 8292.
[38] *Ibid.*, p. 8294.
[39] *Ibid.*
[40] *Ibid.*, pp. 8294–97.
[41] *Ibid.*, p. 8296.
[42] *Ibid.*, pp. 13266–70, 13284.

came to Butterworth's defense by pointing out that, if blame was to be ascribed, it certainly had to be attributed to General Marshall or the State Department rather than to a relatively minor official.[43] On September 27, Butterworth was confirmed by a highly partisan vote.[44] The debate over the confirmation of Butterworth did not make easier the task of subordinate officials charged with implementing a policy of withdrawal. It marked the beginning of a process which led to the appointment during the Eisenhower administration of Walter Robertson as assistant secretary of state for Far Eastern affairs — reportedly the choice of the leading members of the China bloc in Congress.

Approximately one month after the debate in the Senate on June 24, the minister of the Chinese embassy in Washington, Dr. Ch'ên Chih-mai, sent a cable to Generalissimo Chiang, making a specific suggestion on the proper method to influence American policy. Ch'ên recommended:

> As far as our activities in the United States are concerned, it seems that [while] we should cover the administration, as well as the legislative branch, we should especially strive for a closer relationship with the latter. There is no danger at all if our procedure strictly follows the laws of the United States, but Dr. Hu Shih [former ambassador to the United States] is opposed to getting in touch with the legislative branch. His opinion is off the beam.[45]

E. Mao's Policy of Leaning to One Side and Acheson's Search for Methods of Containment

When the officials in the State Department were completing their compilation of a defense of the administration's policy in China and when the senators were debating the nomination of Butterworth, Mao Tse-tung made a historic pronouncement on foreign policy on July 1, 1949. In this paper, *On People's Democratic Dictatorship*, Mao declared that China must ally herself "with the Soviet Union, with every New Democratic country, and with the proletariat and broad masses in all other countries." [46] To make his position unmistakably clear and to anticipate possible objections to a policy of joining one camp in opposition to the other, he wrote:

[43] *Ibid.*, pp. 13290–91.

[44] *Ibid.*, pp. 13293–94.

[45] Ch'ên Chih-mai to Generalissimo Chiang Kai-shek, July 21, 1949, inserted in the *Congressional Record* by Senator Wayne Morse of Oregon (*Congressional Record*, XCVIII, 82d Cong., 2d sess. [1952], 3970). On the question of the authenticity of this and other secret messages from the Chinese embassy to the Chinese government, see the statement by Senator Morse, *ibid.*, p. 3970; the letter from Dr. Ch'ên; and another letter commenting on Dr. Ch'ên's explanation, *ibid.*, pp. 4016–17.

[46] Mao Tse-tung, *On People's Democratic Dictatorship* (Peking: Foreign Language Press, 1952), p. 10.

"You are leaning to one side." Exactly. The forty years' experience of Sun Yat-sen and the twenty-eight years' experience of the
Chinese Communist Party have convinced us that in order to at-
tain victory and consolidate it, we must lean to one side. According to these experiences, the Chinese people must lean either to
the side of imperialism or to that of socialism. There can be no
exception. There can be no sitting on the fence; there is no third
road. We oppose Chiang Kai-shek's reactionary clique, which
leans to the side of imperialism. We also oppose illusions about a
third road. Not only in China but throughout the world, one must
lean either to imperialism or to socialism. There is no exception.
Neutrality is merely a camouflage; a third road does not exist.[47]

Mao was deliberately provocative. For, on the one hand, he did not feel
that in the relations between the revolutionaries and the "reactionaries" it
made any difference whether one was provocative or not. On the other
hand, a clear-cut and provocative statement of position served his purpose
of drawing a sharp line between the revolutionaries and the "reactionaries"
and of "raising our own morale while deflating the enemy's prestige."[48]
Then he proceeded to make explicit the two basic assumptions of his policy
of leaning to one side. On the one hand:

In an era when imperialism still exists, it is impossible for a genuine people's revolution in any country to achieve victory without
various forms of help from the international revolutionary forces.
Even when victory is won, it cannot be made secure without such
help.[49]

On the other hand, Mao did not believe that the United States and Great
Britain would give aid to a "people's state." If they should trade with and
grant a loan to China, they would do so to "ease their own crisis" rather
than to "help the Chinese people."[50] These statements further clarified the
basic assumptions underlying a declaration issued on April 3 by the Chinese
Communists and the leaders of the small parties in China, in which they
condemned the North Atlantic Pact and affirmed their intention to march
hand-in-hand with "our ally, the Soviet Union" in the event of war. Ideological convictions thus combined with hostility toward the United States to
lead Mao to make a sharp break with the age-old Chinese policy of using
barbarians to control barbarians.

Mao's statement did not make it easier for the State Department to im-

[47] *Ibid.*
[48] *Ibid.*
[49] *Ibid.*, p. 11.
[50] *Ibid.*, p. 12. See also p. 13.

plement a program of withdrawal. In printing an article by Chennault which advocated a program of aid to save part of China, the editors of *Life* prefaced it with the observation that Mao's article had "shattered the illusion cherished by many an American — the illusion that China's Communists are 'different.'"

Mao's declaration apparently had a sobering effect on official thinking. In contrast to the first four months of 1949, there were now very few reports that officials in the State Department expected an early development of Titoism in China.[51] On July 18, Secretary Acheson sent Mr. Philip Jessup, ambassador-at-large, a top-secret memorandum setting down the policy of containing communism in Asia and instructing Jessup to draw up possible programs of action to achieve this purpose. Acheson told Jessup of his desire "to make absolutely certain that we are neglecting no opportunity that would be within our capabilities to achieve the purpose of halting the spread of totalitarian communism in Asia."[52] In August, Secretary Acheson invited Mr. Everett Case, president of Colgate University, and Mr. Raymond Fosdick, former president of the Rockefeller Foundation, to serve as consultants to the State Department and to work with Jessup in the search for concrete programs of action.[53]

One alternative which had been ruled out was the conclusion of a Pacific pact similar to the North Atlantic Treaty. Acheson was averse to being drawn into the conflicts between the Southeast Asian countries themselves and between them and the European powers. He was conscious of the limits of American resources and power.[54] Furthermore, India, potentially the most powerful non-Communist nation in South Asia, was averse to participation in any bloc and her government thought all discussions of a Pacific pact premature. Japan was under occupation. The other Asian nations could contribute very little real strength to a common cause. The most active Asian advocate of an anti-Communist alliance was none other than Generalissimo Chiang, from whom the American government was seeking to dissociate itself. On July 5, Generalissimo Chiang declared in an interview with an American correspondent that "regardless of whether I hold

---

[51] On February 14, C. S. Sulzberger reported that the United States clearly recognized "the possibility that while Mr. Mao is a devout Marxist he may also be a 'Titoite' heretic" (*New York Times*, February 14, 1949, p. 10). See also his articles in *ibid.*, February 5, 1949, p. 12; February 18, 1949, p. 8. According to James Reston, some of the American officials believed that Mao Tse-tung and other Communist leaders would rapidly show signs of Titoism once they were in control (*ibid.*, April 24, 1949, Sec. 4, p. 3). See chap. ix, above.

[52] Secretary Acheson's top-secret memorandum for Ambassador Jessup, July 18, 1949, as reprinted in *Nomination of Jessup*, p. 603.

[53] *Ibid.*, pp. 603–4.

[54] See Acheson's statement on May 8, 1949, *Department of State Bulletin*, (May 29, 1949), p. 696; Royal Institute of International Affairs, *Survey of International Affairs, 1949–50* (London: Oxford University Press, 1953), p. 33.

any political office, I cannot give up my revolutionary leadership." [55] At his suggestion, the Kuomintang established in mid-July a new "Extraordinary Committee" with Chiang as the chairman and Acting President Li as one of the two vice-chairmen. This new organization gave Chiang an additional instrument to control political and military affairs in his capacity as the party leader of the Kuomintang. Without even informing Acting President Li beforehand,[56] Generalissimo Chiang flew to the Philippines to pay a visit to President Quirino on July 10.[57] The two Asian leaders announced their intention to issue invitations to a conference for the purpose of discussing an anti-Communist alliance. After his return to Canton, Chiang told the American minister that he had to take the initiative to conclude an anti-Communist alliance because the United States refused to assume the active leadership in Far Eastern affairs.[58] Chiang visited Korea in August, and on August 8 Chiang and President Syngman Rhee urged President Quirino to take steps to summon such a conference. At this time American troops had completed their withdrawal from Korea for more than a month.[59] The previous March, General MacArthur had traced in an interview with a reporter an American line of defense which left out South Korea.[60]

F. The White Paper

While Generalissimo Chiang was flying to Korea to promote his grandiose plan of an anti-Communist alliance, the State Department issued on August 5 the White Paper on China which attributed the failure to counter Communist revolutionary strategy to the basic weakness of Chiang's government. The document was released in the belief that, as Acheson put it subsequently, "the disasters had already overtaken the Nationalist government." [61] The White Paper represented an attempt to justify, before the bar of American opinion, the administration's policy since Pearl Harbor.[62] Acheson's letter of transmittal revealed clearly the dilemma to which the traditional pattern of American policy had led the United States. Acheson conceded that military intervention on a major scale to assist the

[55] *Washington Daily News*, July 5, 1949, as inserted in the *Congressional Record* by Senator Knowland (*Congressional Record*, XCV, 81st Cong., 1st sess. [1949], p. 8820).

[56] Liang, *op. cit.*, pp. 156–63.

[57] Chiang Ching-kuo, *Fu-chung chih-yüan* ["Carrying a Heavy Burden to Reach a Long Distance"] (1960), Part II, pp. 8–10.

[58] *Ibid.*, p. 142.

[59] Harry Truman, *Years of Trial and Hope* (New York: Doubleday & Co., 1956), p. 329. The last of the American troops left Korea on June 29, 1949.

[60] *New York Times*, March 2, 1949, p. 22.

[61] *Military Situation in the Far East*, p. 1770.

[62] Testifying in the MacArthur hearings, Acheson said, "At the time this [*i.e.*, the White Paper] was finally put out, it seemed to me we were in the position where American people had to know what had gone on . . ." (*ibid.*).

Nationalists to destroy the Communists "may look attractive theoretically and in retrospect." But it was "wholly impractical" because "it is obvious that the American people would not have sanctioned such a colossal commitment of our armies in 1945 or later."[63] Acheson's letter also contained an admission that the traditional policy of assisting the Chinese people in resisting domination by any foreign power or powers had failed to achieve its purpose. "In this case," Acheson explained, "the foreign domination has been masked behind the façade of a vast crusading movement which apparently has seemed to many Chinese to be wholly indigenous and national."[64] The only alternative open to the United States was "full-scale intervention in behalf of a Government which had lost the confidence of its own troops and its own people."[65] But intervention "would have been resented by the mass of the Chinese people, would have diametrically reversed our historic policy and would have been condemned by the American people."[66] Acheson concluded:

> The unfortunate but inescapable fact is that the ominous result of the civil war in China was beyond the control of the government of the United States. Nothing that this country did or could have done within the reasonable limits of its capabilities could have changed that result; nothing that was left undone by this country has contributed to it.[67]

Acheson saw no possibility of the development of a Chinese Titoism. As if to answer Mao's flamboyant proclamation of the policy of "leaning to one side," Acheson declared that "the Communist leaders have foresworn their Chinese heritage and have publicly announced their subservience to a foreign power, Russia, which during the last fifty years, under Czars and Communists alike, has been most assiduous in its efforts to extend its control in the Far East."[68] Echoing the policy of containment stated in his July 18 memorandum to Jessup, Acheson warned that "should the [Chinese] Communist regime lend itself to the aims of Soviet Russian imperialism and attempt to engage in aggression against China's neighbors, we and the other members of the United Nations would be confronted by a situation violative of the principles of the United Nations Charter and threatening international peace and security."[69] As for the distant future, Acheson found hope in the belief that "ultimately the profound civilization and the democratic individualism in China will reassert themselves and she will

[63] *United States Relations with China*, p. x.
[64] *Ibid.*, p. xvi.
[65] *Ibid.*, p. xv.
[66] *Ibid.*, p. xvi.
[67] *Ibid.*
[68] *Ibid.*
[69] *Ibid.*, p. xvii.

throw off the foreign yoke."[70] The United States, Acheson submitted, should "encourage all developments in China which now and in the future work toward this end."[71]

If Acheson hoped that the White Paper would silence his critics and win over public opinion, he was soon disappointed. On the very day it was released, both Senator Knowland and Representative Judd made brief statements on the floor of Congress, asserting that the White Paper and the documents reproduced in it substantiated their criticisms of the administration's policy.[72] Two days later, General Hurley issued a statement calling the White Paper "a smooth alibi for the pro-Communists in the State Department who had engineered the overthrow of our ally, the Nationalist Government of the Republic of China and aided in the Communist conquest of China."[73] On August 19, Judd charged that the State Department omitted sixteen documents and facts which would further support the charges made by the critics.[74] The climax was reached when Senators Bridges, Knowland, McCarran, and Wherry issued a lengthy memorandum, bitterly assailing the White Paper as "a 1,054-page whitewash of a wishful, do-nothing policy which has succeeded only in placing Asia in danger of Soviet conquest."[75] The attack was so intense that Secretary Acheson was obliged to issue a statement in answer to Judd's specific charge of sixteen omissions.[76]

Those who opposed the China bloc's demands for a positive policy were also critical of the White Paper but for diametrically opposite reasons.[77] In a series of three articles, Walter Lippmann refused to accept "Acheson's claim that our China policy was essentially right, and that the result was beyond our control."[78] He desired to know "the causes and the remedies for Chiang's stranglehold on American policy."[79] He wanted an inquiry into the disastrous failure which would be "pursued in the manner of statesmen forming a policy rather than of a lawyer seeking a verdict for his client."[80]

[70] *Ibid.*, p. xvi.
[71] *Ibid.*
[72] *Congressional Record*, XCV, 81st Cong., 1st sess. (1949), 10813, 10875.
[73] *Ibid.*, p. 10941.
[74] *Ibid.*, pp. 11881–82.
[75] *Ibid.*, pp. A5451–54. For the most succinct criticism of the publication of the White Paper by a scholar who was also a critic of the administration's policy, see Paul M. A. Linebarger, "The Failure of Secret Diplomacy in China," *Far Eastern Survey,* September 7, 1949, pp. 214 ff.
[76] *Department of State Bulletin*, September 5, 1949, pp. 350–52, 359.
[77] For a survey of the various comments on the White Paper, see Francis Valeo, *The China White Paper* (Washington, D.C.: Legislative Reference Service, 1949).
[78] Walter Lippmann, "The White Paper: The Chiang Stranglehold," September 12, 1949, as reprinted in *Commentaries on American Foreign Policy* (New York: American Institute of Pacific Relations, 1950), p. 7.
[79] *Ibid.*
[80] *Ibid.*

In his opinion, the White Paper "does not even ask, much less does it answer, the crucial questions."[81]

In China, the White Paper proved to be grist to the Communist propaganda mill. The official Communist organ, Jên-min jih-pao, charged on August 19 that the White Paper furnished conclusive evidence of General Hurley's interference in Chinese domestic politics through his policy of supporting Chiang Kai-shek, exposed General Marshall's partiality for the Nationalists in his mediatory efforts, and disclosed the political intrigues of Ambassador Stuart in his attempt to build up the influence of pro-American elements both within and outside the Kuomintang.[82] In five articles written for the Jên-min jih-pao, Mao seized upon the White Paper to intensify his attack on the American government, to launch a campaign to destroy the "illusions" of the Chinese liberals about the United States, and to win them over to his cause. Mao characterized the White Paper as a counterrevolutionary document which openly demonstrated "United States imperialist intervention in China."[83] An old hand at trickery and deception, like British imperialism, would not, he averred, have published such a document but

> the newly arrived, upstart and neurotic United States imperialist group — Truman, Marshall, Acheson, Leighton Stuart and others — have considered it necessary and practicable to reveal publicly some (but not all) of their counter-revolutionary doings in order to argue with opponents in their own camp as to which kind of counter-revolutionary tactics is the more clever.[84]

In revealing many of America's "treasured tricks" of the past, the White Paper had become material for the education of the Chinese people. According to Mao, Acheson had made a clean sweep of the illusions about United States humanity, justice, and virtue which the shortsighted, muddle-headed Chinese liberals and democratic individualists had entertained. "It is," Mao declared, "a bucket of cold water particularly for those who believe that everything American is good and hope that China will model herself on the United States."[85]

As for the future American policy, Mao took seriously Acheson's pious

---

[81] Walter Lippmann, "The White Paper: Mr. Acheson's Conclusion," *ibid.*, p. 1. For an attempt to answer some of the basic questions about the China policy of the United States, see John K. Fairbank, "Toward a Dynamic Far Eastern Policy," *Far Eastern Survey*, September 7, 1949, pp. 209 ff.

[82] *Jên-min jih-pao*, August 19, 1949, p. 2. For an account of other Communist comments on the White Paper, see Knight Biggerstaff, "The Nanking Press: April–September, 1949," *Far Eastern Survey*, March 8, 1950, pp. 53 ff.

[83] Mao Tse-tung, *Selected Works*, IV (Peking: Foreign Languages Press, 1961), (hereafter cited as Mao, *Selected Works*, IV [Peking]).

[84] *Ibid.*

[85] *Ibid.*, p. 430.

declaration that "ultimately the profound civilization and the democratic individualism of China will reassert themselves and she will throw off the foreign yoke." He took it as an indication that the United States would continue to make trouble, placing her hope on the Chinese supporters of "democratic individualism."[86] He declared:

> Make trouble, fail, make trouble again, fail again till their doom; that is the logic of the imperialists and all reactionaries the world over in dealing with the people's cause. . . . This is a Marxist law. When we say "imperialism is ferocious," we mean that its nature will never change.[87]

In contrast, "fight, fail, fight again, fail again, fight again . . . till their victory" was said to be the logic of the people. Mao told the "progressives" that it was their duty to prevent the middle-of-the-roaders and the waverers from being pulled over by the imperialists and to tell the deceived to cast away their illusions about the United States. When these people were won over, "United States imperialism" would be entirely isolated, and Acheson would no longer be able to "play any of his tricks."[88] Let "United States imperialism" and the Kuomintang reactionaries blockade the Chinese Communists for eight or ten years, Mao said, and "by that time all of China's problems will have been solved."[89] Even now, "United States imperialism" and the Kuomintang reactionaries had been defeated. Mao asserted: "It is we who are going to attack them, not they who are coming out to attack us. They will soon be finished."[90]

G. Military Assistance for the "General Area of China"

The China bloc was not deterred by the publication of the White Paper from pressing for military aid to China. Once again it endeavored to use the administration's European program as a peg on which to hang its program for China. In the congressional deliberations on the general military assistance bill implementing the North Atlantic Pact and giving aid to Greece, Turkey, Iran, Korea, and the Philippines, the friends of the Nationalist government both in the Senate and the House proposed amendments to grant military aid to China. In contrast to Marshall's readiness in 1947 and 1948 to make concessions to the China bloc, the congressional supporters of the administration offered strong and effective initial resistance to the China bloc's demands. In the House, two amendments and a

[86] *Ibid.*, p. 428.
[87] *Ibid.*
[88] *Ibid.*
[89] *Ibid.*, p. 438.
[90] *Ibid.*, p. 430.

separate bill to grant military assistance to China failed.[91] In the Senate, Knowland offered an amendment which would grant $125 million for military assistance and provide an American mission to advise the Chinese government.[92] But the combined Committee on Foreign Relations and Committee on Armed Services adopted, by a vote divided strictly along party lines, an amendment offered by Connally granting a $75 million emergency and contingency fund to the President for him to spend or not to spend anywhere in China and the Far East without any detailed accounting to Congress.[93]

Even at this late date, however, the China bloc showed that it was both willing and able to endanger the administration's program for Europe unless it gained some concessions on aid to China. In the House, its defeats on the question of China gave some of its members an additional motive to support an amendment offered by James P. Richards, Democrat of South Carolina, which would cut in half the $1.1 billion requested by the administration for military assistance to the NATO countries with the purpose of prodding them to make integrated arrangements for defense. With strong support from Vorys and Judd, the Richards amendment passed the House by a vote of 209 to 151.[94] In the Senate, some members of the China bloc demonstrated their displeasure by supporting in the combined committees an amendment offered by Senator Walter F. George of Georgia to cut the funds requested for military assistance to Europe by $300 million. George's proposal was defeated by the slim margin of 13 to 10.[95]

Once again a compromise with the China bloc was necessary. The Senate adopted a suggestion offered by Vandenberg, making $75 million available for use in "the general area of China." In the conference committee, the House cut of half the authorization for NATO countries was restored and the Senate provision for $75 million of aid to the "general area of China" was accepted. In the House, both Vorys and Judd reversed their earlier positions and supported the authorization of the amount requested by the administration.[96] The bill passed Congress on September 28, and four weeks later almost the full amount was appropriated. Thus, the United States appeared to the outside world to be tied to the Nationalists by a

[91] *Congressional Record*, XCV, 81st Cong., 1st sess. (1949), 11013, 11782–91; *New York Times*, August 16, 1949, p. 1.

[92] *Congressional Record*, XCV, 81st Cong., 1st sess. (1949), 10737–38.

[93] Westerfield, *op. cit.*, p. 358.

[94] For Vorys' position, see *Congressional Record*, XCV, 81st Cong., 1st sess. (1949), 11666. For Judd's speech, see *ibid.*, pp. 11787–88. For the House action, see *ibid.*, p. 11807.

[95] *New York Times*, September 10, 1949, p. 1. For Knowland's statement of September 9, 1949, see *Congressional Record*, XCV, 81st Cong., 1st sess. (1949), 12757.

[96] For a general account of this episode, see Westerfield, *op. cit.*, pp. 355–59; Holbert Carroll, *The House of Representatives and Foreign Affairs* (Pittsburgh: University of Pittsburgh, 1958), pp. 127–29.

new program of military assistance. But in reality the China bloc won only an empty victory. At the end of December, as we shall see, the National Security Council supported the State Department's view and rejected a proposal made by the Joint Chiefs to give some military assistance to Formosa in addition to the $125 million appropriated in 1948.[97] The $75 million of military assistance to the general area of China was used entirely in places other than Formosa.[98] The adoption of this program did nothing to enhance American prestige. Nor did it serve to delay the Communist advance in China.

H. The Question of Recognizing the Communist Regime

By ordinary logic, one would expect that the State Department's program of disentanglement from the Nationalist government would be accompanied by a policy of recognizing the Chinese Communists as the governing authority in China. Jessup, for one, thought that as a matter of general principle a policy of non-recognition would not serve any useful purpose.[99] Yet contrary to the widespread impression in the autumn and winter of 1949,[100] the top officials of the administration had not decided on an early recognition of Communist China. It is a measure of the predicament confronting the United States that, at a time when her officials were anxiously cutting her remaining ties with the Nationalist government, they also found it impractical and imprudent to seek to establish as quickly as possible normal diplomatic relations with the Chinese Communists — impractical, it would seem, primarily for reasons of domestic politics and imprudent, as the record shows and as officials subsequently stressed, from the standpoint of American prestige and immediate interests.

The question of recognizing a Communist regime in China was posed a few days after the occupation of Nanking by the Chinese Communists on April 24. Ambassador Stuart, who remained in Nanking to give the Communists "the opportunity to discuss relationships with the United States,"[101] was paid an informal visit by Huang Hua, a Communist official who had been active in the tripartite Executive Headquarters during the Marshall mission. In an informal talk, Huang soon broached the subject of recognition. Stuart replied that the question could only be considered when there emerged a new government which had the acceptance of the Chinese

[97] *Military Situation in the Far East,* pp. 1674, 1808. See also pp. 528–29, below.

[98] *Military Situation in the Far East,* pp. 1345–46; *First Semi-annual Report on the Mutual Defense Program,* House Doc. No. 613, 81st Cong., 2d sess. (1950), pp. 9, 11, 20, 36.

[99] *Nomination of Jessup,* pp. 885–86.

[100] For a documentation of this widespread impression, particularly the recollections of Senator H. Alexander Smith and Harold Stassen, see *ibid.,* pp. 616–20, 713–20, 799–802, 836–38, 856–72.

[101] Stuart, *op. cit.,* p. 236.

people and the ability to maintain relations with other nations according to international standards.[102] In Washington, the State Department expected that a central Communist government would be established around October 10. On May 6, it took steps to convince the governments of the major non-Communist powers with interests in the Far East of "(1) the disadvantages of initiating any moves toward recognition or giving the impression through statements by their officials that any approach by the Chinese Communists seeking recognition would be welcomed and (2) the desirability of concerned western powers adopting a common front in this regard."[103] An informal agreement was reached that the non-Communist powers would consult and inform each other before taking action. But the Australian government made known its view that the Communist central government, when established, should be accorded recognition at the earliest possible moment. The Indian government was considering *de facto* recognition of "the Communist government set up in North China."[104]

The State Department's action in seeking to discourage the other powers from granting early recognition must be understood in the light of the fact that only on April 14 had the Congress included in the bill on the European Recovery Program a provision extending the expiration date of $54 million of unexpended funds for economic aid to the Nationalist government until February, 1950. Any indication on the part of the State Department of a willingness to accord early recognition to Communist China would have clearly flouted the wishes of Congress. Here the matter rested while the Communists called a meeting on June 15 of all anti-Kuomintang parties and groups to make preparations for the convening of a "new Political Consultative Conference" and for the establishment of a Communist-dominated "coalition" government.

On June 24, during the debate between Senator Vandenberg and Senator Connally sparked by the confirmation of the nomination of Butterworth, Senator Vandenberg expressed his hope that there would be no consideration of recognition of a Communist government in China without complete preliminary contact and exploration with the Senate Foreign Relations Committee.[105] On this very day, Senator Knowland released a letter to President Truman signed by sixteen Republican and six Democratic senators, asking the President to make it clear that no recognition

[102] *Ibid.*, p. 247.

[103] Jessup's testimony, *Nomination of Jessup*, p. 615; Acheson's testimony befor ' the Foreign Relations Committee, January 10, 1950, as reproduced in *ibid.*, p. 792; Butterworth's statement to the Round Table Conference held in the State Department, October 6, 1949, as reproduced in *Institute of Pacific Relations*, pp. 1565–66.

[104] *Ibid.*, p. 1566.

[105] *Congressional Record*, XCV, 81st Cong., 1st sess. (1949), 8294.

of the Communist forces was presently contemplated.[106] Taking note of congressional sentiments, Secretary Acheson sent a letter to Senator Connally on July 1, giving assurance that the Foreign Relations Committee would be consulted when the subject came up for decision.[107]

On August 2, three days before the publication of the White Paper, Ambassador Stuart left Nanking for the United States, leaving the embassy at Canton in charge of Counselor-Minister Lewis Clark.[108] On August 14, it was announced that the United States intended to maintain her relations with the Nationalist government. On the diplomatic front, the State Department continued its exchanges of views with other governments. During a meeting of the foreign ministers of the United States, Great Britain, and France in Washington, Secretary Acheson in a talk with Mr. Bevin on September 13 again tried to persuade the latter to act in concert with the United States and once more expressed the view that it would be unwise to recognize Communist China.[109] Bevin indicated to Acheson that the British government could not delay recognition of the Communist regime.[110] On October 1, Mao Tse-tung proclaimed the establishment of the "People's Republic of China" and sent out requests for recognition. The Soviet Union extended recognition the next day. The Soviet satellites soon followed the Soviet lead. On October 3, a spokesman for the State Department declared that the American government would not recognize the Chinese Communist government without consulting Congress. He noted that the Chinese message requesting recognition contained no assurance that the regime was prepared to assume its international obligations.[111]

The question of recognizing the Communist government constituted the most important subject discussed in a rather unusual round table conference held on October 6, 7, and 8, which was called by the State Department and attended by twenty-four leading scholars and businessmen interested in China. There was, to use the words of an impartial participant, a "very general agreement about the desirability of recognizing the Communist government in China and recognizing it fairly soon."[112] The minority view was expressed by Harold Stassen, who pleaded for a delay of at least two years and who was certain of the inability of the Communists to consolidate their control.[113] One of the participants made the

---

[106] For the text of the letter, see *ibid.*, p. 8406.

[107] Jessup's testimony, *Nomination of Jessup*, p. 615.

[108] Stuart, *op. cit.*, p. 257.

[109] *Nomination of Jessup*, pp. 924, 928.

[110] *Ibid.*, pp. 615, 930. Butterworth's statement at the Round Table Conference, as reproduced in *Institute of Pacific Relations*, p. 1506.

[111] *New York Times*, October 4, 1949, p. 1.

[112] Professor Edwin O. Reischauer's remark in "Transcript of the Round Table Conference" as reproduced in *Institute of Pacific Relations*, p. 1667.

[113] *Ibid.*, p. 1668.

following significant remark which might explain, in part, the hesitations
of the State Department.

> Sitting in this room arguing and listening, I think I would say
> we had come to a state of mind where we would recognize the
> Communist Government in China but General Marshall has been
> whispering in my ear for the last few days that a lot of things
> we were talking about now you cannot get the American public
> to take right now or the Congress to take. . . . I thing [think?]
> the procedure would be to watch and wait.[114]

Against this background, Secretary Acheson restated in a news conference on October 12 three main tests to be applied in recognizing a new
government: (1) that it control the country it claimed to control; (2) that
it recognize its international obligations; and (3) that it rule with the
acquiescence of the people who were ruled.[115] If the Communist government could be expected to satisfy the first and third conditions soon, there
was little evidence that the second criterion would be met within a very
short time. As early as February 1, 1947, the Central Committee of the
Chinese Communist party declared that it considered invalid all the
treaties, agreements, and loans which the Nationalist government concluded with foreign powers during the civil war. The same point was reiterated on October 10, 1947, in a declaration by the People's Liberation
Army. Abrogation of these treaties and agreements was one of Mao's eight
conditions for a peace settlement with the Nationalist government. Secretary Acheson was fully aware of this fact.[116]

Furthermore, Mao had adopted a policy of "systematically and completely
destroying the imperialist domination of China."[117] He had instructed his
cadres in March, 1949, that upon entering the big cities their first steps
should be to refuse to recognize the legal status of any foreign diplomatic
establishments and personnel, to abolish all imperialist propaganda agencies in China, to take immediate control of foreign trade, and to reform
the customs system. His hatred and suspicion of the West and ignorance
of international affairs had led him to take an extraordinary view on the
question of recognition. He thought that the Chinese Communists should
not and need not be in a hurry to obtain recognition by "the imperialist
countries" even for a fairly long period after total victory over the Kuomintang. He reasoned that "the imperialists, who have always been hostile

[114] Remark by Ernest R. MacNaughton, a banker from Portland, Oregon, *ibid.*, p.
1659. General Marshall, then associated with the Red Cross, attended the conference
as a participant and was asked to present his views.
[115] *Nomination of Jessup*, p. 616.
[116] See Acheson's testimony in an executive session of the Foreign Relations Committee on January 10, 1950, as reproduced in part in *ibid.*, p. 790.
[117] Mao, *Selected Works*, IV (Peking), p. 370.

to the Chinese people, will definitely not be in a hurry to treat us as equals" and "as long as the imperialist countries do not change their hostile attitude, we shall not grant them legal status in China."[118] Carrying out Mao's policy, the Chinese Communists subjected Americans to all sorts of harassment. In July, Vice-Consul William B. Olive was arrested and beaten by police in Shanghai. On August 17, the American government announced that it was evacuating its embassy and consular staff from Canton which was now threatened by the approaching Communist forces. On October 24, Angus Ward, American consul general in Mukden, and four of his staff, were jailed for a month after he and his entire staff had been put under house arrest for nearly a year. This latest action was considered by the United States to be "in clear violation of established principles of international comity and practice respecting the treatment of consular officials."[119] After their release, Ward and his staff were deported from China. The Chinese Communists were apparently using their treatment of American officials and citizens as one way to demonstrate their ability to defy American power and to deal a blow at American prestige. The Republican senators found in the Communist actions an additional issue on which to attack the administration's China policy.[120] American recognition of the Communist government had to await some change in the international behavior of the Chinese Communists and a calmer political atmosphere at home.

There followed in November and December several exchanges of views between the American and the British governments on the subject. The American position continued to be that the Communists must approach a certain standard of international behavior before recognition could be considered and that the non-Communist powers ought to present a common front. But the more extensive economic interests of Great Britain in China and the vulnerability of Hong Kong predisposed the British government toward an early recognition. More important, the hand of the British government was forced by the anxiety of India to establish a friendly relation with her Communist neighbor. On December 16, Mr. Bevin informed Secretary Acheson of a cabinet decision to extend recognition in early January. In reply, Acheson expressed his regret over the British decision and said that there was nothing he could add to the views previously expressed by him.[121] Following the State Department view, Senator Connally declared on December 29 that he was opposed to recognition of the Chinese Communist government before it was able to

[118] *Ibid.*, p. 371.

[119] *Department of State Bulletin*, November 21, 1949, p. 760.

[120] For example, see Knowland's statement, *Congressional Record*, XCV, 81st Cong., 1st sess. (1949), 5238, 9214.

[121] *Nomination of Jessup*, pp. 624–25, 907.

give absolute assurances of respect for international law, including the protection of foreigners.[122] Thus, there was no substance to the charge that the State Department in effect told the British government to go ahead and recognize Communist China and gave it the impression that the United States would soon follow its action. On December 30, India extended formal recognition to the Chinese Communist government. Pakistan took similar action on January 5. On January 5, 1950, the British government withdrew recognition from the Nationalist government and the next day it accorded *de jure* recognition to the Communist regime. Between January 6 and January 18, Norway, Ceylon, Denmark, Israel, Afghanistan, Finland, Sweden, and Switzerland recognized Peking in rapid succession. On January 10, Secretary Acheson informed the Senate Foreign Relations Committee in executive session of the position taken by the State Department on the question of recognition in its exchange of views and consultations with other governments.[123] He gave no indication that the American government was about to recognize Communist China.

On January 14, the Chinese Communist regime seized the property of the American government in Peking which under the Sino-American Treaty of 1943 had been converted from military barracks used by the marines to consular compounds. In protest, the State Department, carrying out its prior warning, immediately recalled all American official personnel from Communist China and closed all American official establishments. On January 14, Senator Knowland declared that the Communist seizure of American properties in Peking underscored the bankruptcy of America's China policy and suggested that "the men responsible for that policy submit their resignations to the President."[124] Senator Bridges asserted that "if our responsible officials cannot change our policy it is time to change our officials."[125] These and other statements were interpreted by the press as demands for the resignation of Secretary Acheson.[126] The opinion in Congress was that American recognition of the Chinese Communist regime could now be considered out of the question. Secretary Acheson told his news conference on January 18 that the seizure of the consular properties made it an obvious conclusion that the Chinese Communists did not want United States recognition.[127] The American government was actually moving away from rather than toward recognition of the Communist regime.

It seems clear from the above account that recognition of the Communist government was an impractical step for the administration to take

[122] *New York Times*, December 30, 1949, p. 1.
[123] *Nomination of Jessup*, pp. 791–92.
[124] *New York Times*, January 15, 1950, p. 1.
[125] *Ibid.*
[126] *Ibid.*
[127] *Ibid.*, January 19, 1950, p. 1.

so long as the American government, in response to congressional pressure, was still giving economic aid to the Nationalist government. While the State Department was trying to disentangle itself from the Nationalists as quickly as domestic politics permitted, it also endeavored to dissuade the other governments from granting recognition so that the United States would not find itself in an isolated position and a common front of the non-Communist powers could be preserved. Moreover, the State Department appears to have been genuinely concerned about the Chinese Communists' attitude toward their international obligations and about their treatment of foreigners, diplomats, and civilians alike.[128] In view of these considerations, the position taken by the State Department is perfectly understandable and is not as surprising as it appears at first glance.[129]

There was very little left for the State Department to do except to avoid, as far as possible, any further involvement in the Chinese civil war and to allow events in China to unfold themselves. The swift onward march of the Chinese Communist forces seemed to indicate that the demise of the Nationalist government was close at hand. On August 4, General Ch'êng Ch'ien, the chairman of Hunan Province, and General Ch'en Ming-jên, commander of the First Group Army, defected to the Communists and surrendered the northern part of the province. Continued disagreement between Generalissimo Chiang and Acting President Li made it impossible to work out a plan for the defense of the province of Kwangtung.[130] On October 13, the Nationalist government evacuated Canton and moved its capital to Chungking. The Communist forces entered

[128] Stuart, *op. cit.*, pp. 255–56.

[129] In the hearings on the nomination of Jessup as United States representative to the General Assembly of the United Nations in October, 1951, Jessup was harassed by some of the Republican senators for the alleged decision of the State Department to grant early recognition to the Communist government in the fall and winter of 1949 and for the important role which Jessup was supposed to have played in that decision. Jessup was able to refute these charges by citing various evidence and producing the memoranda exchanged between the American and British governments. Jessup summarized the position of the State Department in the following words: "I think the essential fact which is documented in the statement I made, supported by the documents you have seen, is that the Department of State did not at any point reach the conclusion, if I may put it this way, that recognition was just around the corner. They never reached the conclusion that if the British, Indian, and other governments recognized, that we would need to follow" (*Nomination of Jessup*, p. 659).

The critics of the State Department and Mr. Jessup found fault even with the State Department's position that recognition would be considered only if the new Communist government passed the three tests mentioned above. This attitude led to the following dialogue between two Democratic Senators, ridiculing the Republicans:

"Senator Fulbright: Unless you say 'never' you are just wrong, and yet nobody expects you to say 'never.'

"Senator Sparkman: If you said 'never,' you would be an imbecile.

"Senator Fulbright: And if you do not say 'never,' nobody is satisfied" (*Nomination of Jessup*, p. 932).

[130] Yin Shih, *op. cit.*, pp. 134–37.

Canton the next day. Three days later, Communist units captured Amoy, the port across the strait from Formosa. On November 20, Acting President Li, a completely defeated man, flew to Hong Kong and shortly afterward arrived in the United States to seek medical care. On December 8, the Nationalist government moved its capital to Taipei, Formosa. Chungking was lost by the Nationalists on December 30. By the end of the year, virtually all of mainland China was in Communist hands. Only a few localities in Southwest China plus Tibet remained to be conquered. On March 1, Generalissimo Chiang resumed the presidency on Formosa.

I. China's Accusation of the Soviet Union in the United Nations

In fighting desperately for its existence, the Nationalist government made a diplomatic move which posed new problems for the State Department. This was the formal complaint which the Nationalist government filed against the Soviet Union in the General Assembly on September 28, 1949, for Soviet violations of the Sino-Soviet Treaty of August, 1945, and the principles of the United Nations Charter.[131] This action was taken by the Nationalist government only three days before the projected inauguration of the "People's Republic of China" on October 1. It was obviously a step to stigmatize the new regime as an illegitimate offspring of Soviet intervention and thus stir up opinions unfavorable to recognition of the Chinese Communist government by the various countries and the United Nations.[132] Concluding a lengthy speech before the Political and Security Committee of the General Assembly on November 25, 1949, Dr. Tsiang expressed his hope (1) that the General Assembly would pronounce judgment on the Soviet Union for obstructing the efforts of the Nationalist government to establish its authority in Manchuria and for giving military and economic aid to the Chinese Communists; (2) that the General Assembly would recognize the cause of China's political independence and territorial integrity as a cause common to all the peoples of the world; (3) that the General Assembly would recommend that all member states desist and refrain from giving further military and economic aid to the Chinese Communists; and (4) that no member state would "accord diplomatic relations" to the Chinese Communist regime.[133]

Subsequently, the Chinese delegation introduced a draft resolution for

[131] *New York Times*, September 28, 1949, p. 3; Wei, *op. cit.*, pp. 237–38.

[132] This was so in spite of the disclaimer by Dr. T. F. Tsiang, the chairman of the Chinese delegation, that the complaint is "not a question between my government and the Chinese Communists. It is a question between my government and the government of the Soviet Union" (Tsiang's statement before the General Assembly, September 29, 1949, in *China Presents Her Case* [New York: Chinese Delegation to the United Nations, December, 1949], p. 5).

[133] *Ibid.*, p. 38; United Nations, *Official Records of the Fourth Session of the General Assembly: First Committee*, 1949, p. 347.

the purpose of translating these hopes, with minor changes, into the findings and recommendations of the General Assembly.[134] Dr. Tsiang explained that, of the four operative clauses of the Chinese draft resolution, the one recommending non-recognition of the Chinese Communists was "the most important." [135]

Meanwhile, the Communist bloc had not been idle. On November 18, Secretary-General Trygve Lie of the United Nations received a cablegram from the Chinese Communist government, demanding that the United Nations immediately deprive the delegation of the Nationalist government of "all rights to further represent the Chinese people in the United Nations so as to conform to the wishes of the Chinese people."[136] This demand by the Chinese Communists furnished the justification for the tactic adopted by the Soviet delegation to counter the Nationalist accusations. On November 15, Mr. Vishinsky declared in the Political and Security Committee that the Nationalist complaint "could not properly be considered since it had been submitted by the Kuomintang ex-Government" and that "his delegation would not participate in the consideration of the question."[137] His position was supported by the Ukrainian, the Polish, the Byelorussian, and the Czech representatives. Ruling on a point of order raised by the Yugoslav delegate, Mr. Lester B. Pearson of Canada, chairman of the committee, upheld the right of the Nationalist delegation to represent China until it was successfully challenged in the proper agency of the General Assembly and in the Assembly itself.[138]

The Chinese draft resolution presented a number of member states in the United Nations with a difficult problem. Most of them had little sympathy with the international behavior of the Soviet Union. But the adoption of the Chinese proposals would limit their freedom of action toward recognition of the Chinese Communist government and thus bar what was thought to be a necessary step to normalize the international situation in the Far East.[139] They were offered a way out of their embarrassment by a joint draft resolution submitted by Philip Jessup and sponsored by the United States, Australia, Mexico, Pakistan, and the Philippines. This joint draft resolution omitted any reference to the issue of recognition of the Communist regime and to the censure of the Soviet Union. It merely

[134] *China Presents Her Case*, pp. 49–50.

[135] Tsiang's statement before the Political and Security Committee, December 1, 1949, *ibid.*, p. 44.

[136] *New York Times*, November 19, 1949, p. 6.

[137] United Nations, *Official Records of the Fourth Session of the General Assembly: First Committee*, 1949, p. 399.

[138] *Ibid.*, p. 340.

[139] In the subsequent debate, the delegates of Australia, Pakistan, and the United Kingdom opposed the Chinese draft resolution on the ground, among others, that member states should not bind themselves for an indefinite period to withholding recognition from the new regime (*ibid.*, pp. 350, 351, 357, 359).

called on all states to be guided by certain general principles in their dealings with China, such as to respect her political independence, to respect the right of the Chinese people to choose their political institutions, to respect existing treaties relating to China, and to refrain from seeking spheres of influence or foreign-controlled regions within the territory of China.[140] There was little doubt that, confronted with the choice between the Chinese draft resolution and the five-power proposal, most member states would opt for the latter. Facing defeat, Dr. Tsiang adroitly asked on December 2 to postpone the vote until December 5.

On December 5, the delegations of Cuba, Ecuador, and Peru came to the rescue of Tsiang by submitting a new joint resolution which would refer the Nationalist complaint to the Interim Committee of the General Assembly.[141] This enabled Tsiang to declare that, if the three-power proposal were adopted, there would be no need to vote on the Chinese draft resolution which would automatically be referred to the Interim Committee.[142] In effect, he withdrew his draft resolution to be reintroduced in the Interim Committee. The three-power proposal, with an amendment submitted by the delegation of Uruguay to strengthen it, was adopted in the Political and Security Committee by a vote of 23 to 19, with the United States in opposition.[143] Since the three-power resolution was procedural in character and was in no way incompatible with the five-power resolution submitted by the United States, the latter was also adopted by 47 votes to 5, with five abstentions.[144] Both of these decisions of the committee were ratified by the General Assembly on December 8. Throughout the debate, Philip Jessup, the principal spokesman of the United States delegation, was unsparing in his attack on Russian imperialism while refraining from condemning the Chinese Communists. No doubt this difference in the American attitude toward the two Communist powers stemmed, in the first instance, from the fact that the Soviet Union rather than the Chinese Communists was the party formally accused by the Nationalist government. But it would seem that the State Department was at this time trying to drive a wedge between the two Communist powers by arousing the nationalistic sentiment of the Chinese against the threat of Soviet imperialism. This intention was also reflected in several official American statements issued in January, 1950. On February 7, 1950, the Interim Committee took up the question of the Chinese appeal but no action was forthcoming.

[140] Ibid., Annex, p. 37.
[141] Ibid., p. 37; United Nations Political and Security Committee, Official Records of the Fourth Session of the General Assembly, 1949, p. 359.
[142] Ibid., December 6, 1949, p. 368.
[143] Ibid., p. 371.
[144] Ibid., p. 372.

J. The Question of Chinese Representation in the United Nations

The question of Chinese representation in the United Nations was closely related to the issue of American recognition of Peking. The actions taken by the State Department toward this question indicated quite clearly a hardening of its attitude toward the Communist regime after the Communist seizure of American properties on January 14 and the announcement of the conclusion of a Sino-Soviet alliance on February 14. The question of Chinese representation in the United Nations came to a head when the Chinese Communist government sent, on January 8, a telegram to the United Nations and the governments of the states represented on the Security Council declaring the presence of the delegate of the "Chinese Kuomintang reactionary remnant clique" in the Security Council to be illegal and demanding his expulsion.[145] Two days later, Mr. Yakov Malik, the Soviet representative on the Security Council, demanded the expulsion of Dr. T. F. Tsiang, the Chinese delegate.

At this time, the United States was not irreconcilably opposed to the admission of the Chinese Communist regime. In the debate, Mr. Ernest Gross, the American delegate, declared that the United States government would vote against the draft resolution submitted by Malik. But he went on to make it clear that the American government considered the question procedural rather than substantive and that his vote against the Soviet motion could not be considered a veto. He declared that his government would "accept the decision of the Security Council on this matter when made by an affirmative vote of seven members." [146] The French delegate also took the same position. On January 13, the Soviet draft resolution was rejected by a vote of six to three with the United Kingdom and Norway abstaining. Thereupon, Malik announced that the U.S.S.R. delegation would not sit on the Council as long as "the representative of the Kuomintang group" had not been excluded from the Council. He reinforced this announcement with the declaration that the Soviet Union "will not recognize as legal any decision of the Security Council adopted with the participation of the representative of the Kuomintang group, and will not be guided by any such decision." [147] His walkout began a Soviet boycott of the United Nations which did not end until one month after the outbreak of the Korean War.

This premature and crude attempt of the Soviet Union to oust the Nationalist delegation from the Security Council was either a grave tactical blunder or a Machiavellian maneuver to isolate Communist China from the West. At this time, five out of the eleven members of the Security Coun-

[145] United Nations Security Council, *Official Records, 459th Meeting*, p. 2.
[146] United Nations Security Council, *Official Records, 460th Meeting*, p. 6.
[147] United Nations Security Council, *Official Records, 461st Meeting*, p. 10.

cil — the U.S.S.R., India, Yugoslavia, Great Britain, and Norway — had already recognized the Chinese Communist government. France and Egypt were expected to extend their recognition soon. If the Soviet delegate had waited a little longer and if the Chinese Communists had subsequently taken no actions to antagonize France and to aggravate the hurt feelings of the United States, the admission of Communist China into the United Nations could not have been delayed.[148] Instead, the Soviet government seemed to many observers to have deliberately courted defeat.[149] The Chinese Communists also took a series of actions which diminished their chance of gaining admission. On January 14, they seized the American consular compound at Peking, as noted. On January 19, Peking radio announced that the Chinese Communist regime had decided to extend diplomatic recognition to the Vietminh government of Ho Chi-minh.[150] In this matter, Peking acted even before Moscow. The effect of this move on French policy was predictable. As Premier Georges Bidault told Trygve Lie later, "France was ready to recognize the new regime, but when Mao and U.S.S.R. recognized Ho Chi-minh recognition on our part was rendered impossible."[151] Likewise, Foreign Minister Robert Schuman confided to Lie that "if it had not been for Peking's support of the Communists in Indochina, France would have voted long since to seat the Chinese Communists."[152]

The Soviet boycott created the gravest crisis confronted by the United Nations up to that time. Secretary-General Lie feared that the Soviet action might be a first step toward the establishment of a rival organization composed of members of the Soviet bloc. He also felt that the Nationalist government, which had already been ousted from the mainland, could no longer represent China in the United Nations.[153] Thus, he took steps to break the deadlock. In a conversation with Secretary of State Acheson on January 21, Lie asked Acheson whether American recognition of Com-

[148] It was thought in the United States that, if the Soviet delegate had not raised the issue prematurely, a proposal to unseat the Nationalist delegate "would certainly be accepted within a few weeks" (*New York Times*, January 11, 1950, p. 1, under the by-line of Thomas Hamilton).

[149] *Ibid.*, January 10, 1950, p. 1. According to Trygve Lie, Secretary-General of the United Nations, Sir Alexander Cadogan, British representative on the Security Council, suspected that "the Soviet attitude was based on a calculated policy of discouraging rather than encouraging recognition of the new Chinese government by either the United States or France. China could thereby be kept more effectively in isolation from the West and under Soviet domination." Sir Alexander expressed these views to Mr. Lie when the latter discussed with him the problem of Chinese representation in the United Nations (Trygve Lie, *In the Cause of Peace* [New York: Macmillan Co., 1954], p. 258).

[150] *New York Times*, January 20, 1950, p. 4.

[151] Lie, *op. cit.*, p. 266.

[152] *Ibid.*

[153] *Ibid.*, pp. 253–54.

munist China would be considered in the foreseeable future. Acheson's answer indicated a hardening of American attitude toward Communist China. He said that the Peking regime scarcely knew what it was doing or what international repercussions its acts had. Recalling the recent seizure of American properties, Acheson declared firmly that the United States would certainly not recognize Peking in such circumstances and was opposed to seating the Communist regime in the United Nations.

After this consultation with Acheson, Lie decided to seek a solution of the issue within the Security Council by trying to persuade two additional members of the council to vote to seat Peking and thus obtain the required majority of seven. But Lie's plan ran into another obstacle. After Malik's walkout on January 13, Peking's seizure of American, French, and Dutch properties on January 14, and Mao's recognition of the Vietminh government on January 19, there was a sudden halt to the rush toward recognition of the Chinese Communist regime which had been gaining momentum since the end of the year when Burma and India had granted diplomatic recognition to Peking. For one reason or another, France, Egypt, Australia, Canada, New Zealand, South Africa, and Mexico – all of whom had been expected to accord recognition soon, withheld their actions. Between January 17, when Switzerland extended recognition, and the outbreak of the Korean War, the Netherlands and Indonesia were the only two nations which recognized Peking. This sudden interruption of the trend toward recognition meant that Peking would not soon be admitted to the United Nations and that the Soviet boycott would not be terminated unless there was a change in the various governments' policies of conditioning a vote in favor of Peking on a prior action of recognition. Thus, the deadlock in the United Nations could be broken only by dissolving the linkage between recognition by the individual governments and representation in the United Nations.

At Secretary-General Lie's request, the Legal Department of the Secretariat prepared in early February a memorandum on the legal aspects of the problem of representation in the United Nations. On the basis of the facts, judicial precedents, and practice, both in the United Nations and in the League of Nations, the memorandum concluded:

> Since recognition of either State or government is an individual act, and either admission to membership or acceptance of representation in the Organization [*i.e.*, the United Nations] are collective acts, it would appear to be legally inadmissible to condition the latter acts by a requirement that they be preceded by individual recognition.[154]

[154] United Nations Security Council, *Official Records, 1950*, Supplement for January 1 through May 31, 1950, Document S/1466, p. 20.

It asserted that the members had made clear by unbroken practice that "a Member could properly vote to accept a representative of a government which it did not recognize, or with which it had no diplomatic relations" and that "such a vote did not imply recognition or a readiness to assume diplomatic relations."[155] As Secretary-General Lie made clear in his memoirs, he hoped that on the basis of this reasoning, France, Egypt, Ecuador, and Cuba — members of the Security Council who did not recognize the Chinese Communist regime — might vote for representation of the Peking government in the council while still withholding recognition.[156] Again, Lie's plan was confounded by another development. On February 14, the conclusion of a Sino-Soviet Treaty of Alliance was announced. The State Department now brought pressure to bear on one of the Latin American countries which, in the light of Lie's memorandum, had planned to support the seating of the Chinese Communists in the Security Council. Neither France nor Egypt gave any sign of preparing to modify their stand.[157]

After the press had learned of Lie's confidential memorandum, Lie made it public on March 8.[158] After its release Mr. Ernest Gross announced that the American government continued to adhere to its earlier position that it would oppose the seating of Peking but would accept a majority decision.[159] In contrast to the situation in January, the State Department now fully realized and had indeed taken steps to make certain that there could not be for the time being a majority in favor of the admission of Peking. Surprisingly enough, the most dispassionate views held by a public figure in the United States were those of John Foster Dulles who subsequently adopted an uncompromising policy toward Communist China when serving as secretary of state in the Eisenhower administration. In a book published on April 18, Dulles wrote that "if the Communist government of China in fact proves its ability to govern China without serious domestic resistance, then it, too, should be admitted to the United Nations."[160] He indorsed the principle of universality and proposed a package deal which would give membership to five nations vetoed by the Soviet Union and three satellite nations opposed by the Western powers.[161] He wrote: "We ought to be willing that all nations should be members without attempting to appraise closely those which are 'good' and those which are

[155] *Ibid.*, p. 22.

[156] Lie, *op. cit.*, pp. 257–58.

[157] *Ibid.*, p. 261.

[158] United Nations Security Council, *Official Records, 1950*, Supplement for January 1 through May 31, p. 18; *New York Times*, March 8, 1950, p. 1.

[159] *Ibid.*, March 9, 1950, p. 16.

[160] John Foster Dulles, *War or Peace* (New York: Macmillan Co., 1950), p. 190; *New York Times*, April 18, 1950, p. 1.

[161] Dulles, *op. cit.*, pp. 189–90.

'bad.' "[162] This was substantially the same position as that taken by Trygve Lie.

Lie's memorandum and the State Department's public position greatly disturbed the congressional supporters of Chiang. Failing to appreciate the subtlety of the State Department's action, Senator Knowland warned the department in a speech on the Senate floor on March 10 that the senators were deeply interested in the question of admitting Peking to the United Nations and demanded that the United States repudiate the actions of Trygve Lie.[163] On May 2, a group of thirty-five senators sent a letter to President Truman, urging him to make clear that the United States had no present intention of recognizing the Communist regime and would actively oppose the Soviet move to unseat the Nationalist representatives and to extend membership to Communist Chinese representatives in the United Nations.[164] To this request, President Truman returned a friendly but noncommittal reply.[165] The American position remained unchanged, as Secretary Acheson told an informal session of Congress meeting on May 31 to hear his report on his trip to Europe.[166]

K. The Question of Formosa

Insofar as America's policy toward China is concerned, the decisive question in this period was whether to defend Formosa by military means. If Formosa should fall, the issue of recognizing the Communist regime and granting it membership in the United Nations would automatically lose its political significance. On the other hand, if the United States should commit herself to the defense of this last Nationalist stronghold by her own armed forces or by military assistance, she could not recognize Peking or allow it to be admitted to the United Nations without opposition, unless there was to be an over-all political settlement with the Chinese Communists in the Far East. As noted in the last chapter, the State Department had in October, 1948, ruled out the use of American armed forces to defend Formosa. On August 4, 1949, Secretary Acheson sent a memorandum to the executive secretary of the National Security Council, stating that the fall of Formosa appeared probable and could not be prevented by political and economic measures alone. On August 16, the Joint Chiefs reaffirmed their previous views that "overt" American military action to deny Formosa to the Communists would not be justified. In a memorandum dated August 26, General Wedemeyer, deputy chief of staff for plans and operations,

---

[162] *Ibid.*, p. 190.
[163] *Congressional Record*, XCVI, 81st Cong., 2d sess. (1950), 3182–84.
[164] *Ibid.*, p. 6492. This request was subsequently indorsed by Herbert Hoover and Senator H. Alexander Smith (*ibid.*, p. 6595).
[165] *Ibid.*, p. 6864.
[166] *New York Times*, June 1, 1950, pp. 1, 5.

suggested to George V. Allen, assistant secretary of state for public affairs, that the latter might consider "information measures" to minimize the "ill effects" of the fall of Formosa on the governments and peoples of western-oriented nations, particularly in the Far East.[167] In September, the Joint Chiefs of Staff advised Secretary of Defense Louis A. Johnson that in their opinion the United States should not even send a military mission to Formosa for the purpose of ascertaining the facts.[168] According to Johnson's retrospective account, he felt that the Joint Chiefs' recommendation was made under political pressure and was influenced by political considerations.[169]

But Republican demands for strong measures to defend Formosa were soon forthcoming. Toward the end of October, Senator H. Alexander Smith of New Jersey returned from the Far East. On November 4, he sent a letter to Secretary Acheson, pleading that the United States should, "under no condition," allow Formosa to fall into the hands of the Chinese Communists. To achieve this purpose, Smith made the following suggestion: if the United States could take the position that Formosa was still technically a part of Japan, the United States, as the occupation power of Japan, could occupy Formosa, with notice to the United Nations that it might be made a trusteeship area. "If this were done," the Republican senator asserted, "the Chinese Communists would be faced with the responsibility of attacking the United States if they attacked Formosa under these conditions."[170] Smith stated these views more positively in his report dated November 29 to the Foreign Relations Committee.[171] He made public his conclusions in a new conference on December 1, implying that General MacArthur supported his position.[172]

On December 8, the Nationalist government moved its capital to Formosa. On the same day, the National Security Council discussed the Formosa situation. The press reported that the American government ruled out any change in its policy not to use American armed forces to defend Formosa.[173] However, Secretary of Defense Johnson asked the Joint Chiefs to make a recommendation from a purely military standpoint without regard to political considerations. The Joint Chiefs reversed their earlier position on the advisability of sending a fact-finding mission to Formosa and suggested that this be done. They also proposed that some military

[167] Wedemeyer's memorandum, "Current Position of the United States with respect to Formosa," *Military Situation in the Far East*, p. 2371.

[168] Johnson's testimony, *ibid.*, p. 2577.

[169] *Ibid.*, pp. 2664–65.

[170] Smith's letter to Acheson, *Congressional Record*, XCVI, 81st Cong., 2d sess. (1950), 150.

[171] *Ibid.*, pp. 156–60. See also *Nomination of Jessup*, pp. 875–85.

[172] *New York Times*, December 2, 1949, p. 15.

[173] *Washington Post*, December 9, 1949, p. 1.

assistance in addition to the $125 million appropriated in 1948 should be given to the Nationalists.[174] On December 15, Johnson sent President Truman a memorandum embodying this recommendation.[175] But the State Department adhered to its original stand, arguing that nothing short of the interposition of American armed forces could save the island and that the dispatch of a fact-finding mission would merely court further damage to American prestige and to the American position in the Far East.[176] On December 27, Johnson learned in a conversation with President Truman that, to use Johnson's words, "I had lost my fight on Formosa. . . . I was told . . . that he wasn't going to argue with me about the military considerations but that on political grounds he would decide with the State Department."[177] On December 23, the State Department, acting on General Wedemeyer's suggestion of August 26, sent out a "policy information paper" on Formosa to its missions abroad and to the Voice of America and other agencies. It advised that the loss of Formosa was widely anticipated and that steps be taken to minimize the importance of Formosa and thus the damage to American prestige.[178] On December 29, the National Security Council formally indorsed the view of the State Department.

While the recommendation of the State Department was accepted by the administration, rising demands for a positive policy came from Republican circles. On December 27, Senator Smith again wrote Acheson, urging the administration to begin conversations immediately with Mr. K. C. Wu, the new governor of Formosa, for the purpose of arranging for the occupation of the island by the United States.[179] On December 30, Senator Knowland, who, like Senator Smith, had also returned from the Far East recently, called for the dispatch of a military mission to Formosa.[180] On

[174] *Military Situation in the Far East*, p. 1674.

[175] Johnson's testimony, *ibid.*, p. 2577.

[176] Acheson's testimony, *ibid.*, pp. 1674–75. Writing on December 18, 1949, Hanson Baldwin stated that "to insure the security of Formosa against both possible external assault and internal subversion would probably take more than the ten divisions that the United States now maintains all over the world" (*New York Times*, December 8, 1949, p. 27). At this time, the Nationalists were reported to have on Formosa some 200,000 to 300,000 combat troops, 500 tanks and armed vehicles, 200 combat planes and a small navy of 150,000 tons. The Communists had approximately 100 combat planes which had passed into their hands through defection of the pilots. Foreign observers in Hong Kong thought that it would require about 500,000 to 750,000 troops to make a successful assault on Formosa. The Communists were busily repairing the cruiser "Chungking" which had defected to the Communists and had been severely damaged by the Nationalist air force. This cruiser had heavier guns than any of the vessels in the Nationalist navy. (*Ibid.*, December 21, 1949, p. 9; December 30, 1949, p. 6).

[177] Johnson's testimony, *Military Situation in the Far East*, p. 2578.

[178] The text was declassified by the combined committees conducting the MacArthur hearings (*ibid.*, pp. 1667–69).

[179] *Congressional Record*, XCVI, 81st Cong., 2d sess. (1950), 154.

[180] *New York Times*, December 31, 1949, p. 1.

the same day, Senator Taft suggested in an interview with a newspaper correspondent that Formosa should be kept out of the hands of the Chinese Communists even if it were necessary to send the United States Navy there.[181] On January 2, Senator Knowland released a letter which former president Herbert Hoover wrote him on December 31 in response to his request for an expression of views on the Chinese situation. Hoover suggested that the United States should, if necessary, give the Nationalist government naval protection for its possessions of Formosa and the Pescadores and possibly Hainan Island.[182] Taft immediately indorsed Hoover's recommendation by reiterating at a news conference his demand for the use of the American navy to prevent the Communists from capturing Formosa.[183]

But the Republicans were by no means united on the advisability of taking such a drastic step. Senator Vandenberg declined to comment on the Hoover-Taft proposal. Senator Henry Cabot Lodge, Jr. expressed grave doubts on the wisdom of drawing the line against Communist expansion along the Formosa Strait. Even Judd was not willing to go so far: he wanted only an American military advisory mission for Formosa.[184] However, Senator Knowland's hand was strengthened by a strange coincidence. The day after the release of Hoover's letter, the State Department information guidance paper on Formosa leaked to the press through General MacArthur's command in Tokyo.[185] Knowland promptly seized this opportunity to denounce the State Department for minimizing the strategic importance of Formosa. Senator H. Alexander Smith immediately supported Knowland's demand for the release of the secret document.[186] To the surprise of many, Representative Charles Eaton, the ranking minority member of the Foreign Affairs Committee, came out in support of United States military action to hold Formosa.[187]

On January 4, Acheson took the initiative to seek a conference with the Senate Foreign Relations Committee on January 10 to explain the Chinese situation and the administration's policy.[188] But the Hoover-Taft proposal had stirred up much speculation. The Chinese Communists charged that the United States had arrived at a secret understanding with the Nation-

[181] *Ibid.*

[182] *Ibid.*, January 3, 1950, p. 1. For the text of the letter, see *Congressional Record*, XCVI, 81st Cong., 2d sess. (1950), 83.

[183] *New York Times*, December 31, 1949, p. 1.

[184] *Ibid.*, January 4, 1950, p. 1.

[185] *Ibid.*, p. 14. For the responsibility for the leak, see Acheson's statement, *Military Situation in the Far East*, p. 1697.

[186] *New York Times*, January 5, 1950, p. 1. Senator Knowland repeated his demands on the Senate floor on the following day (*Congressional Record*, XCVI, 81st Cong., 2d sess. [1950], 82, 86–87).

[187] *New York Times*, January 5, 1950, p. 1.

[188] *Ibid.*

alists for the occupation of Formosa.[189] Against the background of the profound American aversion to war, Taft's and Hoover's proposals for military action to defend Formosa and Knowland's part in arranging for Hoover's letter rendered the position of the China bloc politically vulnerable. The administration decided to clarify its policy prior to consultation with Congress.[190] Without waiting for Acheson's scheduled meeting with the Foreign Relations Committee, President Truman announced in a statement released by the White House on January 5:

> The United States has no desire to obtain special rights or privileges or to establish military bases on Formosa at this time. Nor does it have any intention of utilizing its armed forces to interfere in the present situation. The United States will not pursue a course which will lead to involvement in the civil conflict in China. Similarly, the United States Government will not provide military aid or advice to Chinese forces on Formosa.[191]

Truman's statement stressed the fact that the Cairo Declaration of December 1, 1943, provided for the restoration of Formosa to China and that the United States and the other Allied powers had accepted since V-J Day the exercise of Chinese authority over the island. The administration thus rejected in categorical terms not only the Hoover-Taft proposal and Senator Smith's suggestion; it also made clear that it had no intention of supplying arms to Formosa by spending the $75 million which Congress had, under a compromise worked out by Senator Vandenberg, authorized in September of 1949 for military assistance for the "general area of China." However, the $9 million unexpended balance of the $125 million special fund was still available to the Nationalists for the purchase of military supplies. This was not cut off. The President's statement meant that no further military aid outside of the $125 million would be given.[192] The words "at this time" in the President's statement did leave a loophole for a change in policy toward Formosa. In his press conference on January 5, Acheson explained that "in the unlikely and unhappy event that our forces might be attacked in the Far East, the United States must be completely free to take whatever action in whatever area is necessary for its own security."[193]

[189] *Ibid.*, p. 18.

[190] Secretary Acheson explained in a press conference on January 5 that "it was the *President's desire* to clarify the situation. . . . It was more important to clarify thinking than it was to go on and have the most desirable of all possible things which is consultation [with members of both parties in Congress]" (extemporaneous remarks by Secretary Acheson at his press conference on January 5, 1950, *Department of State Bulletin*, January 16, 1950, p. 80. Emphasis added).

[191] *Ibid.*, p. 79.

[192] *Military Situation in the Far East*, pp. 1808, 1813, 1820, 1829, 1929–30.

[193] *Department of State Bulletin*, January 16, 1950, p. 87.

Truman's statement immediately became the target of united Republican attack on various grounds. On the Senate floor on January 5, Knowland opened the assault by focusing his criticism on the policy of providing no further military aid to Formosa. He called for a major shake-up in the Far Eastern Division in the State Department, the appointment of General MacArthur as the "co-ordinator" of American policy in the Far East, and the dispatch of a military mission under General Wedemeyer to supervise aid to Formosa. He also called for the utilization of the $75 million appropriated by Congress for shipment of arms to Formosa and the $106 million unexpended funds under the China Aid Act for economic assistance.[194] Taft asserted that "the rejection of any idea of using our armed forces to stop the advance of Communism in the area in question [*i.e.*, Formosa] is wholly inconsistent with what we have agreed to do in stopping Communism in Europe." [195] Senator McCarthy entered the China policy debate by characterizing John S. Service as man "who as a representative of the State Department said that the only hope in Asia was Communism."[196] Senator Vandenberg issued a statement to the press expressing regret that the administration had announced its "conclusions regarding Formosa ahead of a realistic consultation on the subject with the appropriate committees of Congress."[197] Senator H. Alexander Smith charged the administration with bad faith for violating an alleged understanding that no action would be taken on the problem of Formosa without consultation with the Foreign Relations Committee.[198]

But the vehement denunciations by the Republican senators of the President's statement could not cover up the very real possibility that any endeavor to deny Formosa to the Chinese Communists would entail a serious risk of war. The alternatives proposed by Hoover, Taft, and Smith, found little support from the public. Thus, in the Senate debate four days later on January 9, the Republican senators were forced to take a defensive position while the spokesmen for the administration launched their counterattack. In a lengthy speech, Senator Smith stressed the "predominantly

---

[194] *Congressional Record*, XCVI, 81st Cong., 2d sess. (1950), 82. The swift advance of the Chinese Communist forces and the rapid contraction of territory under Nationalist control made it impossible to spend the money appropriated under the China Aid Act of 1948 according to plans worked out by the ECA administrators. In the spring of 1949, it was thought $54 million would remain unexpended. In the fall of 1949, the residual funds increased to $94 million. In January, 1950, this figure was $106 million. At this time, the Nationalist government expressed confidence that they could hold Formosa provided they were provided with American economic aid and military supplies (*New York Times*, January 3, 1950, p. 10).

[195] *Congressional Record*, XCVI, 81st Cong., 2d sess. (1950), 89.

[196] *Ibid.*, p. 86.

[197] *Ibid.*, p. 103.

[198] *Ibid.*, p. 102.

peaceful and constructive" character of his proposal. He drew a distinction between his suggestion to occupy Formosa and a policy of committing the United States "in an unlimited military way to the Nationalist cause." He explained that by the word "occupation" he did not mean "to imply the sending of American troops to Formosa, but simply the establishment of a joint political authority and responsibility there between ourselves, the Nationalists, and the Formosan people." He asserted flatly that "I do not think it is necessary to send one soldier there." [199]

This last remark was the object of Senator Connally's ridicule in his rebuttal. Connally asked:

> How are we going to occupy it [Formosa] if we do not send an army there? . . . We cannot occupy it with two or three Senators who went there, who, at the firing of the first gun, would go into a hole somewhere (laughter).[200]

Connally confronted the Republican senators with a clear choice between accepting the administration's hands-off policy and risking a war. He demanded:

> Is there any member of the Senate who wishes to send an army to Formosa? Mr. Hoover wants to send the Navy there. The Senator from Ohio [Mr. Taft] . . . wants to send the Navy there, but they do not have a single spokesman on the floor of this body who will rise and tell the Senate and the country that "I favor sending an army to Formosa."
>
> What do they want to send an army there for? They want to occupy it; they want to take over Formosa. They would say, "According to my formula, in the final analysis we want to intervene in the civil war; we want to run the chance of a war; we want to run the risk of a third world war, on account of Formosa." [201]

As to the idea of "joint occupation," Connally commented: "We would not get very far with joint occupation with Chiang Kai-shek. He would either run the outfit or he would not play, that is all." [202] Furthermore, Connally was now able to link the Republican criticism of the administration's record in China with the Republican proposals for extreme measures. He declared:

> I want to know who the Senators are, and I shall revive the question from time to time, who want to plunge this country, not directly, but possibly, into World War III, in the name of For-

[199] *Ibid.*, pp. 154–55.
[200] *Ibid.*, p. 170.
[201] *Ibid.*
[202] *Ibid.*, p. 172.

mosa, but principally in the name of a bitter attack upon the President of the United States and upon the Department of State.[203]

Connally's attack was so effective that Knowland found it necessary to dissociate himself explicitly from Smith's proposal to occupy Formosa and implicitly from Hoover's suggestion.[204] But Senator Taft held fast to his position. In a Senate speech on January 11, Taft pointed out that the American navy was already deployed in the Formosa Strait and that if the American government should make clear its intention not to permit Communist occupation of Formosa, there would be no Communist attempts at an invasion. Taft explained that such a course of action need not commit the United States to backing the Nationalist government in any prolonged war against the Chinese Communists. He envisaged the possibility of establishing an independent republic of Formosa and was confident of American ability to force the Nationalists to accept such a solution.[205]

While the debate on Formosa was gaining momentum in the United States, Mao Tse-tung arrived in Moscow on December 16 and soon afterward entered into secret negotiations with Stalin himself.[206] These two developments furnished the background for one of the most brilliant as well as the most controversial speeches ever made by Secretary Acheson: his address before the National Press Club on January 12, 1950, entitled "Crisis in Asia — An Examination of United States Policy." Among other things, Acheson defined America's short-term and long-term policy toward China within the general framework of America's basic approach toward Asia. Pointing out that nationalism as the symbol of both freedom from foreign domination and freedom from poverty was the most powerful force in Asia, Acheson asserted that the interests of the United States had been parallel to the interests of the people of Asia. Historically, the United States had always been opposed to the control of China by a foreign power and in favor of the independence of all Asiatic countries. On the other hand, there was a basic conflict between Asiatic nationalism and communism. For "Communism is the most subtle instrument of Soviet foreign policy that has ever been devised and it is really the spearhead of Russian imperialism. . . ."[207] Obviously with an eye on the negotiations in Moscow, Acheson charged:

[203] *Ibid.*

[204] Knowland protested: "The junior Senator from California has not advocated sending American troops to occupy Formosa. In that respect, I disagree with other points of view." He continued to say that he advocated giving the Nationalist government the same kind of assistance which the United States was rendering Greece (*ibid.*, p. 170).

[205] *Ibid.*, pp. 298–99.

[206] Beloff, *op. cit.*, p. 70; Wei, *op. cit.*, p. 266.

[207] *Department of State Bulletin*, January 23, 1950, p. 114.

The Soviet Union is detaching the northern provinces of China from China and is attaching them to the Soviet Union. This process is complete in outer Mongolia. It is nearly complete in Manchuria and I am sure that in inner Mongolia and in Sinkiang there are very happy reports coming from Soviet agents.[208]

This contrast between Russian imperialism and America's traditional friendship for China apparently furnished for Acheson the basic justification of the administration's decision not to intervene in the Chinese civil war and not to defend Formosa. It also led him to base America's long-term policy on the possibility of playing Chinese nationalism against the Soviet Union and the Chinese Communists.

Acheson wrote:

We must not undertake to deflect from the Russians to ourselves the righteous anger, and the wrath, and the hatred of the Chinese people which must develop. It would be folly to deflect it to ourselves. We must take the position we have always taken — that anyone who violates the integrity of China is the enemy of China and is acting contrary to our interests.[209]

He asserted that the consequences of Soviet imperialism in China were saddling the Chinese Communists with the most awful responsibility.[210] Recent events have borne out the prophecy of serious conflict between Communist China and the Soviet Union. But it has taken a form quite different from that envisaged by Acheson. Its primary source is a basic disagreement over revolutionary strategy and tactics against the West, with the Chinese Communists advocating a more militant program, placing a heavier reliance on the use of force, and exhibiting a greater willingness to take militant action than the Soviet Union. The dispute has been conducted in terms of ideology rather than national interest. The border regions have not become a significant issue. Chinese nationalism has turned primarily against the United States instead of the Soviet Union.

To deal with the military threat posed by the Communist bloc, which in his opinion was "not the most immediate" menace, Acheson drew a defensive perimeter in the western Pacific which must and would be held by the United States. This defensive perimeter ran along the Aleutians through Japan and the Ryukyus to the Philippine Islands.[211] Formosa was left out-

---

[208] *Ibid.*, p. 115.
[209] *Ibid.*
[210] *Ibid.*
[211] In his conference with the Senate Foreign Relations Committee on January 10, Acheson had informed the senators of this defense perimeter, and Chairman Connally had told the press about it (*Washington Post*, January 11, 1950, p. 1, under the by-line of Ferdinand Kuhn).

side of this line. The omission of South Korea, which was subsequently thought to have encouraged the North Koreans to launch their attack on June 25, was based on the military assumption that in an all-out war it would be a strategic liability rather than an asset. Apparently, little thought was given to the possibility of local aggression and limited war in that area. The failure to include Southeast Asia indicated that the United States had as yet no firm policy toward its defense. At this time, Ambassador Jessup was on his mission to the Far East and Southeast Asia, searching for a concrete program to contain communism in Asia. He had arrived in Tokyo on January 5 to confer with General MacArthur. He was to meet Generalissimo Chiang on Formosa in the middle of the month and in February to attend a conference at Bangkok, Thailand, of American diplomats stationed in those areas. As to the military security of these areas, Acheson had this to say:

> It must be clear that no person can guarantee these areas against military attack. But it must be clear that such a guarantee is hardly suitable or necessary within the realm of practical relationship. Should such an attack occur — one hesitates to say where such an armed attack could come from — the initial reliance must be on people attacked to resist it and then upon the commitments of the entire civilized world under the Charter of the United Nations which so far has not proved a weak reed to lean on by any people who are determined to protect their independence against outside aggression.[212]

Coming on the heels of Connally's stress of the risk of war in his attack on the proposals of Hoover, Taft, and Smith, Acheson's impressive presentation of the positive aspects of America's Asiatic policy gave the administration considerable advantage. For that policy seemed to avoid any immediate risk of war, drew an easily defensible line to protect America's vital interests, and contained a long-term program for Asia which could be implemented by peaceful means. The Republican critics of the administration had obviously overplayed their hands. As Arthur Krock observed, "Taft, Hoover, Smith and Knowland imperiled their party's campaign against the administration's China policy record by their proposal on Formosa." Moreover, "because of the Republican windfall as to Formosa, Acheson is martially and jubilantly resting a powerful case on administration's policy there."[213] But Acheson's foes quickly found fresh ammunition in a new development. When it was disclosed that the Communists had seized American consular properties in Peking, Knowland and Bridges

[212] *Department of State Bulletin*, January 23, 1950, p. 115.
[213] *New York Times*, January 15, 1950, Sec. 4, p. 3.

demanded indirectly the resignation of Acheson.[214] Again the background of a growing public aversion to adventures in China, the new Republican demands for Acheson's resignation solidified the Democratic ranks. On January 17, the Democratic senators met in a party conference. They were reported to be "practically unanimous in voicing their support for President Truman's hands-off-Formosa policy."[215] The press interpreted the conference to mean "concentrated majority party counterfire to GOP charges of bankruptcy in China policy and Republican demands for Acheson's ouster."[216]

At this point, a group of Republicans in the House under the leadership of Representative Vorys took matters into their own hands. To express their dissatisfaction over the administration's policy in general and its decision on Formosa in particular, they rigorously opposed a bill sponsored by the administration to grant $60 million for economic aid to South Korea for the remaining months of fiscal year 1950. In a debate on the floor, Vorys took the position that in the absence of a comprehensive and sound program for the Far East, economic aid to Korea was money down the "rat hole."[217] Robert Chipperfield, Republican of Illinois, argued that the loss of China rendered South Korea indefensible.[218] Representative Donald L. Jackson, Republican of California, asked: "What kind of policy for the Far East would put économic aid into Korea, which bears no relationship to our national defense, and at the same time refuse a request to put aid into Formosa?"[219] The attack on the aid to Korea bill was so intense that Representative Judd, one of the more responsible and level-headed members of the China bloc, found it necessary to plead with his fellow congressmen that the "mistaken" policies of the administration toward China and Formosa did not justify opposition to aid to Korea even if Formosa was "vital" to the United States and South Korea was not.[220] Joined by economy-minded and non-interventionist Republicans and Southern Democrats, Vorys and his supporters defeated the bill by a margin of one vote. The Republicans opposed it six to one while only three out of four Democrats

---

[214] *Ibid.*, Sec. 1, p. 1. See this chapter, p. 518, above.

[215] Press release, reproduced in *Congressional Record*, XCVI, 81st Cong., 2d sess. (1950), 474.

[216] *Ibid.*, p. 479.

[217] *Ibid.*, p. 636.

[218] *Ibid.*, pp. 639–40.

[219] *Ibid.*, p. 649. Jackson also observed that "South Korea is a Bataan without a Corregidor, a Dunkerque without a flotilla, a dead-end street without an escape" (*ibid.*, p. 644). In contrast, "Formosa is essentially a point in the line of defenses which include Japan, the Philippines, and Okinawa, all essential and vital to the national defense of the United States. Formosa is a tenable position; it is a position which might well be held, it is a position certainly, which should be strengthened if we are going to have any kind of policy at any time in the Pacific area" (*ibid.*, p. 649).

[220] *Ibid.*, p. 651.

supported it.[221] This was the first major setback in Congress for the administration in the field of foreign policy since the end of the war. Once again some members of the China bloc showed their ability to disrupt the administration's program in other areas. Worst of all, the debate publicized the American position that South Korea was indefensible and strategically valueless to the United States. Writing in 1957, Acheson expressed the belief that this action of the House contributed to Soviet miscalculation of the possible American reaction to attack by North Korea.[222] Again, a compromise was worked out. The final bill enacted by Congress combined the Korean aid bill with a provision extending the deadline for the expenditure of the $104 million residual funds under the China Aid Act from February 15 to June 30, 1950.[223] But it was expected that actually only less than $10 million would be spent in Formosa in the extended period and solely for the purpose of continuing the work of the Joint Commission on Rural Reconstruction.[224]

The initial defeat of the Korean aid bill in the House made it clear to the administration that it could do no less than continue economic aid to Formosa in order to insure smooth sailing for its other foreign policy programs. Thus, in the bills passed by both the House and the Senate for general foreign economic assistance for the fiscal year 1951, there was a provision further extending the time limit for the expenditure of the residual funds under the China Aid Act (estimated at $94 million as of June, 1950) from June 30, 1950, to June 30, 1951. The final bill, passed by Congress in May, allocated the residual funds for use "in any place in China and in the general area of China which the President deems to be not under Communist control."[225] It stipulated that "so long as the President deems it practicable, not less than $40,000,000 of such funds shall be available only for such assistance in areas in China (including Formosa)."[226] The ability of the China bloc to influence the administration's policy was weakening. But it was still strong enough to prevent a prompt and complete withdrawal.

L. The Rise of McCarthyism and China Policy

The year which found American policy frozen over the issue of Formosa witnessed the rise of McCarthyism. McCarthyism was fundamentally an underhanded assault on the liberal tradition of America. Given the

[221] Westerfield, op. cit., pp. 353–54, 366–67.

[222] Dean Acheson, A Citizen Looks at Congress (New York: Harper & Bros., 1957), pp. 83–84.

[223] Congressional Record, XCVI, 81st Cong., 2d sess. (1950), 1596.

[224] Ibid., pp. 1596, 1600.

[225] Ibid., Part 6, p. 7520.

[226] Ibid. In April, Hainan was lost to the Communists. Therefore in the final bill, Hainan was not mentioned. See also ibid., p. 7526.

moral unity of the American society, it was natural that a fanatical revolt against the prevailing ethos should take a nihilistic character, attacking the established values, institutions, and policies without presenting affirmative answers to the day's pressing problems. Since many of the traditional liberal perspectives found their fullest expression in America's China policy, it was inevitable that this policy should become a major target of McCarthy's onslaught. Since the misjudgment of the nature of Chinese communism, the minimization of the role of ideology in human affairs and thus of the influence of communism as a vital force, the inability to perceive the existence of irreconcilable conflicts in a society, the overreliance on the efficacy of compromise, the corresponding failure to see the need for the use of force, the elevation of non-intervention as a self-sufficient principle, and the tendency to understand alien things in American terms — all exercised perceptible influence on America's China policy,[227] it is not difficult to see that this policy was highly vulnerable to McCarthy's demagoguery. Nor is it surprising that McCarthy's attack on China policy gained him the support for the first time of powerful and respectable Republican leaders. For Hurley in 1945 and Judd in 1947 had already advanced the theory of conspiracy as an explanation of America's failure in China. Frustrated in their efforts to obtain a program of large-scale aid to China, many Republican leaders had, since 1949, intensified their attack on the State Department, demanded an investigation, and asked for a change in personnel. Failing to realize that the defeat of American policy had its roots in assumptions and attitudes which they themselves shared, many Americans expressed their anxieties over Far Eastern affairs by accepting McCarthy's theory of conspiracy as a salve to their wounded pride and by acclaiming or acquiescing in his hunt for non-existent Communists in the State Department as a substitute for a search for a workable policy.[228]

[227] See chaps. vi and ix, above.

[228] Among the eighty-one cases presented by McCarthy to the Senate as bad security risks or worse, only one employee of the State Department, Mr. Val Lorwin, was ever indicted for perjuring himself in denying past membership in the Communist party. In May, 1954, the Justice Department dropped the charge for lack of evidence (James Rorty and Moshe Decter, *McCarthy and the Communists* [Boston: Beacon Press, 1954], p. 14). Richard H. Rovere reported that at one time McCarthy named an ex-Communist in a government agency, who had concealed his past membership. But McCarthy soon dropped the case. According to Rovere, this was about "the closest" McCarthy ever came to turning up a real Communist in the government. This government employee resigned from the government after Rovere brought the case to the attention of an official of that Government agency (Richard H. Rovere, *Senator Joe McCarthy* [New York: Harcourt, Brace & Co., 1959], p. 159).

According to Rorty and Decter, there had been, besides the much mooted case of Alger Hiss, three Communists in the State Department when McCarthy raised the issue of Communist infiltration of the State Department. But they had either been fired or had left the Department: Carl Aldo Marzani in 1946, Julian Wadleigh in 1946, and George Shaw Wheeler in 1947 (Rorty and Decter, *op. cit.*, p. 56). See also Eric Goldman, *The Crucial Decade* (New York: Alfred A. Knopf, Inc., 1956), pp. 133–37; Jack Anderson

Senator McCarthy discovered the issue of Communist infiltration of the State Department quite accidentally in his search for an issue for his re-election campaign in 1950.[229] In his speech made on February 9 at Wheeling, West Virginia, he did not at once focus his attack on officials and experts concerned with China policy, although he did charge John S. Service by name as a man "who had previously urged that Communism was the best hope of China."[230] On February 20, McCarthy delivered a lengthy speech on the Senate floor in response to demands for an explanation of his charges. In this speech, he presented to the Senate his information regarding the Communist leanings of eight-one State Department employees, past and present, whom he identified by numerals.[231] No. 2 of his eighty-one cases turned out to be John Carter Vincent.[232] He was condemned by McCarthy as one of "the Big Three" of the espionage ring in the State Department.[233] He should, McCarthy urged, "not only be discharged but should be immediately prosecuted."[234] The charges leveled against Vincent were concerned with espionage activities rather than Far Eastern policy.[235] According to Rovere, John S. Service was also one of the numbered cases.[236] But McCarthy did move a step closer to the issue of China policy when he asserted that "Research and Intelligence, the Voice of America, and Far Eastern Affairs seem to be the three prime targets [of Communist infiltration]."[237]

It was inevitable that McCarthy's charge of Communist infiltration would soon be linked with the post-mortem over China policy. In the hearings conducted by a Senate Foreign Relations subcommittee under the chairmanship of Millard E. Tydings, McCarthy accused nine persons by name of Communist leanings. Among them four had been connected by by him with America's China policy in one way or another. Almost casually

and Ronald W. May, *McCarthy: The Man, the Senator, and the Ism* (Boston: Beacon Press, 1952); *New York Times*, January 26, 1950, p. 14; William F. Buckley, Jr., and L. Brent Bozell, *McCarthy and His Enemies* (Chicago: Henry Regnery Co., 1954).

[229] Rovere, *op. cit.*, pp. 122–23.

[230] The complete text of McCarthy's speech at Wheeling was nowhere to be found. McCarthy had no copy of it (*ibid.*, p. 127). Nonetheless, McCarthy read in the Senate on February 20 what purported to be his complete Wheeling speech (*Congressional Record*, XCVI, 81st Cong., 2d sess. [1950], 1954, 1956, 1957).

[231] *Ibid.*, pp. 1954, 1981.

[232] Senate Committee on Foreign Relations, *Report on State Department Employee Loyalty Investigation*, Report No. 2108, 81st Cong., 2d sess. (1950), p. 95 (hereafter cited as *Report on State Department*).

[233] *Congressional Record*, XCVI, 81st Cong., 2d sess. (1950), 1961.

[234] *Ibid.*

[235] *Ibid.*, pp. 1980–81.

[236] Rovere, *op. cit.*, p. 152. Service seems to have been No. 46. The charges against him centered on the *Amerasia* case (*Congressional Record*, XCVI, 81st Cong., 1st sess. [1950], 1967).

[237] *Ibid.*, p. 1960.

he accused Mr. Philip C. Jessup of having "unusual affinity for Communist causes."[238] He characterized Owen Lattimore, director of the Walter Hines Page School of International Relations, Johns Hopkins University, as "an extremely bad security risk" whose "wide knowledge of far eastern affairs and his affinity for the Soviet cause in that area might well have already done this nation incalculable and irreparable harm."[239] He alleged that Lattimore had been "one of the principal architects of our far eastern policy," and had held "numerous positions with the State Department."[240] He elevated John S. Service, then consul general at Calcutta, India, to the position of "one of the dozen top policy makers in the entire State Department on far eastern policy."[241] He declared that "the Communist affiliations of Service are well known."[242] He described Service as "a known associate and collaborator with Communists and pro-Communists . . . consorting with admitted espionage agents."[243] The principal basis of McCarthy's charge was the *Amerasia* case in which Service was arrested in June, 1945, on a complaint that he had transmitted classified material to Philip Jaffe, the editor of *Amerasia*, a periodical specializing in Far Eastern affairs. At that time, a grand jury returned a "no" bill in Service's case by unanimous vote. Up to the time of McCarthy's charge, Service had been cleared thrice by State Department officials looking into his loyalty file.[244]

[238] Senate Committee on Foreign Relations, *Hearings on State Department Employee Loyalty Investigation*, 81st Cong., 2d sess. (1950), p. 28 (hereafter cited as *State Department Employee Loyalty Investigation*).

[239] *Ibid.*, p. 104.

[240] *Ibid.*, p. 92.

[241] *Ibid.*, p. 131.

[242] *Ibid.*

[243] *Ibid.*, p. 140.

[244] It cannot be ascertained whether Jaffe was a Communist. After Service had turned over to Jaffe a number of the reports which he had sent from China to the State Department, he asked Lt. Andrew Roth who had introduced him to Jaffe whether Jaffe was a Communist. Roth answered that Jaffe was not a Communist but "a left-winger and very sympathetic." Harold Isaacs told Service that Jaffe was "bad business" or "bad medicine." The record makes it clear that, soon after Service had given his reports to Jaffe, he began to suspect Jaffe's political affiliation. Service was at least extremely indiscreet in handing over to Jaffe his reports and even more so in continuing his association with Jaffe after he had discovered Jaffe's pro-Communist sympathies. See "Opinion of the Loyalty Review Board in the Case of John Stewart Service," *Institute of Pacific Relations*, pp. 4847–48.

T. A. Bisson testified that Jaffe may have voluntarily and knowingly co-operated or collaborated with Communist party members in furtherance of Communist party objectives. Bisson stated that Jaffe was "connected or associated with Earl Browder" (*ibid.*, p. 4172). For a summary of the *Amerasia* case, see *Report on State Department*, pp. 96–114.

As to the sources of McCarthy's charge, Philip Horton made the following report: "In February, soon after McCarthy's first outburst, Mr. Kohlberg met the Senator for the first time. They needed each other. . . . Over dinner Mr. Kohlberg expounded his thesis that the Institute of Pacific Relations was the instrument of Communist infiltration into the State Department. The Senator was furnished a collection of Mr. Kohl-

Another man named was Haldore Hanson, the chief of the technical co-operation projects staff of the Point Four program. Hanson was charged by McCarthy with entertaining "pro-Communist proclivities" going back to 1938. He was described as "a man with a mission — a mission to communize the world. . . ."[245] The charge arose from the fact that in his capacity as a correspondent for the Associated Press, Hanson had spent four months in 1938 with the Chinese Communist armies and had written a book, which contained some praise for the Communists as well as the Nationalists.[246]

In the first four sessions, McCarthy made little headway in convincing the subcommittee or the public of the validity of his charges against the men named by him. Moreover, it developed that he had no new evidence whatsoever to support the accusations against the eighty-one individuals which he had made on February 20 in the Senate. In contrast, Ambassador Jessup, who had flown back from Pakistan to refute McCarthy's charges, won loud applause from the audience at the end of a lengthy statement before the Tydings subcommittee. Jessup stressed the adverse effects of McCarthy's irresponsible charges on the conduct of the nation's foreign policy. To extricate himself from a difficult position, McCarthy made a desperate move. He declared the next day before the subcommittee that he would stand or fall on the single case of Owen Lattimore.[247] Eight days previously, McCarthy had merely called Lattimore "an extremely bad security risk." Now, he characterized Lattimore as "the top espionage agent,"[248] "the top Russian spy,"[249] and "the top of the whole group of which Hiss was a part."[250] This charge shocked the nation and was reported on the front page of almost all important newspapers.[251]

Lattimore, however, was not and had never been an employee of the State Department in a strict sense, though in his capacities as editor of *Pacific Affairs*, a prolific writer, American adviser to Generalissimo Chiang, and deputy director of the Office of War Information in charge of Pacific operations, he had undoubtedly had some influence, to a degree difficult to define, on official policy. The charge that he was the top espionage agent was completely groundless. Freda Utley, the first person to expound fully in an official hearing the thesis that Lattimore followed the Communist party line in his writing, was forced to say:

berg's favorite articles and releases, including 'The State Department Espionage Case' by Emmanuel S. Larsen. . ." (Philip Horton, "The China Lobby," *Reporter*, April 29, 1952, p. 2).

[245] *State Department Employee Loyalty Investigation*, pp. 74, 82.
[246] *Report on State Department*, pp. 32–37.
[247] *State Department Employee Loyalty Investigation*, pp. 284–85.
[248] *Ibid.*, p. 285.
[249] *Ibid.*
[250] *Ibid.*, p. 281.
[251] Anderson and May, *op. cit.*, p. 213; Goldman, *op. cit.*, p. 143.

I think that Senator McCarthy was wrong in his original statement that Owen Lattimore is the Soviet Government's top espionage agent in America. I think the Senator underestimated Lattimore. Mr. Lattimore is such a renowned scholar, such an excellent writer, so adept at teaching the American people that they ought to stop opposing the great, good, and progressive Soviet Government, that it is impossible to believe that Moscow would regard him as expendable, as all spies are. To suggest that Mr. Lattimore's great talents have been utilized in espionage seems to me as absurd as to suggest that Mr. Gromyko or Mr. Molotov employ their leisure hours at Lake Success, or at international conferences, in snatching documents.[252]

Senator McCarthy himself was to admit on March 30: "I fear in the case of Lattimore, I may have perhaps placed too much stress on the question of whether or not he has been an espionage agent."[253]

But regardless of the question of its validity, McCarthy's characterization of Lattimore as the top espionage agent raised all the issues of America's China policy. McCarthy now allied himself without reservation with the China bloc in and out of Congress. His charges of Communist infiltration of the State Department found a focus. After an inauspicious beginning in February, it was gaining support by late March.[254] Taft's early reaction to McCarthy's attack had been that "it was a perfectly reckless performance."[255] But on March 22, the very day after McCarthy had charged Lattimore as the top espionage agent before the Tydings subcommittee, the Senate Republican Policy Committee moved toward an indorsement of McCarthy. After a meeting of the Senate Policy Committee of the Republican party, Taft announced that McCarthy's charges were "not a matter of party policy" but that Republican senators were helping him "in his fight" and "reaction seems to be pretty good on the whole."[256] Taft was reported to have said that "if one case doesn't work, try another."[257] On March 25, Senator Bridges told reporters that a group of Republicans would "go after" Acheson in a series of public attacks.[258] Two days later, he delivered a speech in the Senate strongly attacking Acheson. He charged that the Tydings subcommittee was opening "a white-wash factory to make camouflage for the failures of a diplomatic dean of

[252] *State Department Employee Loyalty Investigation*, p. 768.
[253] *Congressional Record*, XCVI, 81st Cong., 2d sess. (1950), 4385.
[254] Goldman, *op. cit.*, p. 144.
[255] Rovere, *op. cit.*, p. 135.
[256] *New York Times*, March 23, 1950, p. 1. Compare Westerfield's interpretation of Taft's statement with that of Rovere (Westerfield, *op. cit.*, pp. 376–77; Rovere, *op. cit.*, p. 135).
[257] *Ibid.*, p. 136.
[258] *New York Times*, March 26, 1950, p. 1.

fashion." He declared that the wreckage of our diplomatic and military efforts in Europe and Asia was no accident and that "Stalin had help from inside our ranks." He demanded that the Tydings sub-committee find out from Acheson who was responsible for the decision to abandon China.[259]

On March 30, McCarthy made a lengthy speech in Congress, restating his charges of Communist influence in the government. He now centered his attack exclusively on Lattimore, Jessup, Service, Hanson, and the Institute of Pacific Relations, and on the China policy of the United States.[260] He adopted Utley's thesis that Lattimore served Communist interests by propagating the party line. Of Lattimore he said:

> In view of his position of tremendous power in the State Department as the "architect" of our far eastern policy, the more important aspect of his case deals with his aims and what he advocates; whether his aims are American aims or whether they coincide with the aims of Soviet Russia.[261]

He charged that Lattimore's views were followed by the State Department[262] and that "Acheson takes the same position as his counselors on far-eastern affairs — Lattimore, Jessup, and Service."[263] He concluded his speech with the assertion:

> It was not Chinese democracy under Mao that conquered China, as Acheson, Lattimore, Jessup, and Hanson contend. Soviet Russia conquered China and an important ally of the conquerors was this small left-wing element in our Department of State.[264]

The theory of conspiracy which General Hurley had originated was in full blossom.[265] McCarthy not only could draw on the ideas of Alfred Kohlberg (the founder of the American China Policy Association), Mrs. Freda Utley, and a growing body of anti-Communist writers on both the extreme right and left. But in concentrating his attack on the officials and scholars connected with China policy in one way or another, his infamous

[259] *Congressional Record*, XCVI, 81st Cong., 1st sess. (1950), 4118–21.
[260] *Ibid.*, pp. 4372–4408.
[261] *Ibid.*, p. 4385.
[262] *Ibid.*, p. 4386.
[263] *Ibid.*, p. 4407.
[264] *Ibid.*, p. 4407–8.
[265] Hurley had charged that a group of career officials in China and in Washington were "disloyal to the American policy." Hurley's testimony before the Senate Foreign Relations Committee investigating Far Eastern policy in December, 1945, p. 160, as quoted in *Report on State Department*, p. 146.
In his letter of resignation dated November 26, 1945, Hurley said: "The professional foreign service men sided with the Chinese Communist armed party and the imperialist block of nations whose policy it was to keep China divided against itself" (*United States Relations with China*, p. 582). See Part II, chap. viii, above.

crusade also fed upon what the Tydings subcommittee called "the vague uneasiness of many Americans concerning the ascendency of the Communists in China and the decline of the Nationalist government."[266]

Senator Knowland also caught the spirit of the times. As late as March 2, he had attacked Lattimore merely for advocating "a policy of appeasement."[267] Yet on April 5, Senator Knowland delivered a speech in the Senate in which he compared Lattimore's writings with the theses and resolutions of the Sixth World Congress of the Communist International adopted in December, 1928; the Constitution of the Chinese Communist party adopted in July, 1945; a statement on China policy issued in January, 1949, by a front organization of the American Communist party; and an Associated Press report on April 4 of an article in *Pravda*. Knowland asked in what way Lattimore's recommendations differed from the objectives, programs, and policies set forth in the Communist documents.[268] Being an upright man, Knowland refused to be drawn by McCarthy into a discussion of Lattimore's motives, but he did stress "the strange coincidence" between these two sets of views.[269] On June 1, Knowland lent further support to McCarthy by demanding a reopening of the *Amerasia* case.[270] This sustained generalized assault nullified much of the partisan advantage which the administration had gained on the specific issue of Formosa in January. It made disengagement from Chiang more difficult than ever.[271]

At this time, the officials and scholars under McCarthy's attack were still in a strong enough position to launch a forceful counterattack. In his appearance before the Tydings sub-committee, Lattimore openly challenged McCarthy to a debate on China policy.[272] He was able to produce the testimonies of 170 distinguished scholars and experts on his personal integrity and loyalty. He won applause from the audience when he declared that his obligation was to refute McCarthy's charges and establish beyond further challenge the right of American scholars to express their views freely without fear.[273] The Tydings subcommittee issued a report on July 20 totally refuting McCarthy's charges of Communist infiltration and influence in the State Department. It cleared Lattimore, Jessup, Service, Hanson, and Vincent of all of McCarthy's accusations.[274] The Tydings

[266] *Report on State Department*, p. 151.
[267] *Congressional Record*, XCVI, 81st Cong., 2d sess. (1950), 2642.
[268] *Ibid*., pp. 4804–6.
[269] *Ibid*., pp. 4828–29.
[270] *Ibid*., p. 7785.
[271] Westerfield, *op. cit.*, p. 368.
[272] *State Department Employee Loyalty Investigation*, p. 419.
[273] *Ibid*., p. 826.
[274] It conceded that Service was "extremely indiscreet" in his dealings with Jaffe (*Report on State Department*, pp. 93–94).

report and America's preoccupation with the national crisis ushered in by the Korean War brought about a brief period of eclipse for McCarthy.[275]

M. The Collapse of American Policy and the Traditional Dilemma

The years 1949 and 1950 witnessed the triumph of the Chinese Communists on the mainland, Mao's proclamation of his policy of leaning to one side, and the conclusion of the Sino-Soviet Treaty of Alliance. Formosa was expected soon to fall. A half-century's policy was reaching a point of collapse.

The latest phase in the cycles of advance and retreat of the United States in China, the Marshall-Acheson program of gradual disengagement paralleled Theodore Roosevelt's acquiescence in Russia's and Japan's special positions in Manchuria, Secretary Bryan's note to Japan of March 13, 1915, the Lansing-Ishii Agreement, Hoover's inaction after the Manchurian crisis, and finally the Yalta Agreement. These retreats usually followed a previous advance and were the products of the inconsistency between ends and means in American policy. Throughout the fifty-year period, traditional American methods, which ruled out the purposeful use of military power, were sooner or later found to be incompatible with the avowed objectives of maintaining the Open Door and preserving the territorial integrity of China. Diplomatic support, moral encouragement, and limited assistance proved unavailing. When the United States was confronted with a choice between the use of force and the acceptance of a situation created by the actual or potential use of military power by the other side, retreat followed.

In contrast, all major American advances in China were accomplished after the United States had taken part in war or had resorted to strong measures on issues not immediately related to China. The dispatch of Hay's notes and circular followed the Spanish–American War. The Washington Conference followed the First World War. The refusal to compromise with Japan on the issue of stationing Japanese troops in China followed the imposition of the total embargo on oil — a measure taken not so much to defend China as to deter Japan from cutting the British trade routes and seizing the rich resources in Southeast Asia. The policy of making China a great power followed Japan's attack on Pearl Harbor. The landing of American marines and the dispatch of the Marshall mission followed the end of the Pacific war. These advances were rendered possible when the United States displayed her actual or potential military power or when her unwillingness to use force on behalf of China was overcome by a crisis centered elsewhere.

But none of these advances brought about lasting results. In the course

[275] Rovere, *op. cit.*, p. 158.

of time, the United States had to face situations which could not be controlled by peaceful means or by a policy of limited assistance. If the traditional policy was bound to suffer one temporary setback after another before the Second World War, it was doomed to eventual failure by the transformation of the multiple balance of power into the bipolar system. Under the bipolar system, both a policy of containment and a policy of liberation required, in typical cases, a readiness to use military power for their successful implementation. But willingness to use force in China was absent. It was no accident that when the policy of containment was adopted in March, 1947, that policy was not applied to China. It was not until Secretary Acheson had begun to implement the policy of disengagement from China that he instructed Jessup to work out a program to contain the Communists within the boundaries of China. Furthermore, the bipolar system sharpened the inconsistency between the objective of supporting an existing government and the principle of non-intervention. For the bipolar system, together with the theory and practice of the international Communist movement, put a premium on the policy of intervention as a component in either an offensive or defensive strategy. In contrast, the traditional principle of non-intervention inhibited American action. Acheson's letter of transmittal contained an admission of the inadequacy of the traditional policy to deal with a popular movement in China which owed its allegiance to international communism.

While Marshall and Acheson ruled out armed intervention, they did not have the freedom necessary to adopt and implement a policy of prompt withdrawal from China, even if they had desired to do so. The traditional attachment to China, now reinforced by the perception of the threat posed by international communism, found expression in the China bloc's demands for positive action in China. By the first half of 1950, the administration and the friends of Chiang reached a stalemate over China policy. This partisan deadlock was the reflection of the inherent contradiction, now brought to the fore by events, between the two elements of American policy: the objective of supporting China and the unwillingness to use force. In the proposals of Hoover and Taft, there were for the first time suggestions of using American military power to intervene in the Chinese civil war. Subsequent events proved that Taft was right in his belief that the Chinese Communists would not dare challenge the American navy in the Formosa Strait. But these proposals ran into America's aversion to war. Mainland China had been lost. Formosa was not considered important enough to American security to warrant a last-minute armed intervention. The proposals of Hoover and Taft succeeded merely in making the position of the China bloc politically vulnerable, with the result that the Republicans failed to force the administration to undertake military commitments in Formosa.

On the other hand, the administration could not refuse to continue arms shipments and economic aid to the Nationalists without running the risk of jeopardizing its other foreign policy programs. The critics of the administration who held tenaciously to the objective of supporting the Nationalists had demonstrated their capacity for causing trouble. Economic aid and shipment of arms under the unexpended balance of the $125 million special fund would not apparently entail the danger of war. Under these circumstances, the United States continued to be entangled in China and American policy was immobilized at the center. She could not take any initiative because she was unwilling either to use force or to give up her objective. With the United States at odds with herself, the moves of other powers would tip the unstable balance of her policies in one direction or another. If it had come about, Mao's projected assault on Formosa would have enabled the United States to disentangle herself from Chiang. But, in the event, the North Korean aggression on South Korea led to a decision to defend Formosa by force.

Meanwhile, another persistent feature of America's traditional policy reappeared in a new form. Just as it had been in the past, non-recognition as a policy was born of the contradiction between the nation's reluctance to forsake an objective and her incapacity to achieve it by the purposeful use of military power. The friends of the Nationalists advocated non-recognition passionately. The administration adopted it without much conviction as a temporary measure, partly in response to Republican pressure and partly in response to Mao's policy of deliberately provoking the Western powers. Mao's provocative actions and pronouncements stemmed basically from his Marxist-Leninist ideology. But the American policy of sustaining the Nationalist government reinforced his distorted views of the United States while the policy of limited assistance failed to impress on him American strength and determination. It was no accident that Mao responded to the White Paper by fully developing his theme of the unchanging nature of imperialism and by showing his utter contempt for American power. To the extent that the administration was deterred by the provocative acts of the Chinese Communists from recognizing their regime, it was reaping the consequences of its attempt to achieve the objective of sustaining the Nationalist government while ruling out the use of force. It was also harvesting the fruits of its inability to withdraw promptly from China.

Important as was the partisan stalemate in preventing a prompt and complete withdrawal, there was still another related factor, much less obvious but of some significance. When one carefully reflects on the development of American policy from the vantage point of today, one discerns an elusive fact: While American officials were intensely conscious of the immediate dangers of armed intervention, there was no comparable awareness and thus few public discussions of the possibility that a Communist victory could lay the foundation, and continued American entanglement in China could increase the chance, of an eventual armed clash between the Chinese Communists and the United States. Without foreknowledge of the seriousness of a possible Sino-American clash, the very real and ever-present difficulties involved in a policy of prompt disengagement could not have been overcome.

As we have seen, prompt and complete withdrawal would have meant abrupt severance of the ties to a government long supported by the United States, cutting off arms shipments, economic aid, and political bonds. It would have required the abandonment of illusions that parts of China could somehow be denied to the Chinese Communists by a program of limited assistance. It would have involved the relinquishment of any advantage which might have been gained from delaying the total conquest of China by the Communists. It would have entailed the renunciation of a nation to which the United States had been emotionally attached for over a century. It would have had to be undertaken in the face of the Communists' open hostility, defiant challenges, and deliberate affronts.

These emotional attitudes and practical considerations which hindered prompt withdrawal found expression in the views and proposals of the American friends of the Nationalists and their attacks on the administration's policies and its officials. These difficulties could not have been easily and completely outweighed by those disadvantages of continued entanglement which could be seen at the time and which were used as arguments in favor of withdrawal. The capture by Communists of American-supplied arms seemed a trivial matter, involving readily replaceable matériel. The amount of economic aid appropriated but unexpended was small and not a serious drain on American resources. The further loss of American prestige was a serious concern but became less significant in the light of the long American identification with the Nationalists. The rise of anti-Americanism worried American officials, but they continued nonetheless to rely on the supposedly deep-rooted traditional friendship between the United States and China. The argument that continued entanglement would drive the Chinese Communists into the arms of the Soviet Union but withdrawal would promote Chinese Titoism was rapidly weakened and then destroyed by Chinese pronouncements and actions.

All the disadvantages of continued entanglement would have been judged to be as serious as they turned out to be only if the potentiality of China for good or evil had been adequately recognized and the role of ideology in Chinese Communist foreign policy had been correctly judged. Only then could the United States have perceived that the loss of American prestige, the intensified Chinese hostility against the United States, the Chinese Communist leaders' ties with the Soviet Union, and the lack of normal diplomatic relations between the United States and Communist China might lead to an armed clash which might entail a major military effort on the part of the United States. A correct estimate of the dangers involved might in turn have increased the chance of a successful program of prompt withdrawal. But, in the event, American officials and scholars who recommended a program of withdrawal were generally those who did not regard China as a serious menace to the United States or else did not consider ideology a paramount element in future Chinese international behavior. The political figures who did regard a Communist China as a formidable enemy were those who advocated a program of continued assistance to the Nationalists in the vain hope that the Communist advance could be halted or delayed by limited means. While the administration vigorously and successfully opposed any new program of aid to China in 1949 and 1950, it did not advocate and implement a program of prompt and total disengagement with a sense of urgency. This absence of a sense of urgency stemmed from the same basic assumption underlying Marshall's refusal to undertake armed intervention — that China could not soon develop into a strong state and could not readily become a serious threat to the United States. It was also derived from the judgment that the traditional Chinese suspicion of Russian imperialism and the historic Sino-American friendship would soon overcome the ideological bias which bound China to the Soviet Union and engendered hostility to the United States.

The expectation of Chinese Communist impotence or moderation in foreign affairs has turned out to be false. But it was only the last of many unfounded hopes regarding China. It followed the wish that China under the Nationalists could become a great power, the judgment that the Chinese Communists were not dedicated Communists, and the hope that a coalition government could be established. These overly optimistic expectations arose to satisfy a psychological need created by the pattern of America's China policy. For the gap between America's objectives and meager means brought about situations in the Far East over which the United States had no real influence. Yet she could not but hope that somehow things could work out satisfactorily. If Japan had to be eliminated as a significant factor and the United States did not plan to maintain a military presence in China, the only hope for stability in the Far East lay in the possibility of China's emergence as a great and friendly power. If a strife-ridden China could not become a great power and the Kuomintang could not bring about political progress, the only hope lay in a coalition government in which the "so-called Communists" would take part. If the coalition government could not be established and a third force could not be fashioned, the only hope lay in the weakness or moderation of the Chinese Communists. These hopes obviated the necessity of making difficult choices or of accepting what would have looked like impending catastrophe. Many of these illusions also had their roots in America's political tradition.

Up to June, 1950, American policy did achieve one negative result: the avoidance of armed intervention in the Chinese civil war and thus of an immediate military conflict with the Chinese Communists on the mainland of China. But the North Korean aggression against South Korea was to bring about a sudden reversal of the policy of not defending Formosa by force which had been dramatically reaffirmed by Truman and Acheson less than six months before. Despite all its endeavors to avoid that contingency, the administration was to find it necessary to intervene militarily in the Chinese civil war. Once again, the United States was to make a new advance in China as a result of the pressure of events occurring elsewhere. The neutralization of the Formosa Strait was to render an armed conflict with Communist China likely sooner or later, unless it could lead to a political settlement with Peking over the question of Formosa. The crossing of the 38th Parallel and Peking's intervention in the Korean War were to precipitate that conflict sooner than anyone could have expected. The ground for this military confrontation was prepared by the erratic shifts of policy in 1947 and 1948, the partisan debate and deadlock in 1949 and 1950, and the failure to effect a prompt disengagement, which were in turn the expression of the contradictions inherent in American policy. In short, the inconsistencies of the traditional policy did not enable the United States either to achieve her objectives or to avoid the use of her armed forces in dealing with issues relating to China. With the military conflict between Communist China and the United States in Korea, the misfortune of American policy was to become complete.

PART FOUR

THE

IRONIC

FULFILMENT

CHAPTER XIII

THE KOREAN WAR

AND

THE EMERGENCE OF

COMMUNIST CHINA

AS A

GREAT POWER

A. The Soviet Move and the American Reaction

On June 25, 1950, North Korean forces launched a large-scale, carefully planned attack on South Korea. This North Korean aggression was inspired and planned by the Soviet Union,[1] and it appears to have been designed primarily to disrupt the American plan for concluding a separate peace treaty with Japan and to frighten Japan away from America by a demonstration of Communist strength and American weakness. In Soviet calculations, even if it should fail to achieve this principal aim, the conquest of South Korea would improve the defensive and offensive position of the Communist bloc against an eventual American-Japanese alliance.[2] The Soviet plan apparently rested on the assumption that the United

[1] Harry S. Truman, *Years of Trial and Hope* (Garden City, N.Y.: Doubleday & Co., 1956), p. 335. For the testimonies of General Omar Bradley, the chairman of the Joint Chiefs of Staff, and Secretary of State Dean Acheson in the MacArthur hearings, see Senate Committee on Armed Services and Committee on Foreign Relations, *Hearings on the Military Situation in the Far East*, 82d Cong., 1st sess. (1951), pp. 210–11, 1935–36 (hereafter cited as *Military Situation in the Far East*). See also John Foster Dulles, "A Militaristic Experiment," *Department of State Bulletin*, July 10, 1950, p. 49, and his speech before the Commonwealth Club of San Francisco, *ibid.*, p. 207; Alexander L. George, "American Policy-Making and the North Korean Aggression," *World Politics*, January, 1955, pp. 209–32; Allen S. Whiting, *China Crosses the Yalu* (New York: Macmillan Co., 1960), chap. iv; John W. Spanier, *The Truman–MacArthur Controversy and the Korean War* (Cambridge, Mass.: Harvard University Press, 1959), chap. ii.

For a statement of the opposite view, see Wilbur H. Hitchcock, "North Korea Jumps the Gun," *Current History*, March, 1951, pp. 136–4?.

[2] Whiting, *op. cit.*, pp. 37–38; George, *loc. cit.*, pp. 214–15; Dulles, *loc. cit.*, pp. 50, 208.

States would not defend South Korea with her armed forces. This assumption found support in American actions and statements concerning Korea since 1948.

American commitments in Korea stemmed from actions taken during the Pacific war. In the Cairo Declaration of December 1, 1943, Roosevelt, Churchill, and Chiang Kai-shek announced that "in due course Korea shall become free and independent." The Cairo Declaration was reaffirmed in the Potsdam Declaration of June 26, 1945, to which the Soviet Union adhered upon her entry into the Pacific war. As for the period prior to the establishment of Korean independence, President Roosevelt envisaged, as early as March, 1943, an international trusteeship.[3] This proposal for a transitional arrangement was accepted by Stalin at both the Teheran and the Yalta conferences.[4] In his conversations with Harry Hopkins in May, 1944, Stalin agreed that Korea should be placed under a trusteeship composed of the United States, China, Great Britain, and the Soviet Union.[5] At the time of Japan's surrender, the United States and the Soviet Union agreed on the 38th Parallel as the dividing line for the purpose of accepting the surrender of the Japanese forces in Korea. In the next two years, negotiations between the United States and the Soviet Union to establish a four-power trusteeship for a unified Korea met with no results. After the breakdown of bilateral negotiations, the United States in September, 1947, brought the Korean problem to the General Assembly of the United Nations. The United States now discarded the idea of a four-power trusteeship, and her avowed objective became the establishment of an independent, united Korea.[6] Within the month, however, the Joint Chiefs of Staff were to conclude that, from the standpoint of military security, the United States had little interest in maintaining troops and bases in Korea and that the two American divisions there could well be used elsewhere. Shortly before, General Wedemeyer, in his now famous report, had recommended that American forces be withdrawn concurrently with the withdrawal of Soviet forces from North Korea.[7]

In other words, the United States, by ostensibly emphasizing the ambitious, long-term goal of a united Korea and by bringing the problem to the United Nations, was actually trying to provide a cover for the contem-

[3] Cordell Hull, *Memoirs* (New York, Macmillan Co., 1948), II, 1596.

[4] Department of State, *Foreign Relations of the United States: The Conferences at Cairo and Teheran, 1943* (Washington, D.C.: Government Printing Office, 1961), p. 869; Department of State,*Foreign Relations of the United States: The Conferences at Malta and Yalta, 1945* (Washington, D.C.: Government Printing Office, 1955), p. 770.

[5] Robert E. Sherwood, *Roosevelt and Hopkins* (New York: Harper & Bros., 1948), p. 903.

[6] Leland M. Goodrich, *Korea: A Study of United States Policy in the United Nations* (New York: Council on Foreign Relations, 1956), pp. 7–41.

[7] General Albert C. Wedemeyer, *Wedemeyer Reports!* (New York: Henry Holt & Co., 1958), p. 479; Truman, *op. cit.*, pp. 325–26.

plated reduction of military commitment in South Korea which was judged to be of little importance to her security. As a substitute for military power, the United States sought to invoke the support of the United Nations to uphold her position in South Korea. This structure of avowed objective, actual purpose, prescribed means, and underlying assumption bore a close resemblance to the traditional policy toward China. It was to produce consequences fairly similar to those flowing from the Open Door policy before 1941. It was to invite attack by another power, which the United States would then be obliged to counter with her armed forces. Not long after the United States was to use strong measures, the verbal policy would be transformed into a program to be implemented by force. It was to confront the United States with the dilemma of forsaking an objective to which she had committed her prestige or employing in Korea more manpower and resources than she thought prudent.

After the government in South Korea had been formally inaugurated on August 15, 1948, the American forces began their withdrawal on September 15 as noted in the last chapter. General MacArthur in an interview in early March, 1949, traced an American line of defense which left out South Korea. By the end of June, all American troops had left Korea. In an address on January 12, 1950, Secretary Acheson drew a defense perimeter in the western Pacific which omitted South Korea. All these actions and pronouncements apparently suggested to the Russians that the United States would not defend South Korea against an attack by the North Korean regime. But the well-planned, large-scale attack by North Korean forces across an established boundary suddenly confronted the United States with the clear-cut moral issue of upholding the system of collective security and defending a weak state against armed aggression. It created a crisis which forcefully impressed upon American officials the possibly disastrous consequences of inaction.

The North Korean attack was widely interpreted as a test by the Soviet Union of America's determination to resist open, armed attack by Communist forces. It was assumed that, if the United States failed to resist, other local aggressions would quickly follow and might lead to a general war.[8] President Truman viewed the North Korean attack in terms of Japan's attack on Manchuria, Mussolini's conquest of Ethiopia, and Hitler's aggressions in the thirties.[9] To Secretary Acheson, if the North Korean attack was not repelled, the whole system of collective security would begin to disintegrate; and the system of collective security was one of the bases of American security.[10] To John Foster Dulles, a North Korean success would place Japan "between the upper and lower jaws of the Rus-

[8] George, *op. cit.*, pp. 213, 215–16.
[9] Truman, *op. cit.*, pp. 332–33.
[10] *Military Situation in the Far East*, pp. 1818–19.

sian bear."[11] Truman also felt that if the United States failed to protect a country established under American auspices, the peoples in countries adjacent to the Soviet Union not only in Asia but in Europe, the Middle East, and elsewhere would be adversely affected.[12]

This new evaluation of America's security interests in Korea, reinforced by a clear-cut moral issue, led the United States to reverse suddenly her military strategy in the Far East. On June 27, General MacArthur was authorized to use American naval and air forces to prevent the Inchon-Kimpo-Seoul area from falling into unfriendly hands.[13] On June 30, Truman accepted MacArthur's recommendation to employ American ground forces in Korea.[14] In recommending the use of ground forces in Korea, MacArthur envisaged "an early offensive action in accordance with his mission of clearing South Korea of North Korean forces."[15] The commitment of American ground forces on a large scale in Korea constituted not only a reversal of the strategic plan symbolized by the withdrawal of American forces from South Korea in 1949. It also represented a departure from one of the strongly held views of General Marshall to the effect that American ground forces should not be used on the continent of Asia[16] — a view which contributed to his refusal to intervene in the Chinese civil war.[17]

B. The Neutralization of the Formosa Strait

One of the first decisions made after the North Korean attack was the dispatch of the Seventh Fleet to neutralize the Formosa Strait. Notwithstanding the testimony of Secretary of Defense Johnson to the contrary,[18] this decision was taken in the first day after the North Korean attack, upon the joint recommendation of the Department of State and the Joint Chiefs of Staff. According to Secretary Acheson's testimony, the of-

[11] Dulles, "A Militaristic Experiment," loc. cit., p. 50.

[12] Truman, op. cit., p. 339.

[13] Military Situation in the Far East, p. 3192.

[14] Truman, op. cit., pp. 342–43. For the official statement announcing this decision, see press release by the White House, June 30, 1950, Department of State, United States Policy in the Korea Crisis (Washington, D.C.: Government Printing Office, 1950), p. 25.

[15] Military Situation in the Far East, p. 1012.

[16] George, op. cit., p. 224.

[17] See chap. ix, above.

[18] Johnson's restrospective account can be summarized as follows: It was he who injected the issue of Formosa into the deliberations in the evening of June 25 at the first Blair House meeting. He insisted that "relatively the security of the United States was more affected by Formosa than Korea." Johnson and Secretary Acheson had a brief but "really violent" discussion. Then Truman indicated that the question of Formosa would be discussed later. The decision to dispatch the Seventh Fleet was made the next day (Military Situation in the Far East, p. 2580). See also Albert L. Warner, "How the Korean Decision was Made," Harper's, June, 1957, pp. 99–106.

ficials in the State Department and from the Joint Chiefs of Staff worked out together a series of recommendations which included the dispatch of the Seventh Fleet to the Formosa Strait. At the President's request, these recommendations were presented by Secretary Acheson himself at the Blair House meeting on June 25.[19] In his memoirs, President Truman stated that Acheson recommended making a statement that the Fleet would repel any attack on Formosa and that no attacks should be made from Formosa on the mainland.[20] These recommendations were accepted by Truman. The next evening at the second Blair House meeting, the President directed Secretary Johnson to give General MacArthur the instructions regarding the Seventh Fleet.[21] It was also at this meeting that Truman approved the State Department's recommendation to use air and naval force to support the South Korean army—a move which, according to Johnson, "the military neither recommended nor opposed."[22] Truman also approved recommendations for the strengthening of American forces in the Philippines and for increased aid to the French in Indochina. All these decisions were announced by President Truman in a public statement on June 27.

One cannot ascertain from published records whether it was the officials of the State Department or the officers representing the Joint Chiefs who, in their meeting to prepare a joint recommendation, initiated the idea of sending the Seventh Fleet to the Formosa Strait.[23] There is no question that even before the Korean attack, there had been continued pressure on the administration for a change of its policy toward Formosa. When Secretary Johnson and General Bradley came back from a ten-day tour of the Far East just before the North Korean aggression, they brought back with them a memorandum on Formosa prepared by MacArthur which stressed the strategic interest of the United States in denying Formosa to the Communists.[24] How much weight MacArthur's memorandum carried in the deliberations on June 25 cannot be determined.

[19] *Military Situation in the Far East*, p. 2055.

[20] Truman, *op. cit.*, p. 334; *New York Times*, June 28, 1950, p. 1, under the by-line of James Reston.

[21] Truman, *op. cit.*, p. 337.

[22] *Military Situation in the Far East*, p. 2580.

[23] Goodrich observed: "It is quite possible that the neutralization of Formosa was a condition set by the Joint Chiefs for their consent to the State Department's proposal to come to the assistance of the Republic of Korea with armed forces" (Goodrich, *op. cit.*, p. 111).

[24] *New York Times*, June 28, 1950, p. 12, under the by-line of James Reston.

This memorandum was read by General Bradley at the request of Secretary Johnson at the Blair House meeting on the evening of June 25 (Johnson's testimony, *Military Situation in the Far East*, pp. 2579–80; see also Acheson's testimony, *ibid.*, p. 2055). Brigadier General L. Joseph Fortier, director of Theater Intelligence Division of the

There is reason to believe, however, that after the North Korean aggression, Secretary Acheson was quite ready to reverse his policy toward Formosa. The neutralization of the Formosa Strait as well as American actions in South Korea was a step to discourage Communist moves elsewhere, to localize the conflict, and to induce Communist withdrawal in Korea by demonstrating American strength and determination.[25] Thus President Truman, in his statement of June 27, 1950, declared: "The attack upon Korea makes it plain beyond all doubts that Communism has passed beyond the use of subversion to conquer independent nations and will now use armed invasion and war. . . . In these circumstances the occupation of Formosa by Communist forces would be a direct threat to the security of the Pacific area. . . ."[26] Significantly, the President announced at the same time a program of accelerating military assistance to Indochina and the Philippines. Furthermore, domestic politics and the necessity to win wholehearted Republican support for the State Department's policy in Korea made it highly desirable for the administration to reverse its position on Formosa. In sending the Seventh Fleet to prevent an attack on Formosa, the administration adopted, at least as a temporary measure, the policy advocated by Senator Taft and Mr. Hoover. It took a step which was momentarily in line with Senator H. Alexander Smith's suggestion for joint United States–Nationalist occupation of Formosa and went beyond Knowland's and Judd's proposal of sending a military mission and giving military

Far Eastern Command from February, 1949, to September, 1950, flew to Formosa at the invitation of Generalissimo Chiang Kai-shek in late May or early June, 1950. He spent three days in Formosa and stayed in a "very comfortable cottage near where the Generalissimo lived." His mission was to get a first-hand estimate of the situation on Formosa. At the time, the United States government had a consul general and military, air, and naval attachés stationed on the island (General Fortier's testimony, Senate Committee on the Judiciary, *Hearings on the Institute of Pacific Relations*, 82d Cong., 1st and 2d sess. [1951–52], pp. 848–52).

It cannot be ascertained from published records whether or not General Fortier's trip was one of the steps leading to the preparation of General MacArthur's memorandum on Formosa. According to the testimony of Admiral Charles M. Cooke, commander of the Seventh Fleet from December, 1945, to February, 1948, military attachés and diplomatic representatives believed in May, 1950, that Formosa would probably fall before July 15 and a new warning was issued for all Americans to leave Formosa. This appreciation of the military situation was challenged by Admiral Cooke who was in Formosa as a representative of the International News Service. Later, Admiral Cooke served in Formosa as the co-ordinator of the Commerce International–China, an American corporation retaining a group of retired officers, reserve officers, and ex-officers to furnish technical services to the Nationalist government. General Fortier's trip and General MacArthur's memorandum obviously arose from the uncertain situation confronting Formosa (*ibid.*, pp. 1540–41). In the two weeks before the North Korean attack, the Chinese Communist troops opposite Formosa increased from about 40,000 to about 156,000 (*Military Situation in the Far East*, p. 2621).

[25] George, *op. cit.*, pp. 229–30.
[26] *United States Policy in the Korea Crisis*, p. 18.

aid to Formosa.[27] The neutralization of the Formosa Strait temporarily produced bipartisan co-operation on Far Eastern affairs.[28]

Once more, a crisis centered elsewhere overcame America's unwillingness to use force on an issue relating to China. The United States was compelled by the pressure of global events to halt her retreat, to intervene in the Chinese civil war at the last moment, and, temporarily at least, to make a new advance in China. By this time, however, the Chinese Communists were no longer an armed party seeking to seize power; they were the masters of mainland China with a strong alliance with the Soviet Union.

Peking reacted more forcefully than Moscow to President Truman's statement of June 27. For the American government not only abruptly thwarted the Chinese Communists' plan for an early invasion of Formosa but also reopened the whole question of Formosa. President Truman specifically declared that "the determination of the future status of Formosa must await the restoration of security in the Pacific, a peaceful settlement with Japan or consideration by the United Nations."[29] This declaration stood in contrast to his statement of January 5, 1950, announcing the "hands-off" policy and stressing the Cairo Declaration of December 1, 1943, in which President Roosevelt, Prime Minister Churchill, and Generalissimo Chiang Kai-shek stated that Formosa would be returned to the Republic of China.

Mao Tse-tung's immediate reaction was to assert that the American President himself now proved that "his statement [of January 5] was false."[30] Looking through his Marxist-Leninist prism, Mao interpreted this American change in policy to meet a new situation as an "open exposure by the United States of its true imperialist face."[31] In a formal statement on June 28, Foreign Minister Chou En-lai declared: "The fact that Taiwan is part of China will remain unchanged forever. This is not only a historical fact but has been affirmed by the Cairo Declaration, the Potsdam Declaration, and the existing conditions after Japan's surrender."[32] He charged

---

[27] James Reston reported: "When President Truman on June 27 ordered the United States Seventh Fleet to prevent any attack on Formosa, he had several things in mind. He wanted to localize the Korean War by neutralizing Formosa, and to minimize the political opposition to the Korean War by neutralizing Senators Taft, Knowland, Smith of New Jersey and others who had been condemning his 'hands-off Formosa' policy" (*New York Times*, July 28, 1950, p. 5).

[28] Spanier, *op. cit.*, pp. 62–64.

[29] *United States Policy in the Korea Crisis*, p. 18.

[30] Chairman Mao Tse-tung's comment on President Truman's statement of June 27, a brief talk given on June 28, 1950, at the eighth meeting of the Central People's Government Council in Chang Tao-li, *Why China Helps Korea* (Bombay: People's Publishing House, 1951), pp. 31–32.

[31] *Ibid.*

[32] For the Chinese text see, *Hsin-hua yüeh-pao*, II, No. 3 (July, 1950), 525.

that Truman's statement and the actions of the American navy "constitute armed aggression against the territory of China and total violation of the United Nations Charter." [33] He declared defiantly that "the Chinese people . . . will surely be victorious in driving off American aggressors and in recovering Taiwan." [34] It was apparent from his declaration that Peking would not allow the question of Formosa to be decided at a peace conference over Japan which was then under American occupation or by the United Nations in which the Communist countries were in the minority. An editorial in the *Jên-min jih-pao* on June 29 pointed out that, as late as June 23, Acheson declared that Truman's January 5 statement was still valid.[35] It argued that the Korean situation could not justify the American action in the Taiwan Strait. It appears quite possible that the Chinese Communists had counted on the United States to adhere to the hands-off policy and had derived considerable assurance from every American pronouncement that could be interpreted as a reaffirmation of that policy. The sudden reversal of American policy further increased their distrust of American intentions and their doubt about the reliability of American declarations.

The intensified hostility and distrust toward the United States apparently strengthened Peking's disposition to push its revolutionary interests and to oppose American policies elsewhere in Asia. Both Mao and Chou did not confine their attacks to the reversal of American policy toward Formosa. They viewed American actions in the broad context of Asian affairs. Mao seized upon Truman's statement to denounce American intervention in the "internal affairs" not only of China but also "Korea, the Philippines, Vietnam and other countries." [36] Assuming the role of leadership in Asian affairs, Mao declared that "the affairs of Asia should be administered by the peoples of Asia themselves and not by the United States." He asserted that "United States aggression in Asia will only arouse the extensive and resolute resistance of the people of Asia." He called on the people throughout China and the world to unite and make "adequate preparations to defeat any provocation of American imperialism" which was "outwardly strong but feeble within, because it has no support among the people." [37] Chou charged that "the attack by the puppet Korean government of Syngman Rhee on the Korean People's Democratic Republic at the instigation of the United States government was a premeditated move by the United States, designed to create a pretext for the United

[33] *Ibid.*

[34] *Ibid.*

[35] *Wei-ta ti k'ang Mei yüan Chao yiin-tung* ["The Great Movement to Resist the United States and To Help Korea"], (Peking: Jên-min ch'u-pan-shê, 1954), pp. 649–51 (hereafter cited as *K'ang Mei*).

[36] Chang Toa-li, *op. cit.*, pp. 32–33.

[37] *Ibid.*

States to invade Taiwan, Korea, Vietnam and the Philippines." [38] Thus from the outset the Chinese Communists did not look at American action in the Formosa Strait in the narrow context of American intervention in the Chinese civil war, but in the broad framework of what they called the "new, premeditated aggressions" of "American imperialism" against the Asian people. They did not define their task as merely taking over Formosa but also as rallying "the people throughout the world who love peace, justice and freedom, particularly the oppressed nationalities and peoples of the East, to rise up and check the new aggressions of American imperialism in the Orient." [39] They took the neutralization of the Formosa Strait as an additional confirmation of their distorted view of the United States. The revolutionary fervor, the ideological perspective, and the mental image of the United States which characterized both Mao's informal talk and Chou's formal statement inevitably affected the Chinese Communist regime's conception of its interests and its duties, its estimate of the external threat, and its appraisal of American intentions. These appraisals were to play an important part in Peking's intervention in Korea after the American forces crossed the 38th Parallel.

The tone and content of Mao's and Chou's statements re-emphasized the Chinese Communists' policy of "joining with revolutionaries" in other countries which was formulated in 1948–49.[40] In turn, this policy was partly the outgrowth of the new aggressive line of international communism which encouraged the resort to armed actions. This new line was inaugurated at the end of 1947 by A. A. Zhdanov's speech at the opening conference of the Cominform.[41] By the summer of 1949, Russian leaders began to stress the importance of the Chinese example for Communist movements in Southeast Asia and allowed the Chinese Communists to take the lead in co-ordinating or guiding them. Flushed with revolutionary fervor and emboldened by their smashing victory over the Nationalists against overwhelming odds, the Chinese Communists accepted without hesitation their new role of leadership in Asian affairs.

In an address to the Trade Union Conference of Asian and Australian countries in Peking on November 16, 1949, Liu Shao-ch'i, a member of the Politbureau, claimed for Communist China the leadership of national revolutionary movements in all other countries of Asia on the basis of the success of the political-military program worked out by Mao Tse-tung. Liu declared: "The path taken by the Chinese people in defeating im-

[39] *Ibid.*, p. 32.

[39] *Ibid.*

[40] H. Arthur Steiner, *The International Position of Communist China* (New York: Institute of Pacific Relations, 1958), pp. 10–11.

[41] Max Beloff, *Soviet Policy in the Far East, 1944–1951* (London: Oxford University Press, 1953), pp. 208–10; Captain Malcolm Kennedy, *A History of Communism in East Asia* (New York: Praeger, 1957), pp. 358–60.

perialism and its lackeys and in founding the People's Republic of China is the path that should be taken by the peoples of various colonial and semi-colonial countries in their fight for national independence and people's democracy." [42] Communist China was the first Communist regime to grant diplomatic recognition to the Democratic Republic of Vietnam on January 18,[43] anticipating a similar action by the Soviet Union on January 30. By 1950 the influence of the Maoist strategy was clearly discernible in the revolutionary program of the Communist parties in Vietnam, the Philippines, and Burma.[44] Up to August of 1950, the Chinese Communists followed a policy hostile, not only to the United States, but also to the established governments in such countries as India, Burma, and Indonesia which had recognized the Peking regime.

At the time the neutralization of the Formosa Strait was thought to be a temporary measure taken in the face of an emergency. It left open the question of the future status of Formosa.[45] But, as we have noted, Chou proclaimed Peking's confidence in driving out "the American aggressors" and in recovering Taiwan.[46] Thus, the neutralization of the Formosa Strait created a new issue between Peking and Washington and produced a basic change in the pattern of conflict among Peking, Washington, and Moscow. The United States had now directly opposed with her armed forces the national interest of China and the revolutionary interests of the Chinese Communist movement. The tension between Peking and Washington was immeasurably heightened. It made insignificant any possible disagreement between Peking and Moscow which may have existed at that time. It even overshadowed any conflict of interests between Moscow and Washington in the Far East. It doomed to failure Acheson's attempt to turn Chinese nationalism against the Soviet Union.

C. The Renewed Conflict over China Policy

Within the United States, the neutralization of the Formosa Strait only temporarily pacified the American friends of Generalissimo Chiang. It enlisted their support for the administration's actions in Korea but did not bring about unity on China policy. It did not make Secretary Acheson

[42] Steiner, op. cit., Appendix A, p. 34.

[43] On January 14, 1950, Ho Chi-minh, the chairman of the Democratic Republic, announced his regime's willingness to establish diplomatic relations with all countries. The next day, the foreign minister of the North Vietnam regime cabled Chou En-lai with a similar request. Chou replied favorably on January 18. For documents, see Hsin-hua yüeh-pao, I, No. 4 (February 15, 1950), 1081.

[44] Shen-yu Dai, Peking, Moscow and the Communist Parties of Colonial Asia (Cambridge, Mass.: Center for International Studies, Massachusetts Institute of Technology, 1954).

[45] Truman, op. cit., p. 339.

[46] P. 562, above.

immune to further attacks. Even at the moment when political unity was momentarily restored, Senator Taft interpreted the neutralization of the Formosa Strait as a reversal by the President of Acheson's policy, attributed to Acheson's hands-off Formosa policy the cause of the Korean War, and demanded the Secretary's resignation.[47] The dispatch of the Seventh Fleet merely marked a turning point after which the United States again became increasingly involved in the Chinese civil war, the heretofore weakening influence of the China bloc was revived and strengthened, and the conflict over China policy was sharpened by the developments in the Korean War.

This conflict over China policy found its most forceful expression in the controversy between the administration and General MacArthur over three issues: the degree of American commitment to Chiang, the neutralized status of the Formosa Strait, and the future of that island. The administration desired to limit its ties to Chiang so as to preserve its freedom of action, while MacArthur wanted an all-out commitment. The administration believed that there was a "basic conflict of interest" between the United States and Chiang; for it was feared that in his burning ambition to use Formosa as a steppingstone for his re-entry to the mainland, Chiang might drag the United States into a war with the Chinese Communists.[48] The administration felt that the adoption of a wrong approach to Chiang and Formosa might destroy the unity of the United Nations. In contrast, MacArthur thought that the United States should back anyone who would fight communism, that Chiang's determination to resist Communist control paralleled the interests and purposes of the American people, and that the administration's policies and the hostile attitudes of the State Department were undermining Chiang.[49]

The administration employed the Seventh Fleet to prevent Nationalist actions against the mainland as well as the projected Communist assault on Formosa. MacArthur felt from the very beginning that the neutralization of the Formosa Strait had given the Chinese Communists "complete immunity" from any countermeasure while they were building up their forces for an attack against Formosa. He suggested that the President withdraw the prohibition against attacking the airfields on the mainland if the Chinese Communists continued to construct airstrips or to build up their position along the Formosa Strait.[50]

Insofar as one can ascertain from published materials, the administration did not have a clear-cut substantive policy for the future of Formosa.

[47] *Congressional Record*, XCVI, 81st Cong., 2d sess. (1950), 9319–23.

[48] Truman, *op. cit.*, p. 351.

[49] *Ibid.*, pp. 352–53; Major General Courtney Whitney, *MacArthur: His Rendezvous with History* (New York: Alfred A. Knopf, Inc., 1956), pp. 373–75.

[50] *Ibid.*, pp. 369–70; Truman, *op. cit.*, p. 353.

It seems to have desired to prevent Formosa from falling into hostile hands by the establishment of "an independent government . . . through the medium of the United Nations." [51] It may have been thinking of an independent Formosa with Formosan self-rule.[52] In contrast, MacArthur could find no evidence for the desire of Formosans for independence. He attributed far greater strategic importance to Formosa than the Joint Chiefs. In his opinion, Formosa in the hands of a hostile power could be used to breach and neutralize America's defense system in the Pacific Ocean. The loss of this defense perimeter "would shift any future battle area 5,000 miles eastward to the coast of American continent, our own home." [53] MacArthur subsequently made this point even more emphatically when he testified in the hearings on his dismissal that "from our standpoint we practically lose the Pacific Ocean if we give up or lose Formosa." [54] His public views at the time implied even to Admiral Forrest Sherman, chief of naval operations, that "we are going to use that [Formosa] as a base from which we would be able to attack objectives in Asia and so on." [55] In contrast, the administration merely wanted to deny Formosa to a hostile power and had no intention to use it for offensive operation. It did not believe that the loss of Formosa to an enemy, to use General Bradley's words, "would jeopardize our position to the extent that we would lose all our other positions in the Pacific." [56]

These conflicts over policy manifested themselves in two significant incidents. On July 31, MacArthur visited Formosa with the prior approval of the Joint Chiefs but not the State Department, which had apparently tried to dissuade him from going at that time. This visit took place six days after Yakob Malik, the Soviet representative on the Security Council, announced that he proposed to return to the council, thus ending the Soviet boycott of seven months. It increased the allies' and neutrals' anxiety over American policy toward China. It played into the hands of Malik's peace offensive. It was considered in Lake Success "a triumph of mistiming." [57] It was also thought to be evidence of lack of co-ordination in American diplomacy. This incident ended when Truman obtained through his emissary, Averell Harriman, a soldier's pledge from MacArthur to support his policy.

The second incident was MacArthur's message to the Veterans of For-

[51] *Ibid.*, p. 352.

[52] For indirect evidence on this point, see MacArthur's comment on Harriman's remarks as reported by the latter, *ibid.*; General Bradley's testimony, *Military Situation in the Far East*, p. 984.

[53] Whitney, *op. cit.*, pp. 377–80.

[54] *Military Situation in the Far East*, p. 53.

[55] *Ibid.*, p. 1591.

[56] *Ibid.*, p. 985.

[57] *New York Times*, August 11, 1950, p. 11, under the by-line of James Reston. See also his dispatch in *ibid.*, August 6, 1950, p. E3.

eign Wars in which MacArthur stated his views on the strategic importance of Formosa.[58] The full text of this message was carried in an American weekly magazine which appeared on August 26. It was sent without
the advance knowledge of President Truman, Secretary Acheson, Secretary
Johnson, or the Joint Chiefs.[59] It was made known to the world only one
day after Ambassador Warren Austin had repeated, in a lengthy letter to
Secretary-General Lie, America's strong indorsement of United Nations
consideration of the case of Formosa, pledging American support for a full
United Nations investigation. Austin's letter was an adroit maneuver to
counter Peking's complaint of August 24 of American "aggression" on
Taiwan. It represented an effort to gain through the United Nations the
allies' and neutrals' support for America's position on Formosa. Successfully executed, it would have extricated the United States from her isolated and vulnerable position on this divisive issue.

MacArthur's message contradicted Austin's letter and gave credence
to Peking's charge of American aggression on Taiwan. On August 29, the
Peking radio declared that MacArthur's statement constituted a "formal
and public admission that Formosa was an indispensable part of America's
Pacific line of defense." [60] On September 1, the Soviet radio declared that
MacArthur had torn the cover from the real intention of America which
was to seize Formosa for the United States.[61] The State Department was
distressed not only by the propaganda advantage which MacArthur's message gave the Communists; it was also concerned that to friendly and
neutral nations the United States appeared to be speaking with two voices.
At the order of President Truman, MacArthur's message was officially
withdrawn. But as a result of its publication in the magazine, its full text
was known to the world. The Chinese Communists were not impressed by
Truman's action in directing MacArthur to withdraw his message. They
cited David Lawrence of the *New York Herald Tribune* to the effect that
General MacArthur's message was not incompatible with the policy of the
State Department and that it was only ill-timed.[62]

Paralleling the growing conflict between the administration and MacArthur, the bipartisan unity temporarily restored at the outbreak of the Korean War was fast breaking down. On August 1, Chairman Guy Gabrielson
of the Republican party announced that his party would back American
policy in Korea in the November election campaign but would criticize
the Truman administration.[63] On August 7, Senator Kenneth S. Wherry
of Nebraska, the Republican floor leader, declared that he planned to fix

[58] For the full text, see Whitney, *op. cit.*, pp. 377–80.
[59] Truman, *op. cit.*, p. 356.
[60] *New York Times*, August 29, 1950, p. 17.
[61] *Military Situation in the Far East*, p. 2002.
[62] *Hsin-hua yüeh-pao*, III, No. 1 (November, 1950), 16.
[63] *New York Times*, August 1, 1950, p. 1.

responsibility for the blunder in not recognizing the danger of a Communist invasion of South Korea and demanded the dismissal of Secretary Acheson.[64] A few days later, Senator Taft charged again that the administration's policy in Asia had encouraged the North Korean attack. In a statement made public on August 13, four out of five Republican members of the Foreign Relations Committee accused Truman and Acheson of having invited the Communist assault on Korea.[65] Senator Vandenberg, the ranking Republican member of the committee and the symbol of bipartisanship in foreign policy, was ill. But he saw the text and was "in general agreement with it." [66] The next day, Senator Wherry again demanded the resignation of Acheson and called on President Truman to "get rid of the alien-minded radicals and moral perverts in his administration." [67] Two days later, he followed up his attack on Acheson with the statement that "the blood of our boys in Korea is on his shoulders, and no one else." [68]

Louis Johnson's resignation on September 12 as secretary of defense and the appointment of General Marshall to that post touched off a new round of Republican denunciations. In the debate on September 15 in the Senate over the bill granting President Truman authority to appoint General Marshall, Senator William E. Jenner, Republican from Indiana, shocked that august body by his denunciation of Marshall as "a front man for the traitors," a "living lie," and "either an unsuspecting stooge or an actual co-conspirator with the most treasonable array of political cutthroats ever turned loose in the executive branch of the government." [69] He charged that Marshall had been appointed as secretary of defense for the "frightening purpose of providing the front of respectability to the vicious sell-out not only of Chiang, not only of Formosa . . . but of the American GI's who are fighting and dying even now because of one treachery." [70] The enabling bill was passed on September 15 in both houses, and Marshall's nomination was confirmed by the Senate on September 20 by votes divided almost strictly along party lines.[71] Bipartisanship in foreign policy reached

[64] *Ibid.*, August 7, 1950, p. 2.
[65] *Ibid.*, August 14, 1950, pp. 1 and 10. The four senators were Alexander Wiley of Wisconsin, H. Alexander Smith of New Jersey, Bourke B. Hickenlooper of Iowa, and Henry Cabot Lodge, Jr., of Massachusetts.
[66] *Ibid.*
[67] *Ibid.*, August 15, 1950, p. 1.
[68] *Ibid.*, August 17, 1950, p. 1.
[69] *Ibid.*, September 16, 1950, p. 1. See also, *Congressional Record*, XCVI, (1950), pp. 14913–21. As reprinted in the *Congressional Record* the last part of Jenner's characterization of Marshall reads as follows: "An errand boy, a front man, a stooge, or a co-conspirator for this administration's crazy assortment of collective cutthroat crackpots and Communist fellow-travelling appeasers" (*ibid.*, p. 14917).
[70] *Ibid.*, p. 14916.
[71] *Ibid.*, pp. 14931, 14972–73, 15182; *New York Times*, September 20, 1950, p. 1.

a new low. Secretary Acheson's position was as vulnerable as ever. He had avoided any recommendations which could be considered appeasement of the Communists.[72] But his policies toward Korea and Formosa did not avert Republican attacks on him and on the administration. Only a smashing victory over the Communist bloc could restore the prestige of the administration, brighten its political outlook, and enhance its freedom to seek a diplomatic solution of the question of Formosa.

D. The Crossing of the 38th Parallel

With the neutralization of the Formosa Strait, the American Seventh Fleet and Chinese Communist forces confronted each other. The preponderance of American naval and air power effectively deterred the Communists from attacking Formosa. Soon afterward, Peking moved approximately 30,000 troops from the area opposite Formosa to Shantung. The projected invasion of Formosa was postponed.[73] In retrospect, however, it is clear that given Peking's distrust of American intentions, her determination to occupy Formosa eventually, and her assumption of revolutionary leadership in Asia, a clash between Communist China and the United States was sooner or later likely to occur, if not over Formosa then at other places where terrain, lines of supply, and other geopolitical factors gave Peking a better chance of successfully challenging the United States. What brought this clash about sooner than anyone could have expected was the crossing of the 38th Parallel. What enabled Peking to score a surprising, epochal victory was MacArthur's headlong drive toward the Yalu River. At the roots of the decision to cross the 38th Parallel was a pattern of calculations characteristic of the China policy of the United States. At the root of MacArthur's drive beyond the narrow neck of the Korean peninsula were the same misjudgments underlying the crossing of the parallel, plus MacArthur's pride in his military prowess and the administration's inability to restrain his military movements in spite of the misgivings of the Joint Chiefs and the State Department.

In the early days of the Korean War, the political objective of the United States was merely the restoration of the *status quo ante bellum*.[74] There are indications, however, that as early as the beginning of August the idea of crossing the 38th Parallel came into the mind of important officials. General MacArthur seems to have taken the lead in advocating this idea. In a conference with Harriman on August 6 and 8, MacArthur, who had

[72] *Ibid.*, November 16, 1950, p. 6.
[73] Whiting, *op. cit.*, pp. 62–65.
[74] Truman's remarks at the National Security Council meeting on June 29, Truman, *op. cit.*, p. 341; Secretary Acheson's address before the convention of the American Newspaper Guild June 29, 1950, *Department of State Bulletin*, July 10, 1950, p. 24; *New York Times*, July 15, 1950, p. 1.

conceived of his plan for a landing at Inchon in the first week of the war, told the President's confidant that United Nations-supervised elections could be held within two months after Syngman Rhee's government was re-established in Seoul and that the North Koreans would vote for a non-Communist government when they were sure of no Russian or Communist intervention. He continued that there was no need to change the constitution of the Republic of Korea which provided for 100 seats for the North.[75] The General was obviously thinking of the unification of Korea under the government of Syngman Rhee, for which a military occupation of North Korea would be a prerequisite. Interestingly enough, MacArthur's remarks on Korea drew no adverse comments from Harriman, whose report to Truman showed no sign of hesitancy in criticizing the General's other views.

In a debate in the Security Council on August 17, Ambassador Austin declared that the General Assembly, in adopting its resolutions on Korea in 1947, 1948, and 1949, had sought the establishment by the Korean people of a free, unified, and independent nation, and the holding of free elections throughout all of Korea under the supervision of the United Nations. The United Nations would not want to turn from these objectives now. If all the members of the United Nations would support these objectives, many of the issues would be resolved. Austin ended his speech with these statements: "The opportunity is here. The place is here. The time is at hand. Only the word and the deed are lacking. We are waiting. And while we wait, the strength of the United Nations increases. Its resolution will neither flag nor fail." [76] According to Thomas J. Hamilton of the *New York Times*, this speech by Austin indicated that the United States delegation to the United Nations was entertaining the idea that the resolutions of the General Assembly, together with the Security Council's resolution of June 25, constituted authorization for General MacArthur to continue his advance up to the Soviet border.[77] On September 7, Secretary Acheson declared that crushing the North Korean aggression was by no means the end of the task of the United Nations.[78] Two days later, Dean Rusk, assistant secretary for Far Eastern affairs, stated in a general review of America's Far Eastern policy that "the United Nations must have an opportunity to give effect to its long-standing policy in favor of a free and united Korea along the lines set forth in the resolutions of the General Assembly over the past three years." [79] At the same time, Secretary-General Lie asserted that it would "not be enough" to bring about

[75] Truman, *op. cit.*, p. 357.

[76] United Nations Security Council, *Official Records, 488th Meeting*, August 17, 1950, p. 8.

[77] *New York Times*, August 24, 1950, p. 5.

[78] *Department of State Bulletin*, September 18, 1950, pp. 450–51.

[79] *Ibid.*, p. 467.

the withdrawal of the North Koreans to the 38th Parallel and that "the aim of the United Nations is and must be a united and independent Korea in which all of the people of Korea are able freely to select a government of their own choosing." [80]

MacArthur's remark, Harriman's silence, and the statements by Austin, Acheson, and Rusk were natural developments of American policy. After all, the long-range political objective of the United States since 1947 had been an independent, united Korea through elections supervised by the United Nations. This aim had been frustrated by Soviet obstructions which could not be removed without resorting to force. But the use of American military power to counter the North Korean aggression now opened up the possibility that this long-range objective could be realized. So after a brief interval and with no public debate and apparently insufficient deliberations in official circles, American officials and the public were beginning to think of the Korean War in terms of the unification of Korea even though this objective meant very little in the scheme of American purposes. A verbal policy was in the process of being transformed into a program to be implemented by force, just as the Open Door policy was in 1941. This development came so naturally that American officials and the public gave very little thought to the risks and costs involved.

In a conference in late August with General J. Lawton Collins, army chief of staff, and Admiral Sherman, General MacArthur won their approval for a landing at Inchon.[81] He also secured at this time their agreement that, for the purpose of destroying the North Korean forces, the 38th Parallel would have to be crossed.[82] On the highest level, the formal decision to cross the 38th Parallel was made on September 11 when President Truman approved a recommendation of the National Security Council that "General MacArthur was to extend his operations north of the parallel and to make plans for the occupation of North Korea, if there was no indication or threat of entry of Soviet or Chinese Communist elements in force." [83] On September 15, the day of the Inchon landing, the Joint Chiefs of Staff sent General MacArthur a directive based on the decision of the National Security Council. The Truman administration's program of containment thus did not preclude a policy of liberation which the Republican party later proclaimed with much fanfare but never implemented.

At the time there was overwhelming sentiment for crossing the 38th Parallel in non-Communist circles in the United States, not only on the

[80] *New York Times*, September 9, 1950, p. 1.

[81] Whitney, *op. cit.*, pp. 345–50.

[82] Martin Lichterman, "Korea: Problems in Limited War," *National Security in the Nuclear Age*, ed. Gordon B. Turner and Richard D. Challener (New York: Praeger, 1960), p. 34.

[83] Truman, *op. cit.*, p. 359. Lichterman noted that this was not an order to Mac-Arthur to cross the 38th Parallel, in *loc cit.*

right but also on the left.[84] On September 24, former Attorney General Francis Biddle, national chairman of Americans for Democratic Action, urged continuation "to its conclusion" of the military campaign, to be followed by the setting up of a unified Korea.[85] American officials were almost unanimous in recommending similar action. America's allies and friends also lent their support to this plan. It was only subsequently revealed that George Kennan was opposed to the crossing of the 38th Parallel on the grounds that it would bring Communist counteraction.[86]

General MacArthur's brilliant amphibious attack on Inchon and the total collapse of the North Korean army opened up the immediate possibility of crossing the 38th Parallel. An eight-nation resolution giving tacit approval to the United Nations forces to move into North Korea was submitted to the General Assembly. On September 30, Ambassador Austin declared that "the aggressor's forces should not be permitted to have refuge behind an imaginary line" and that "the artificial barrier which has divided North and South Korea has no basis for existence either in law or in reason." [87]

From Peking, these military and political developments brought increasingly specific warnings against the crossing of the parallel by American forces. On September 22, Peking admitted MacArthur's charge that Communist China had, prior to the North Korean aggression, "furnished substantial if not decisive military assistance to North Korea by releasing a vast pool of combat-seasoned troops of Korean ethnic origin" for service in the North Korean army.[88] She reaffirmed her support for Pyongyang, implying that further assistance would be given. On September 25, General Nieh Jung-chên, the acting chief of staff of the People's Liberation Army, told the Indian ambassador, K. M. Panikkar, that the Chinese did not intend to sit back with folded hands and let the Americans come up to their border.[89] On September 30, Premier Chou En-lai declared in a speech:

> The Chinese people absolutely will not tolerate foreign aggression, nor will they supinely tolerate seeing their neighbors being savagely invaded. Whoever attempt to exclude the nearly 500

[84] *New York Times*, September 24, 1950, pp. E1, E3.

[85] *Ibid.*, September 25, 1950, p. 5. He also urged that the United States should withdraw recognition of Chiang's regime but should grant it recognition as the *de facto* government of Formosa only. The Peking regime would be recognized only if it gave concrete assurance not to intervene in Korea and not to attack Formosa.

[86] *Ibid.*, November 16, 1950, p. 6, under the by-line of James Reston.

[87] Goodrich, *op. cit.*, pp. 130–31.

[88] Statement by spokesman of the foreign ministry, September 22, 1950, as reprinted in *Hsin-hua yüeh-pao*, II, No. 6 (October, 1950), 1961. For MacArthur's charge, see *Military Situation in the Far East*, pp. 1218–22.

[89] K. M. Panikkar, *In Two Chinas* (London: Allen & Unwin, 1955), p. 108.

million people from the United Nations and whoever ignore and violate the interests of this one-fourth of mankind and fancy vainly to solve arbitrarily any Far Eastern problem directly concerned with China, will certainly break their skulls.[90]

On October 1, the South Korean troops had, on the Eighth Army's order, penetrated seven miles into North Korea.[91] On the same day, MacArthur issued his ultimatum, ordering Pyongyang to surrender.[92] The next day, Peking fully defined the *casus belli* in a dramatic manner which was probably intended to convey her sense of urgency. Chou summoned Panikkar to a midnight conference and told the Indian ambassador that if the American forces crossed the 38th Parallel China would be forced to intervene.[93]

Washington dismissed Chou's midnight warning as merely a gambit to influence the pending vote in the General Assembly on the eight-nation resolution.[94] It did not believe that Peking would intervene. On October 7, the General Assembly approved the eight-nation resolution. The next day, American troops crossed the 38th Parallel in force. Less than two months later, they were to run into a gigantic trap carefully laid by the Chinese Communist forces which had begun their movement across the Yalu River in mid-October.

The administration's miscalculation of Peking's intentions does not seem to have stemmed from Acheson's belief that the Chinese Communists were deeply involved in conflict with the Soviet Union and, for that reason, neither would nor could intervene in Korea. There is no doubt that Acheson's long-range policy was to exploit the alleged conflicts between Chinese nationalism and Soviet imperialism. But his actions, such as the neutralization of the Formosa Strait and the attempt to seek a solution of the future status of that island through the United Nations, were dictated by the strategy of containment and were based on the assumption that Peking and Moscow were firm allies, acting in concert at least for the time being. His various statements playing up Sino-Soviet conflict were designed to arouse Chinese nationalism against Moscow, to make more difficult the Russian task of instigating the Chinese Communists to enter the Korean War, and to dissuade Peking from yielding to Soviet pressure or persuasion. Probably they were made also to convince the neutrals at the United Nations that Peking would not intervene and that there was little danger in United Nations' approval of the crossing of the 38th Parallel. The rea-

[90] Chang Tao-li, *op. cit.*, p. 16. For the complete text in Chinese, see *Hsin-hua yüeh-pao*, II, No. 6 (October, 1950), 1218–22.

[91] *New York Times*, October 2, 1950, p. 1.

[92] For text of the ultimatum, see *Military Situation in the Far East*, p. 3482.

[93] Panikkar, *op. cit.*, pp. 109–10.

[94] Acheson's testimony, *Military Situation in the Far East*, p. 1833; Truman, *op. cit.*, p. 362.

sons for the administration's miscalculation must be sought in other, deeper sources.

In his testimony during the MacArthur hearings, Secretary Acheson gave two explanations of the administration's underestimation of the probability of Chinese intervention. The first relates to the administration's estimate of Peking's intentions. The administration realized, Acheson declared, that Communist China had the military capability to intervene in the Korean War.[95] But the administration thought, and quite correctly, that intervention would require the utmost military effort from Peking and that it would entail serious political risks inside China. Above all, the administration was convinced that intervention would weaken rather than strengthen Peking internationally and bring no real advantage to the regime.[96]

The second explanation given by Acheson concerns the administration's estimate of the probable outcome of China's intervention.[97] Prior to the Inchon landing, American observers had credited China with the military capability to tip the balance of victory to the North Koreans and even to push American forces off the peninsula altogether.[98] The brilliant success at Inchon and the smashing victory following it brought about a complete change in the estimate of the military effectiveness of Chinese Communist troops vis-à-vis the United Nations forces. On October 2, one highly placed official in Washington was reported to have said: "I don't think that China wants to be chopped up."[99] Describing Washington's reaction to the warnings transmitted through the Indian government, James Reston wrote: "In spite of the Republican Party's conviction that the Chinese Communists always do the Kremlin's bidding, the chances are that Mao Tse-tung will hesitate to commit suicide."[100] Confidence in the ability of American forces to cope with Peking's intervention was reflected in a directive sent to General MacArthur by the Joint Chiefs of Staff on October 9. This reads in part: "Hereafter in the event of the open or covert employment anywhere in Korea of major Chinese Communist units, without prior announcement, you should continue the action as long as, in your judgment, action by forces now under your control offers a reasonable chance of success."[101] Washington's estimate was later confirmed by

[95] Acheson's testimony, *Military Situation in the Far East*, pp. 1832–35, 2100. For General Bradley's testimony on the same point, see *ibid.*, p. 759.

[96] Acheson's testimony, *ibid.*, p. 2101.

[97] *Ibid.*, p. 1835.

[98] *New York Times*, September 3, 1950, p. E5; September 11, 1950, p. 6, under the by-line of Hanson Baldwin. See also September 3, 1950, p. E3; September 11, 1950, p. 4.

[99] *Ibid.*, October 2, 1950, p. 3.

[100] *Ibid.*, October 1, 1950, p. E3.

[101] Truman, *op. cit.*, p. 362. See also Whiting, *op. cit.*, p. 111; Richard E. Neustadt, *Presidential Leadership* (New York: John Wiley & Sons, 1960), pp. 137–38.

General MacArthur's appraisals. At the conference at Wake Island on October 15, General MacArthur told President Truman and his top advisers, "Had they [the Chinese Communists] interfered in the first or second months, it would have been decisive. We are no longer fearful of their intervention. We no longer stand hat in hand. . . . They have no Air Force. Now that we have bases for our Air Force in Korea, if the Chinese tried to get down to Pyongyang, there would be the greatest slaughter." [102] Since American officials gave Peking the credit of being wise enough not to court disaster, they thought Chinese intervention unlikely. Thus, the impact of Peking's increasingly specific warnings on American calculations and policy was offset by Washington's enhanced confidence in American military might, particularly in the effectiveness of air power to deal with the Chinese forces.

Although the administration miscalculated the intentions of Peking, some of the reasons it gave for its mistake were, to some extent, valid. They also entered into the calculations of the Chinese Communists, as far as we can find out from various published materials. Mr. Chou Ch'ing-wên, the vice secretary-general of the Democratic League, who broke with the Peking regime and fled to Hong Kong in December, 1956, reported that for several days after Chou issued his warning on September 30, high officials in Peking discussed the question whether China should enter the Korean War. Those who opposed Chinese intervention argued that the newly established regime needed peace for reconstruction, particularly when its enemy was a first-rate power. This view was shared even by some generals in the People's Liberation Army.[103] Chou Ch'ing-wên's account was substantiated by contemporary evidence. An editorial in the Jên-min jih-pao on November 6, 1950, found it necessary to state and then to refute the view of those who opposed Chinese intervention.[104]

It emerges from Chou Ch'ing-wên's report that the Chinese Communists carefully weighed the serious risks involved in Chinese participation in the Korean War. The possibility of a Chinese defeat in Korea was taken into account. So was the contingency of an American invasion of the Chinese mainland. According to Chou Ch'ing-wên, Premier Chou En-lai told a group of officials at the time that "if necessary, we are prepared to retreat from the coast to the interior of China and to use the Northwest and the

[102] Senate Committee on Armed Services and Committee on Foreign Relations, *Substance of Statements Made at Wake Island Conference*, 82d Cong., 1st sess. (1951), p. 5.

[103] Chou Ch'ing-wên, *Fêng-pao shih nien* ["Ten Years of Storm"] (2d ed.; Hong Kong: Shih-tai p'i-p'ing shê, 1959), p. 193. An English translation of this book has since appeared. Chou Ching-wen, *Ten Years of Storm* (New York: Holt, Rinehart, and Winston, 1960), pp. 116, 117.

[104] Reprinted in *Hsin-hua yüeh-pao*, III, No. 1 (November, 1950), 3–4.

Southwest as the bases for a prolonged war." [105] Peking also took into consideration the possibility of the United States using the atomic bomb.[106] It will be recalled that on September 25 General Nieh gave Ambassador Panikkar the first indication of Peking's intention to enter the Korean War. On that occasion, the Indian ambassador endeavored to impress upon the Communist deputy chief of staff the ability of the United States to destroy China's industry and cities by aerial bombing and naval bombardment. Nieh replied: "We have calculated all that. They [the Americans] may even drop atom bombs on us. What then? They may kill a few million people. . . . After all, China lives on the farms. What can atom bombs do there?" [107] In early November, the Chinese Communists published no less than three widely distributed articles which contained statements disparaging the effectiveness of the atomic bomb, particularly when dropped in such a country as China. In one of these, Mao Tse-tung was quoted as having said in September, 1946: "The atomic bomb is a paper tiger. It looks fierce but is actually not so." [108] In the early part of November, the Chinese Communists took extraordinary precautions against the possibility of retaliatory air raids. Vital machinery, including rolling mills, was shifted from the South Manchurian industrial region. Peking even issued orders to its regional agencies in Central-South China to prepare for the removal of state-owned industrial components.[109]

What made the Chinese Communists willing to take these grave risks, thus upsetting the administration's calculations, appears to have been their estimate of the threat to their security posed by an American victory in North Korea. In making this estimate, they were influenced not only by the geopolitical importance of Korea to China but also by their image of the United States as the foremost imperialist power. This can be easily seen in several statements published in early November. A joint declaration issued on November 4 by all parties participating in the Peking regime asserted that there were no limits to the aggressive ambitions of imperialists and that, in launching the aggressive war against Korea, the American imperialists certainly did not confine their design to the destruction of the North Korean government but also wanted to invade China, extend their rule over Asia, and conquer the whole world.[110] An editorial in the *Jên-min jih-pao* on November 6 took President Truman's statement of June 27 as proof that the United States had decided to attack China from three

[105] Chou Ch'ing-wên, *op. cit.*, pp. 117, 195.
[106] *Ibid.*, p. 195.
[107] Panikkar, *op. cit.*, p. 108.
[108] *Shih-shih shou-ts'ê* ["Handbook on Current Affairs"], November 5, 1950, p. 45. (hereafter cited as *Shih-shih shou-ts'ê*). Mao made this remark in his interview with Anna Louise Strong in August, 1946.
[109] *New York Times*, November 11, 1950, p. 3; Chou Ch'ing-wên, *op. cit.*, p. 195.
[110] Reprinted in *Hsin-hua yüeh-pao*, III, No. 1 (November, 1950), 6.

directions: Korea, Formosa, and Indochina. Of these three fronts, Korea was, the editorial averred, the most important one. "After the United States will have completed her aggression against Korea, she will then be able to thrust a dagger into China's chest." [111] An outline for propaganda issued by the Chinese Communists pointed out that the United States had already built a network of bases which, according to MacArthur's public admission, had China and the Soviet Union as their targets.[112] President Truman's action in directing MacArthur to withdraw his statement was interpreted as an attempt to cover up America's real intention. The aggressive designs of the United States were said to have arisen out of her endeavor to extricate herself from the crisis created by the rapid decline of the capitalistic world on the one hand and the unprecedented growth of the socialist camp on the other.

With this grim, ideologically colored view of American intentions, the Chinese Communists saw American actions in Korea as a repetition of Japan's course of aggression in the fifty years before the collapse of Japan at the end of the Pacific war. Their ideological perspective did not permit them to distinguish between Japan of yesterday as an expansionist nation and the United States of today as a status quo power. In their eyes, the United States inherited Japan's position in the Far East and was following Tanaka's plan of conquering China and the world. The only difference between the United States of today and the Japan of yesterday was that the United States would not have to stop and consolidate her gains in Korea for as long a period of time as Japan did before attempting to invade Manchuria.[113] The Chinese Communists thus came to the conclusion that China's security was intimately related to the existence of the North Korean regime, that to save one's neighbor was to save onself, and that to defend the fatherland required giving help to the people of Korea.[114] It was this sense of immediate danger which impelled the Chinese Communists to take "voluntary actions to oppose the United States and to help Korea; to protect our homes and to defend our nation." [115] It is probable that this sense of immediate danger was enhanced by MacArthur's pronouncements and actions, and that "the cumulative anxieties of China's leaders may well have focused in their image of an aggressive General MacArthur."[116]

But the Chinese Communists did not enter the Korean War without hope of military victory and political gains. One prominent element of

[111] Reprinted in *ibid.*, pp. 1–4. The quotation was taken from p. 2.

[112] "How To Understand the United States," *Shih-shih shou-ts'ê*, pp. 9–27.

[113] Editorial, *Jên-min jih-pao*, November 6, 1950, as reprinted in *Hsin-hua yüeh-pao*, III, No. 1 (November, 1950), 2–4.

[114] "Joint Declaration of All Democratic Parties," as printed in *ibid.*, p. 6.

[115] Editorial, *Jên-min jih-pao*, November 6, 1950, as reprinted in *ibid.*, pp. 3–4.

[116] Whiting, *op. cit.*, p. 159.

Chinese Communist mentality was the paradoxical combination of a deep sense of insecurity and a tremendous confidence in ultimate victory. This combination was partly a product of ideology and was nurtured by their revolutionary experience. Their sense of insecurity stemmed from their intense hatred and fear of their class enemy. Their confidence in ultimate victory, which found expression in their scorn and contempt for their foe, was derived from their faith in the "scientific" laws of history. This combination of fear and confidence underlay their caution and patience which constituted important factors in their success in the revolutionary war. It was now brought to the fore by their sense of serious danger and the possibility of great gain. Characteristically, the Chinese Communists told the Chinese people in their propaganda to hate, to scorn, and to despise the United States. The Chinese people must hate the United States because she was their implacable enemy. While Secretary Acheson was talking about the traditional friendship of America, the Chinese Communists were teaching their compatriots that from the early nineteenth century onward the United States had consistently followed an aggressive policy toward China which culminated in her support for Chiang Kai-shek in the civil war and her present actions in Korea and Taiwan.[117] The Chinese people were told to treat the United States with scorn because she was a decaying capitalist nation and the headquarters of the declining reactionary camp. They should despise the United States because she was a paper tiger and "certainly" could be defeated.

An earlier article pointed out that the strategic thinking of the United States rested on the use of the atomic bomb and the air force and neglected the ground forces. The army was "the weakest link" in America's military power and the "fatal weakness" was the lack of a sufficient number of troops. The United States could not wage ground warfare on a large scale.[118] The Chinese Communists thus concluded in early November that "the voluntary actions of the Chinese people [i.e., the actions of the Chinese "volunteers"] will give the Korean people boundless encouragement and confidence, and probably can enable them to effect a change in the entire military situation, to annihilate or repulse the American forces which have not yet established a firm foothold, and to force the aggressors to accept a just and peaceful solution of the Korean question."[119] Mao Tse-tung was reported to have given the following retrospective explanation of his decision to intervene in Korea: a victory would

[117] "How To Understand the United States," *Shih-shih shou-ts'ê*, pp. 9–15. This theme, as applied to American policies and activities before 1900, was elaborated in a two-volume work, entitled *Mei-kuo ch'in Hua shih* ["A History of U.S. Aggression against China"], by Ch'ing Ju-chieh (Peking: San lien shu-t'ien, 1952).

[118] "The Strategic Weakness of the American Imperialism," as reprinted in *Hsin-hua yüeh-pao*, III, No. 1 (November, 1950), 11–14.

[119] Editorial, *Jên-min jih-pao,* as reprinted in *ibid.*, p. 4.

at once raise China's international status to a new height; a stalemate between a backward China and a first-rate power would be a victory for China; a defeat would merely entail a repetition of China's war of resistance against Japan.[120] Mao's statement suggests that, in addition to the defense of the Yalu boundary against the imaginary threat of United States "aggression," Peking entered the war to enhance its international prestige, particularly in Asia.

If the pronouncements of the Chinese Communists reflect, in some degree of accuracy, their thinking and if the above analysis is anywhere near the truth, one can conclude that the administration's miscalculations of Chinese intentions rested on an underestimation of the force of ideology in shaping the policies of the Chinese Communists. It did not judge correctly the intensity of their distrust and hostility toward the United States. It failed to gauge their willingness to take well-calculated risks to achieve political gains while warding off serious dangers, a trait which had been planted by their ideology, strengthened by their revolutionary experience, and which had become deeply imbedded in their mentality. Beyond this, there was the inability to take China seriously once the tide of battle in Korea was turned by the brilliant landing at Inchon. American officials apparently refused to believe that China, having been for a hundred years "the sick man of Asia," would dare to oppose or could successfully challenge the triumphant army of the foremost power. The failure to understand fully the nature of the Chinese Communist movement and the underestimation of China's political and military potentiality were the ultimate basis of Truman's and the Joint Chief's assent to MacArthur's proposal to cross the 38th Parallel and of Acheson's hesitant agreement to go along. These misjudgments explained why the decision was not modified in the face of Peking's warnings. American officials still could not free themselves completely from these two basic miscalculations. The first of these had found the most forceful expression in the recommendations of John S. Service and John P. Davies. The second, which had flowered from American disillusionment with Nationalist performance during the Pacific War, had constituted the fundamental reason for General Marshall's decision not to intervene in the Chinese civil war by the use of American troops. If there remained, after the neutralization of the Formosa Strait, any chance for Secretary Acheson to implement successfully his long-range policy of turning Chinese nationalism against Russia, it was destroyed by the administration's decision to cross the 38th Parallel.

It would seem that American officials also were insufficiently aware of the changing pattern of Peking-Moscow-Washington relations which the neutralization of the Formosa Strait had brought about. Acheson and other

[120] Chou ch'ing-wên, *op. cit.*, p. 395.

American officials had time and again sought to play China against the Soviet Union, relying on America's traditional friendship for China and pointing to Russia's past intrusions into China's border regions. Yet in the developing pattern, Peking's anxieties over "America's occupation of Formosa" greatly outweighed any possible concern over Soviet influence in her borderland. The crossing of the 38th Parallel and the subsequent clash between Chinese and American forces were to harden this changing pattern whose significance American officials were slow to recognize.

E. MacArthur's Drive toward the Yalu

General MacArthur's operations in North Korea were initially governed by a directive dated September 27. Under this directive, MacArthur's military objective was "the destruction of the North Korea armed forces." But he was told that "as a matter of policy, no non-Korean ground forces were to be used in the provinces bordering on the Soviet Union or in the area along the Manchurian border." [121] In conformity with this directive, MacArthur envisaged, in his plan of operations submitted the next day, a halt of the non-Korean forces at the Chongju-Yongwon-Hungnam line (see map). This line ran along the narrow neck of the Korean peninsula, ranging roughly from fifty to a hundred miles below the Manchurian border at various points.[122] However, by the time American forces were approaching the restraining line, it was no longer there. For one of the results of the Wake Island Conference, attended by Truman and MacArthur on October 15, was the General's modification and then elimination of the restraining line. On October 17, MacArthur issued a new order moving the restraining line for American forces to a lateral drawn through Chongsanjangsi-Huichon-Pyongwon-Toksili-Pungsan-Songjin, a line which was, at some places, as much as sixty miles north of the original line.[123] This new order was still in accord with the vague directive of September 27. It evoked no adverse reaction from Washington. In retrospect, however, the modification of the restraining line was a move of great military significance. By this order, General MacArthur abandoned the shortest possible line of defense above the 38th Parallel. It was largely in the area between the new and the old lines that the American forces suffered their decisive defeat in late November in the battle for North Korea.

On October 24, MacArthur did away with the restraining line altogether. He advised his field commanders that the initial restrictions were based upon "the possibility of enemy capitulation." He now authorized them "to use any and all ground forces at their commands, as necessary, in

---

[121] Truman, op. cit., p. 359.

[122] Whitney, op. cit., p. 398; Lynn Montross and Captain Nicholas A. Canzona, The Chosin Reservoir Campaign (Washington, D.C.: U. S. Marine Corps, 1957), pp. 8–9.

[123] Ibid., p. 36.

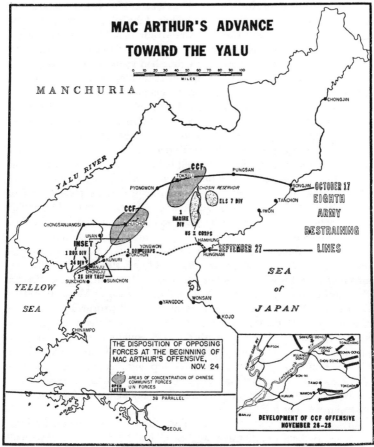

Sources. — This map is obtained by combining the following three maps: (1) "Eighth Army Advances and Restraining Lines," in Lynn Montrose and Captain Nicholas A. Canzona, *The Chosin Reservoir Campaign* (Washington, D.C.: United States Marine Corps, 1957), p. 4; (2) S. L. A. Marshall, *The River and the Gauntlet* (New York: William Morrow & Co., 1953), p. 15; (3) *ibid.*, p. 181. Used with permission.

order to capture all of North Korea." [124] General MacArthur issued his order of October 24 without having first advised the Joint Chiefs. On October
25, the Joint Chiefs told General MacArthur that his order was not in
consonance with their instructions of September 27. They further stated
that, while they realized that MacArthur had sound reasons for his new
order, they would like to be informed of these reasons. Later in the Mac-
Arthur hearings, General Collins cited General MacArthur's order as the
one case in which MacArthur violated a directive of the Joint Chiefs, or
at least a policy laid down in a directive.[125] General MacArthur immediately replied that the lifting of the restriction was "a matter of military
necessity because the Republic of Korea forces were not of sufficient
strength and were not sufficiently well led to be able to handle the situation." He explained that he had been given the necessary latitude for modifying the directive of September 27 by a message dated September 30 from
Secretary of Defense Marshall. This stated: "We want you to feel unham-
pered tactically and strategically to proceed north of the 38th Parallel."
MacArthur concluded, "I am fully cognizant of the basic purpose and
intent of your directive, and every possible precaution is being taken in the
premises. The very reverse, however, would be fostered and tactical haz-
ards might even result from other action than that which I have directed.
This entire subject was covered in my conference at Wake Island." [126]
Once again, President Truman was as much taken by surprise as everybody
else. As late as October 26, he reiterated at a press conference that "it was
his understanding" that only South Koreans would approach the northern
provinces.[127] If Truman's purpose in meeting MacArthur at Wake Island
was to establish a more cordial relationship with his field commander, to
make certain of MacArthur's faithful implementation of Washington's
policies, and to prevent the General from taking provocative action,[128]
that aim was not fulfilled.

In late October and early December, the Chinese Communist forces
launched two counteroffensives against United Nation troops. Meanwhile
the Communist regime started a mass campaign in China, featuring the
theme of "hating, despising, and scorning" the United States. All the
parties taking part in the regime issued on November 4 a joint declaration
vowing support for the movement to oppose America and help Korea "on
a voluntary basis." This represented the indorsement by all the parties
of the intervention in Korea which was already an accomplished fact. An
editorial of the *Jên-min jih-pao* on November 6, scornfully rejected any

[124] *Military Situation in the Far East*, p. 1240.
[125] *Ibid.*, pp. 1216, 1230–31, 1239–41, 1314.
[126] Truman, *op. cit.*, p. 372; *Military Situation in the Far East*, p. 1241.
[127] *New York Times*, October 27, 1950, p. 1.
[128] Spanier, *op. cit.*, pp. 107–10.

idea that the United States forces might halt at the Sino-Korean border. It noted that, when American forces were approaching the 38th Parallel, the United States created the impression that American forces would stop at that line. Later, the United States created the impression that American forces would stop some distance from the borders of the Soviet Union and China. But, the editorial charged, events proved these statements to be lies. Now, American troops were approaching the Yalu River. Once again, American spokesmen were laying down a smokescreen by giving verbal assurances that MacArthur's armies would not push beyond the Korean border. The editorial asked: In the light of past experience, were not these statements precisely the sign that American aggressors would push beyond the Korean borders? [129]

On November 7, Chinese and North Korean troops suddenly broke contact with the United Nations forces. This tactical disengagement ushered in a lull on the Korean battlefield. Chinese intervention was now a fact. But there remained the question: What was the purpose and extent of Chinese intervention? Neither Washington nor MacArthur knew. But the administration was much more concerned than MacArthur over a clash with the Chinese Communists. It therefore sought to settle the problem of Chinese Communist intervention by political means while leaving MacArthur's military missions unchanged.[130] It endeavored to reassure Peking of Washington's intention to respect the Manchurian frontier through a six-nation resolution introduced in the United Nations on November 10 and through the public statements made by Acheson on November 15 and by the President himself the next day.[131] It explored the possibility of establishing a buffer zone along the Yalu River. It was prepared to respect China's legitimate interests near the frontier and to grant Peking access to the hydroelectric power generated by installations on Korean soil.[132] Diplomacy was now put ahead of military operations as a means to achieve the unification of Korea.[133] This policy of exploring the possibility of negotiations while leaving MacArthur's directive unchanged rested on two assumptions. First, the Chinese Communists would be willing to negotiate on the basis of a buffer zone and access to power supply in North Korea. Second, General MacArthur's military operations would be successful. Both assumptions turned out to be false.

MacArthur violently opposed any attempt to negotiate with the Chinese

[129] Reprinted in *Hsin-hua yüeh-pao*, III, No. 1 (November, 1950), 3.

[130] Truman, *op. cit.*, pp. 378–80.

[131] *Department of State Bulletin*, November 27, 1950, p. 855; *ibid.*, pp. 852–53. See also U.S. Security Council, *Official Minutes, 530th Meeting*, pp. 22–23.

[132] See the statement by Assistant Secretary of State Dean Rusk, *New York Times*, November 11, 1950, p. 1; *Department of State Bulletin*, December 4, 1950, p. 89; Panikkar, *op. cit.*, p. 115.

[133] Neustadt, *op. cit.*, pp. 140–41.

Communists or to make a conciliatory gesture. He dismissed the importance of the hydroelectric system as a consideration in Peking's calculations. He objected to the idea of a buffer zone on moral and political grounds. He cabled Washington: "To give up a portion of North Korea to the aggression of the Chinese Communists would be the greatest defeat of the free world in recent times; to yield to so immoral a proposition would bankrupt our leadership and influence in Asia and render untenable our position, both politically and militarily." [134] He did not believe that Peking would intervene in full force. He was convinced that a rapid occupation of all Korea would check the Soviet Union's and Communist China's aggressive designs, "before these countries are committed [to a course of action] from which, for political reasons, they cannot withdraw." [135] If the Chinese Communist forces did intervene on a full scale, he was confident that his air power would destroy them.[136] MacArthur was so certain of the overwhelming might of the forces under his command that he launched his final offensive to win the war on November 24, telling his troops that they would be home by Christmas. He split his forces into two groups under two separate commands, with a gap of 20 to 35 air miles between them.[137]

Three days later, the Chinese Communists and North Korean forces met MacArthur's general assault with an all-out counteroffensive. The blow landed "with full speed, full surprise and full shock" against the Republic of Korea II Corps in the central sector.[138] The disintegration of the South Korean forces exposed the right flank of the Eighth Army. With this knowledge and under pressure from numerically superior Chinese Communist forces, the Eighth Army began its withdrawal on November 27. All along the line, the Chinese Communist troops smashed at the United Nations forces. The enemy proved to have amassed a much larger force than previous estimates had indicated. On November 25, Eighth Army intelligence put the enemy strength on its front at 149,000, an increase of

[134] Whitney, op. cit., p. 412.

[135] Ibid., p. 419.

[136] Roy E. Appleman, South to the Naktong, North to the Yalu (Washington, D.C.: Government Printing Office, 1961), pp. 757–65. In reviewing these events, one always wonders to what extent the disagreement between the administration and MacArthur over the method of preventing full-scale Chinese intervention stemmed, as did other controversies, from a fundamental difference in outlook on China policy. As Anthony Leviero of the New York Times pointed out in October, MacArthur disagreed in important respects with the administration's Far Eastern policy, favoring strong acts backed by military force, but the fundamental principle of the administration's Far Eastern policy was that communism, especially in China, could not be overcome by force (New York Times, October 12, 1950, pp. 1 and 6).

[137] Appleman, op. cit., p. 745.

[138] S. L. A. Marshall, The River and the Gauntlet (New York: William Morrow & Co., 1953), pp. 169–70, 172–73, 176; New York Times, November 26, 1950, p. 1; Montross and Canzona, op. cit., p. 146.

95,000 from its estimate of the day before.[139] Three days later the strength of Chinese Communist forces in Korea was put at 200,000. There were actually 300,000 Chinese troops.[140] In a special communiqué on November 28, General MacArthur announced that "we face an entirely new war." This new war began with what S. L. A. Marshall called "one of the major decisive battles of the present century followed by the longest retreat in American history."[141]

Peking accompanied its counterattack in Korea with a diplomatic offensive in Lake Success. On November 24, General Wu Hsiu-ch'üan, the chief delegate of the Peking regime to the Security Council, arrived in New York to attend the Security Council meeting to discuss Peking's complaint of "armed invasion of Taiwan." In a lengthy speech on November 28, Wu ruled out any compromise solution of the question of Formosa. He declared:

> Whatever decision the United Nations General Assembly may take on the so-called question of the status of Taiwan, whether it be to hand over the island to the United States so that it might administer it openly [or] under the disguise of "trusteeship," or "neutralization," or whether it be to procrastinate by the way of "investigation," thereby maintaining the present state of actual United States occupation, it will, in substance, be stealing China's legitimate territory and supporting United States aggression against Taiwan in opposition to the Chinese people. Any such action would in no way shake the resolve of the Chinese people to liberate Taiwan, nor would it prevent action by the Chinese people to liberate Taiwan.[142]

Wu demanded that the Security Council "take concrete steps to apply severe sanctions against the United States for its criminal acts of armed

[139] *Ibid.*, p. 140.

[140] Appleman, *op. cit.*, p. 768.

[141] Marshall, *op. cit.*, p. 1. General Whitney asserted that MacArthur had directed his staff to prepare a detailed program for disengagement and withdrawal to be implemented in case of full-scale Chinese intervention (Whitney, *op. cit.*, p. 414). If such a plan existed, no one so far has been able to uncover it. S. L. A. Marshall's meticulous account of the Eighth Army's retreat made no mention of it. On the contrary, he revealed that it was not until November 29 that Major General Lawrence B. Keiser, commander of the Second Division which bore the brunt of the Chinese attack, learned, indirectly and quite accidentally, of the Eighth Army headquarters' plan for withdrawal. Even then, "he did not get a direct order to withdraw and the road by which he should take the division out was not specified" (*op. cit.*, pp. 263–64). On the eastern sector, it was not until November 30 that General Almond directed his divisional commander to draw up a plan and time schedule for extricating the American forces east of the Chosin reservoir area (Montross and Canzona, *op. cit.*, p. 239).

[142] United Nations Security Council, *Official Records, 527th Meeting*, November 28, 1950, p. 10.

aggression against the territory of China, Taiwan, and armed intervention in Korea," and "that the Security Council adopt effective measures to bring about complete withdrawal of American forces from Taiwan and Korea." [143] The violence of Wu's attack on the United States matched the fury of the Chinese Communist assault against the American forces in Korea.

Later, on December 11, Premier Chou En-lai rejected an Indian plea that the Chinese forces halt at the 38th Parallel. He told Ambassador Panikkar that his terms of settlement included the withdrawal of American forces from Taiwan, China's admission to the United Nations, and withdrawal of all foreign troops from Korea.[144] Just as American officials before him, Chou in his hour of victory overestimated his military strength. On December 16, President Truman proclaimed the existence of a national emergency. Only a further test of strength on the battlefield could bring about a restoration of peace.

F. The Korean War and the Demise of the Administration's China Policy

With Peking's intervention and the subsequent stalemate in the Korean War, the neutralization of the Formosa Strait lost its temporary character. These developments spelled the total failure of the administration's policy of disengagement. This failure had its origins in the partisan controversy in the United States. The China bloc's demands for a positive program of aid to the Nationalists and its sentimental attachment to China had necessitated the adoption of a policy of limited assistance in 1947. They had immobilized America's China policy for a year and a half after Marshall had for all practical purposes written off both mainland China and Formosa in October, 1948. This immobility and continued entanglement in China provided the Soviet Union with ample time to prepare for and implement new moves in China and in Korea in order to counter America's policy of building up Japan. Whatever the calculations of the Soviet Union may have been in scheduling the attack on South Korea ahead of Peking's projected assault on Formosa, the aggression in Korea led to the neutralization of the Formosa Strait which further aroused Peking's hostility toward the United States. After American forces crossed the 38th Parallel, Peking intervened. After scoring a surprise victory in North Korea, Communist China, like the United States, refused to halt her forces at the 38th Parallel. We may never know what precise effect the neutralization of the Formosa Strait had on Peking's decision to enter the Korean War or on her subsequent refusal to halt her forces at the 38th Parallel. It may very well be that the crossing of the 38th Parallel by American forces was the sufficient condition for the decisions and actions

[143] *Ibid.*, p. 25.
[144] Panikkar, *op. cit.*, pp. 118–19.

taken by Peking. But one must also remember that the neutralization of the Formosa Strait was one of the most significant events preceding Peking's intervention. It could not but have influenced Peking's decisions. It could not but have lightened Moscow's task in persuading Peking to intervene and to drive American forces out of Korea, if such persuasion was necessary. In any case, the temporary neutralization of the Formosa Strait was followed by the crossing of the 38th Parallel and Chinese intervention which, in turn, basically altered Sino-American relations.

Thus, by the end of 1950, the whole edifice of the administration's policy toward China lay in ruins. The administration had acted to disentangle the United States from the Chinese civil war, but events forced it to intervene at the last moment by neutralizing the Formosa Strait. It had endeavored to dissuade Peking from intervening in Korea, but MacArthur's drive across the 38th Parallel, assented to by the Joint Chiefs and hesitantly by Acheson, brought Peking into the war. It had tried hard to avoid a military conflict between the United States and Communist China, but the decision to march into North Korea paved the way for the defeat of the technologically modern army of the United States by the poorly equipped Chinese soldiers in a terrain even more favorable to the latter than the Chinese mainland. It had attempted to limit America's commitments to the Nationalist government, but the developments of the Korean War after November, 1950, led to a sharp and rapid increase in military aid to Formosa. It had sought a compromise solution of the question of Formosa through the United Nations, but Peking underscored her rejection of any such program by pressing her attack in Korea across the 38th Parallel. It had apparently wished to establish normal diplomatic relations with Peking eventually, but found itself increasingly opposed to recognition of the Communist regime and its admission to the United Nations.[145] It had based its long-term policy on the hope of splitting the Sino-Soviet alliance by turning Chinese nationalism against Russia, but the neutralization of the Formosa Strait and the Chinese intervention in Korea greatly increased Peking's dependence on Moscow and, for the next few years, solidified the unity of the two leading Communist partners.

The decision to cross the 38th Parallel need not have led to the humiliating defeat suffered by American forces if the administration had taken steps to halt MacArthur's drive toward the Yalu. President Truman or the Joint Chiefs could have insisted on maintaining the restraining line

[145] According to James Reston, Acheson was opposed to a British proposal for trying to negotiate a cease-fire at the 38th Parallel in December, 1950. He told the British that, even if the Chinese Communists were brought into the United Nations, recognized by the United States as the government of China, and handed Formosa, they would then probably make demands upon French Indochina and demand a voice in the Japanese peace settlement (*New York Times*, December 6, 1950, p. 8).

for American forces near the narrow neck of Korea.[146] He or they could have countermanded MacArthur's order on October 17 which moved the restraining line sixty miles northward at some points. At the shortest possible line of defense near the narrow neck, the United Nations' forces might have had a better chance of warding off an all-out Chinese assault. Or Truman and the Joint Chiefs of Staff could have countermanded Mac-Arthur's order of October 24 eliminating the restraining line altogether — an order which violated the Joint Chiefs' directive of September 27 or at least a policy laid down in it. Such a step might have prevented some advance elements of the American forces from marching too far into the Chinese trap. In November, the administration might have changed its directive to MacArthur when its diplomatic overtures to Peking met with rebuff. None of these steps was taken because the political objective remained the ambitious one of unification of Korea and the military risks were apparently not thought to be as serious as they turned out to be. After all, China, be it Communist or Nationalist, was not a serious factor in American calculations. The sentimental attachment of the United States to China was not coupled with a respect for Chinese power. Moreover, the administration was in a weak position politically to restrain MacArthur because its China policy had been under severe attack for several years and MacArthur was the symbol of a new approach to Far Eastern affairs. Thus, America's defeat in North Korea had its roots in her policy toward China.

Perhaps a military clash between Communist China and the United States was inevitable because of the ideological component in Peking's foreign policy and the quest for greatness which had always been deeply imbedded in Chinese history and culture and which was reactivated by a revived sense of power and unity after a century of humiliation and defeat. But the failure to withdraw promptly from China between 1947 and 1950, the neutralization of the Formosa Strait, and the decision to cross the 38th Parallel turned potentiality into immediate actuality. It thus deprived the United States of room for maneuver and time for adjustment to the new configuration of power in the Far East. This new configuration of power would in all probability have come into existence over a period of time even if the Korean War had not occurred. For the revolutionary and national interests of an awakened China under Communist leadership clashed sharply with the American policy of containment and with American efforts to bolster non-Communist regimes in Asia. But the Korean War precipitated this emergent international configuration and added to the equation of power new political and emotional factors which otherwise would not have existed.

[146] Neustadt, *op. cit.*, pp. 137–47.

The new configuration of power as it evolved out of the Korean War consists of two main elements. The first is the emergence of China as a powerful nation in the Far East, and the second is a new pattern of conflict among Peking, Moscow, and Washington. The battle in North Korea was the first great victory won by Chinese forces over a major power which had a lasting effect on the outcome of an international war since the Opium War opened the modern era in China.[147] It marked the ironic, partial fulfilment of President Roosevelt's wartime policy of making China a great power. Since the Korean War the balance of power in the Far East has rested on a confrontation between the ground forces of the Communist bloc on the Asiatic mainland and the air and naval power of the United States based on the island perimeter. The Korean peninsula and Southeast Asia have become the objects of the political-military struggle between the two blocs.

Second, the neutralization of the Formosa Strait and Chinese intervention has precipitated a new pattern of relations among Peking, Moscow, and Washington. The unresolved question of Formosa became an obsession with Communist China. As a result, the clash of interests over Formosa between Peking and Washington has tended to overshadow the conflicts between the Soviet Union and the United States. The antagonism between a junior partner in the Communist bloc and the leading nation in the free world has become sharper than the expected tension between the most powerful countries in the two rival camps. The respective positions of Moscow and Peking in the Sino-Soviet alliance have also been basically altered. Moscow's reliance on Peking to promote her foreign policies in Asia has been eclipsed by Peking's dependence on Moscow's support to achieve her most important political objective: the elimination of a rival regime and the attainment of national unity. Peking's diplomatic isolation from the United States has been nearly complete, but Moscow's freedom of maneuver has been greatly enhanced. This change doomed to failure Acheson's policy of playing China against the Soviet Union. It has put the United States in the position of making Peking rather than Moscow the major antagonist with whom no improvement in relations has so far been possible.

Peking's amazing success in a surprise attack and the subsequent prolonged stalemate have been taken by her as confirmation of Mao's concept of the United States as a paper tiger. They have been considered a vindication of his formula of "taking the enemy lightly strategically and

[147] In early 1938, General Li Tsung-jên defeated the Japanese forces at Taiêrh-chuang (F. F. Liu, *A Military History of Modern China* [Princeton, N. J.: Princeton University Press, 1956], pp. 199–200). But this Chinese victory in a major battle only temporarily delayed the Japanese advance. It did not constitute the turning point of a war.

taking him seriously tactically," which had always been an important part of Mao's thought but which was to be concisely stated in these terms in November, 1957.[148] The strengthened conviction of the correctness of these ideas was to lead Mao to overestimate the significance of the possession of intercontinental ballistic missiles by the Soviet Union, to attribute strategic superiority to the Communist bloc, and to proclaim that the East wind prevailed over the West wind.[149] This misjudgment in the realm of strategic calculations has not been fully compensated by Peking's caution in tactics. Peking has been advocating a militant policy against the United States wherever and whenever the opportunity has presented itself.

On the part of the United States, the initial defeat and subsequent frustrations aroused deep fear and hostility toward the Chinese Communist regime, all the more because of the previous sentimental attachment to China. This fear and hostility has since replaced traditional friendship as the dominant mood in the American attitude toward China. The United States thus reciprocates Peking's phobia and hatred for Washington. Emotional attitudes and unresolved problems reinforce each other to harden Sino-American antagonism which, in day-to-day struggles, overshadow the long-term Soviet-American rivalry for world leadership.

The courses of action adopted by the Eisenhower administration flowed naturally from the collapse of the Truman administration's policy. To many, the only alternative to a policy that had failed was its logical opposite. The policy of maximum isolation of Peking replaced that of seeking a modus vivendi. The policy of rehabilitating the Nationalist government as a foremost ally in the Far East replaced the policy of limiting America's commitment. Up to at least the end of 1958, the supposition that the Chinese Communist regime was not a lasting phenomenon replaced the assumption that it was here to stay. The policy of going to the brink of war to deter Peking's new moves replaced efforts to reassure China about America's present intentions and to remind her of traditional friendship. The exertion of maximum pressure on the Sino-Soviet bloc as a measure to split the alliance replaced the hope of making Russia the primary target of Chinese nationalism. Meanwhile, Peking has taken upon herself the role of the most uncompromising enemy of the United States in the Communist bloc.

Thus, it has come to pass that after half a century the Open Door policy of John Hay has ended in a confrontation between a bamboo curtain on one side and a total trade embargo on the other. The principle of preserv-

[148] *Comrade Mao Tse-tung on "Imperialism and All Reactionaries Are Paper Tigers"* (Peking: Foreign Language Press, 1958), p. 25.

[149] Donald Zagoria, *The Sino-Soviet Conflict, 1956–1961* (Princeton, N.J.: Princeton University Press, 1962) pp. 164–65, 202, 326; Alice Langley Hsieh, *Communist China's Strategy in the Nuclear Era* (Englewood Cliffs, N.J.: Prentice-Hall, 1962), pp. 76–166.

ing Chinese territorial and administrative integrity has terminated in the reality of two Chinas. Non-intervention in Chinese affairs has passed into an American-enforced *de facto* cease-fire in the civil war. Traditional sympathy for the underdog of the Far East has been superseded by fear of the awakened giant of Asia. Pride in America's moral leadership in China has been replaced by apprehension about Chinese ideological influence in Asia. Missionary and philanthropic activities have given place to political and propaganda warfare. Neighborly dialogue has been supplanted by mutual denunciation. Historic friendship has been consummated in reciprocal hostility. On the horizon looms an ever-present chance of war. One could hardly find a more sobering example of the tragic results produced by a policy of good intentions and high ideals which lacked the foundation of a correlative estimate of self-interest and which was not supported by military power equal to the noble tasks.